Reading Women

MATERIAL TEXTS

A complete list of books in the series is available from the publisher.

Reading Women

Literacy, Authorship, and Culture in the Atlantic World, 1500–1800

EDITED BY
HEIDI BRAYMAN HACKEL AND
CATHERINE E. KELLY

PENN

University of Pennsylvania Press
Philadelphia

Published by
University of Pennsylvania Press
Philadelphia, Pennsylvania 19104–4112

Printed in the United States of America on acid-free paper

10 9 8 7 6 5 4 3 2 1

A Cataloging-in-Publication record is available from the Library of Congress
ISBN-13: 978-0-8122-4054-2
ISBN-10: 0-8122-4054-5

In memory of Sasha Roberts

Contents

Illustrations

Introduction

Heidi Brayman Hackel and Catherine E. Kelly

The Virgin Mary pores over a book of devotion, oblivious to the angel standing before her. A merchant's wife titters and flushes as she reads a French romance, slipping toward sexual ecstasy as she fingers the pages. A matron in a gauzy Empire dress reads a history of ancient Rome and ponders her nation's prospects. A mouse of a girl curls up in a window seat, lost in an enormous book.

These are familiar images. In the four hundred years since significant numbers of Western women began to read, such pictorial and textual representations of women reading have become part of our cultural wallpaper. They are the stuff of Renaissance paintings and nineteenth-century novels; they figure equally in exemplary lives and cautionary tales. In recent decades these same images have gained new complexity and generated new questions, thanks to the work of a generation of feminist scholars who have illuminated the multiple, often conflicting, representations of the female reader. The essays collected in this volume aim to further their investigations both by turning toward more empirically based accounts of women's reading and by problematizing the dynamic relation between representation and recorded experience. We do not pretend to offer a definitive history of women reading, convinced as we are of the impossibility of such a narrative at this moment. Instead, the following essays aspire to advance a conversation across disciplinary fields and across national borders. They offer new data about the gendered realities of reading on both sides of the Atlantic, and they pose fresh questions about the relationship between those realities and the representations that were intended to shape them. Taken together, these essays help us track the dramatic emergence of girls and women as important participants in the production and consumption of texts and as statistically meaningful possessors of literacy.

It is no exaggeration to call this process dramatic. In England in 1500, as much as 99 percent of women may have been illiterate, and girls of all social backgrounds were the objects of purposeful efforts to restrict their access to full literacy. Three centuries later, in 1800, nearly half of English and Anglo-American women demonstrated alphabetic literacy and the female reader had emerged as a cultural ideal and market force. By the middle of the nineteenth century, the U.S. census reported that 90 percent of white men and women were literate.[1] The protean expansion of a female readership shaped the history of publishing and the development of literary culture. We can see its impact in the steadily increasing numbers of texts aimed at least partly at female readers-cum-consumers and in the popularity of novels whose plots revolve around heroines who are *themselves* avid readers: fictional readers such as Jane Eyre, Dorothea Brooke, and Jo March resulted from and encouraged a capacious culture of women's reading.

These heroines, along with their contemporary readers, have drawn critical attention. Some twenty years after the publication of pathbreaking studies by Janice Radway and Cathy Davidson, we now know a good deal about the past two hundred years of Anglo-American women's reading.[2] However, if scholars have written extensively about women's reading in the nineteenth and twentieth centuries, they have generally overlooked female readers at the critical moment when their reading assumed significant cultural and economic power. This problem has not gone unremarked. David McKitterick deems the field of early modern women's book ownership as "long overdue for a book" and still awaiting "its historian," and Kevin Sharpe concedes, "Nearly all the readers about whom we have information are male." Indeed, even as the field of early modern reading has burgeoned, the readers who have emerged most visibly are elite men: Gabriel Harvey, John Dee, Ben Jonson, Sir William Drake. David Hall has similarly observed a gap in Americanist scholarship, noting that where women's reading is concerned, "an adequately historical description has taken second place to ideological criticism."[3]

Although historians of reading have not sufficiently understood women's reading, one might expect more discoveries from scholars of women writers. Yet, most studies that have attempted to glimpse women readers have more often attended to women writers, not only turning to women's works for the evidence but also directing such evidence, finally, toward a history of a female literary tradition. Even a study aspiring to offer an as-yet-unsketched "group portrait" of eighteenth-century female readers of Alexander Pope, for example, settles into a study of women's poetry and literary criticism in the period.[4] Certainly, a female literary tradition has emerged from the shadows because of the efforts of two generations of feminist scholars who have recovered and edited hundreds of texts by early modern Englishwomen, documenting along the way the cultural habits that obscured this history and made it possible for Virginia Woolf to imagine in 1928 that "no woman could have written poetry" in the Elizabethan period.[5] A similar effort must now be made to rediscover the landscape of women's reading in these formative periods. As scholars have begun to demonstrate, it is an overgrown landscape, not an imaginary one, for long before Jane Eyre "mounted into the window-seat" to read, girls and women were reading—sometimes furtively, often voraciously, and rarely with the full support of their culture.

Although the field of women's reading is comparatively undeveloped for the periods before 1800, several contributors to this volume—Mary Ellen Lamb, Sasha Roberts, Margaret Ferguson—have directed scholarly attention to the role of gender in early modern reading and advocated for a more carefully theorized account of the gendering of literacy. Taken together, their work has suggested a rough trajectory for the development of early modern Englishwomen's reading. Notwithstanding variations among households and fluctuations over time, female literacy increased and female literary engagement intensified markedly in the two centuries after 1500. In the sixteenth century a literate woman in a gentry household might have had access to a housewifery manual, a devotional text or two, and the Bible; depending on exactly where and when she lived, she might have been prohibited from reading the Bible without the direct supervision of her father or husband. By the late seventeenth century this same woman might well have counted among her books a Bible, a French dictionary, Katherine Philips's poems, a couple volumes of English plays, and a book of geography. However, this cultural shift developed within and against strong constraints. If many women gained new access to secular texts, their brothers and husbands almost always had more and better access. Barred from acquiring classical languages, women were at a marked disadvantage for reading their culture's most intellectually prestigious texts. In addition, the figure of the female reader, whether exalted or caricatured, became a lightning rod for anxieties about sexuality, gender, class, and power. Precisely because early modern women's reading, as both a daily practice and a cultural barometer, was so fraught, it has been obscured and overlooked in the historical record. If it is true that female readers, like nonelite male ones, left *fewer* records to document their reading habits than did elite males, it is also true that female readers left *different* records. Scholars who would recover the complex world of the early modern reader—much less the women who operated within that world—must therefore think creatively about sources and evidence. Signature literacy, the standard measure which equates a signature with literacy and a mark on a public document with its absence, does not begin to reveal the extent of women's literacy not only because these measures conflate reading and writing but also because they conflate reading and signing in public. As scholars have demonstrated, a woman who wrote a good italic hand in private might well choose to witness a legal document with an *X.* Rather than continuing to attempt to quantify female literacy with such inadequate measures, Ferguson urges scholars to expand the "archive of materials" and not to lament their inconclusiveness but rather to consider the "fuzziness of the information . . . as an asset to a model of cultural interpretation that interrogates scholarly claims to epistemological certainty or closure."[6]

While scholars now insist on the fundamental invisibility of many literate women in the historical record, it is also increasingly clear that the "Female Reader" is a fiction. Like their male peers, women brought a range of experiences, skills, and associations to their engagement with texts. Balancing this "multiplicity of interests and experiences that make up the female perspective," however, is the "common ground . . . that sets women apart from men."[7] Accordingly, as Sasha Roberts reminds us in her essay, gender is "a surprisingly problematic category of critical analysis—both definitive and reductive, enabling and restricting." The crux of much feminist debate, particularly around the gendering of reading, has been a fundamental disagreement about the category of "woman" itself. To ask if women read differently from men is to ask, after all, where gender falls in the hierarchy of motivations and constraints in a human life. Feminist theorists have struggled to reconcile the assumptions of a recuperative paradigm, which seeks to reclaim women's voices from the past, with poststructuralist rejections of "woman" as an essentialist category.[8] Many feminists have agreed finally to acknowledge the constructedness of gender and the variousness of its effects while still presuming its power: "The texts of our selves," Sandra Gilbert explains in a representative assertion, "as much as the texts we write or read, are variously but inexorably marked by the imperatives of gender, at least as much as by those of class and race."[9] Other feminist scholars have theorized the ways in which modern readers may reclaim texts through explicitly gendered readings: Judith Fetterly proposes, for example, a resisting female reader.[10] While this important work has opened up new readings of canonical texts and disarmed the canon itself, it has not, finally, moved us closer to an understanding of the particularities of girls' and women's reading in earlier periods, for reading, along with literacy, is never a transhistorical phenomenon. To uncover what it meant to read as a woman, one might best examine what it meant to read as a seventeenth-century Yorkshire merchant's young wife or as an eighteenth-century Philadelphia widow.

If, then, one cannot speak of a singular, unilegible "Female Reader," this volume nevertheless asserts that gender was an organizing—and often the dominant—factor shaping women's reading in the Atlantic world during the period from 1500 to 1800. Certainly, the historical record is peopled by "ordinary exceptions," some of whom figure in the essays that follow. Yet it also documents a period in which most of the conditions of textual consumption and production were indeed gendered. Access to texts, education, and literacy was responsive to cultural ideals and norms; early in the period, legal and institutional constraints further narrowed the range of girls' and women's experiences as readers. As the essays in the final section of the volume describe, the critical relationship between reading and writing, consumption and production was more fragmented and less automatic for women than for men. If men's reading was often preparatory for writing, many women were discouraged altogether from writing.

The chronological parameters of our book are 1500–1800, with some spillover into earlier and later periods. On the one hand, there is surely something arbitrary about locating beginning and end points: the lives of individual readers almost never coincide neatly with historical periods, and scholars have successfully challenged the very notion of periodization. On the other hand, Western women's reading emerged in tandem with the modern world and specific cultural and historical phenomena identified with it. The year 1500 symbolically marks the end of the incunabular period or infancy of print, and we end near the introduction of wood-based paper and books mass-produced on a scale unimaginable to the handful of Continental printers just setting up shop in London in 1500. In a volume committed to crossing national boundaries, it is nevertheless worth observing that we begin contemporaneously with the Tudor dynasty, which would usher in a new consolidation of monarchal power and a new era of self-presentation, and we end with the creation of the United States, which yoked reading and gender to the republican project.

Precisely because women's reading was so closely connected to the emergence of the modern world, it defied the boundaries of emergent nations, complicating the creation of national cultures on both sides of the Atlantic. To be sure, men's and women's reading surely contributed to the creation of imagined national communities, and some texts and practices remained insistently local. But—like persons—literacies, identities, and texts crossed borders and oceans. Readers in early modern France and England devoured *novelles* in translation and in the original languages. Some two hundred years later, readers in the United States loaded their bookshelves with imprints from across Europe, using those texts to elaborate a distinctive American culture. Individuals who were propelled across Europe and around the Atlantic world for religious, political, and economic reasons migrated with books in hand. Moreover, this circulation of people and texts created a kind of cosmopolitan imaginary, one that enabled readers who stayed put to consume the exotic customs and landscapes of distant lands. If this unprecedented movement of texts and readers was part of Europe's expansion, it entailed far more than an inexorable move from center to periphery. On the contrary, readers and especially texts moved from center to periphery and back again, following routes that were circuitous as often as they were direct. Texts and readers moved with the market, circulating through a protean market economy that was explicitly transatlantic, even global. As scholars working in literary, historical, and cultural studies have discovered, the emergent "modern world" is best viewed in a transnational, transatlantic context.[11] Taken together, the essays in this volume demonstrate that isolating our explorations of women's reading within the boundaries of a single nation distorts important stories and obscures pressing questions.

At the same time, the following essays simultaneously direct our attention to the institutions that structured women's reading in the past and to the contemporary scholarly and methodological approaches that enhance our understanding of it. A strikingly wide variety of institutions competed to determine the kinds of texts that women read as well as the images of and experiences of female readers. Some—most obviously churches and schools—championed protocols and texts that aligned certain forms of reading and specific categories of readers with a distinctly feminine piety and respectability; not surprisingly, readers and texts that transgressed those conventions portended an equally feminized form of religious, cultural, economic, and sexual disorder. However, these hegemonic institutions were themselves situated alongside and sometimes challenged by a far more heterodox constellation of discursive practices and texts than scholars have allowed. Women's reading was shaped not only by the wisdom of clerics and pedagogues but also by the polite and often heterosocial conversations of early modern courts, eighteenth-century tea tables, and nineteenth-century parlors. Scripture and conduct manuals competed not only with poetry, drama, and a cacophonous press but also with scientific and aesthetic treatises and unpublished, privately circulated manuscripts. This plurality, visible as early as the fifteenth century, was only exacerbated by the consumer revolution of the long eighteenth century, which placed multiple institutions and texts within the reach of increasing numbers of readers, female and male alike. The broad outlines of this trajectory—more sites of consumption and reception, more texts, more readers—have become familiar to scholars working in a variety of disciplines.[12] Nevertheless, the essays in this volume bring new levels of specificity and nuance to our understanding of that narrative by showing how it unfolded across space as well as over time.

As the essays collected here alert us to the range of texts and contexts that shaped women's reading, they also underscore the need to think more inventively about the sources that document it. Most obviously, they remind us of the ways in which the textual is imbricated in the material. Whether precious folios or mass-market novels, intimate letters or schoolgirls' commonplace books, the texts women consumed, circulated, and created were also objects. These textual objects simultaneously created and drew meaning from the constellation of things that surrounded them: pulpits and lutes, writing desks and parlor tables, tambour hoops and curiosity cabinets. From the sixteenth through the eighteenth centuries, women's reading took shape in a remarkably rich material world. To apprehend the complexity of that world and its effect on reading, scholars must look beyond the transformations wrought by the consumer revolution writ large: they must do more than document the increasing numbers of titles available to women. After all, the objects that women and men read acquired meaning partly from the texts they contained and partly from their relation to other textual objects. An eighteenth-century Bible, for example, might signify both because of the Scripture it contained and because of its potential to counter the secular, eroticized worlds projected by novels and plays. However, as several contributors contend, textual objects also acquired meaning from and bestowed meaning upon artifacts not usually associated with reading. Their essays demonstrate that we can learn a great deal from exploring the connections between, say, learning to read a book and sewing a sampler or between assembling a curiosity cabinet and creating a commonplace book. Further, with women's reading, more surely even than with that of their male peers, not all textual objects were printed ones. Just as early modern women's writing circulated—or at least was recorded—more often in manuscript than in print, so women's experience of textuality often extended beyond the page itself. Texts that were sewn in samplers, engraved on rings, chalked on walls, and inscribed on trenchers constituted the beginnings of female literacy and rooted it in the domestic and material sphere. In an early modern world that was "paper-short" and in which the whitewashed domestic wall may well have been the "primary scene of writing" (and thus reading), we must look beyond the printed and even manuscript page for a full sense of textuality, literacy, and reading practice.[13]

Just as we cannot divorce the texts that women read from their material context, neither can we divorce reading from the social and cultural practices that surrounded it. Images of solitary women poring over devotional manuals or curled up with novels reflect some aspects of women's reading but certainly not all of them. In practice, women's reading was very often embedded in other practices. Most obviously, from the seventeenth century, the reading woman was associated with the shopping woman. By the eighteenth and early nineteenth centuries, the reading woman was positioned, however uneasily, alongside the writing woman. Even so, as the following essays suggest, women's reading emerged in concert with practices less frequently associated with reading in general and books in particular. Reading was bound up with performance, spectatorship, and listening. It resonated with collecting, painting, and embroidery. It prompted storytelling and translation as well as writing. Moreover, these practices were gendered in reciprocal ways. The *female* reader (be she wanton or judicious) was figured in relation to an equally *female* consumer or writer or needleworker.

The essays collected are clustered to explore three broad sets of questions generated by the historical emergence of women's reading as well as by contemporary efforts to recover the history of reading in general. The essays in "Pleasures and Prohibitions" focus both on women's contested access to a variety of texts and on how and why particular kinds of texts were deemed appropriate for female readers. In "Practices and Accomplishment" we turn our attention to the material and explicitly social dimensions of women's reading. The final section, "Translation and Authorship," raises questions about the relationship between different, and differently gendered, forms of reading and writing.

Notes

1. David Cressy, *Literacy and the Social Order: Reading in Tudor and Stuart England* (Cambridge: Cambridge University Press, 1980), graph 8.1. Cressy's equation of signing with literacy has been widely challenged, though scholars generally accept the narrative of progressively increasing literacy for women, always lagging behind their male peers. See Margaret W. Ferguson, *Dido's Daughters: Literacies and Ideologies of Empire in England and France, 1400–1690* (Chicago: University of Chicago Press, 2003); Frances Dolan, "Reading, Writing, and Other Crimes," in *Feminist Readings of Early Modern Culture: Emerging Subjects*, ed. Valerie Traub, M. Lindsay Kaplan, and Dympna Callaghan, (Cambridge: Cambridge University Press, 1996), 142–67; and Eve Rachelle Sanders, *Gender and Literacy on the Early Modern Stage* (Cambridge: Cambridge University Press, 1998). For figures on New England, see Kenneth Lockridge, *Literacy in Colonial New England: An Inquiry into the Social Context of Literacy in the Early Modern West* (New York: Norton, 1974); and Candy Gunther Brown, *The Word in the World: Evangelical Writing, Publishing, and Reading in America, 1789–1880* (Chapel Hill: University of North Carolina Press, 2004), 10. For useful corrections to Lockridge, see E. Jennifer Monaghan, "Literacy Instruction and Gender in Colonial New England," in *Reading in America: Literature and Social History*, ed. Cathy Davidson (London: Johns Hopkins University Press, 1989), 53–80; and David D. Hall, *Cultures of Print: Essays in the History of the Book* (Amherst: University of Massachusetts

Press, 1996), 172–73n9. For an articulation of the later obscuring of female literary production, see Pamela Joseph Benson and Victoria Kirkham, eds., *Strong Voices, Weak History: Early Women Writers and Canons in England, France, and Italy* (Ann Arbor: University of Michigan Press, 2005).

2. Janice Radway, *Reading the Romance: Women, Patriarchy, and Popular Literature* (Chapel Hill: University of North Carolina Press, 1984); Cathy N. Davidson, *Revolution and the Word: The Rise of the Novel in America* (Oxford: Oxford University Press, 1986).

3. David McKitterick, "Women and Their Books in Seventeenth-Century England: The Case of Elizabeth Puckering," *Library* 7.1 (2000): 359, 363; Kevin Sharpe, *Reading Revolutions: The Politics of Reading in Early Modern England* (New Haven, Conn.: Yale University Press, 2000), 297; Hall, *Cultures of Print*, 182. For an exceptional early attempt to open the field of women's reading, see Suzanne W. Hull, *Chaste, Silent and Obedient: English Books for Women, 1475–1640* (San Marino, Calif.: Huntington Library, 1982).

4. Claudia N. Thomas, *Alexander Pope and His Eighteenth-Century Women Readers* (Carbondale: Southern Illinois University Press, 1994), 16.

5. Virginia Woolf, *A Room of One's Own*, quoted in Margaret J. M. Ezell, *Writing Women's Literary History* (Baltimore: Johns Hopkins University Press, 1993), 66. For a useful overview of the dramatic recovery of early modern women writers, see Benson and Kirkham, *Strong Voices, Weak History*, 1–13. Also see Tina Krontiris, *Oppositional Voices: Women as Writers and Translators of Literature in the English Renaissance* (London: Routledge, 1992). For a history of the "soft canon" of American women writers, see Karen L. Kilcup, ed., *Soft Canons: American Women Writers and Masculine Tradition* (Iowa City: University of Iowa Press, 1999), 1–24.

6. Margaret Spufford, *Small Books and Pleasant Histories: Popular Fiction and Its Readership in Seventeenth-Century England* (Cambridge: Cambridge University Press, 1981), 21–22, 34–35; Ferguson, *Dido's Daughters*, 61–82, quotation on 81.

7. Elizabeth A. Flynn and Patrocinio P. Schweickart, eds., *Gender and Reading: Essays on Readers, Texts, and Contexts* (Baltimore: Johns Hopkins University Press, 1986), xiii–xiv.

8. Carla Kaplan, "Reading Feminist Readings: Recuperative Reading and the Silent Heroine of Feminist Criticism," in *Listening to Silences: New Essays in Feminist Criticism*, ed. Elaine Hedges and Shelley Fisher Fishkin (New York: Oxford University Press, 1994), 169–71. For a critical overview of the debate over "reading as woman," specifically the conflict between feminism and deconstruction, see Diana Fuss, "Reading Like a Feminist," in *The Essential Difference*, ed. Naomi Schor and Elizabeth Weed (Bloomington: Indiana University Press, 1994), 98–115.

9. Sandra M. Gilbert, Foreword to *Engendering the Word: Feminist Essays in Psychosexual Poetics*, ed. Temma F. Berg (Urbana: University of Illinois Press, 1989), xi.

10. Judith Fetterly, *The Resisting Reader: A Feminist Approach to American Fiction* (Bloomington: Indiana University Press, 1978).

11. On reading, print culture, and the construction of national identities, see Benedict Anderson, *Imagined Communities: Reflections on the Origin and Spread of Nationalism* (London: Verso, 1991). On the conceptualization of Atlantic history, see David Armitage, "Three Concepts of Atlantic History," in *The British Atlantic World, 1500–1800*, ed. David Armitage and Michael J. Braddick (New York: Palgrave Macmillan, 2002). Recent studies that attend to the movement of readers and texts include Elizabeth L. Eisenstein, *Grub Street Abroad: Aspects of the French*

Cosmopolitan Press from the Age of Louis XIV to the French Revolution (Oxford: Clarendon Press, 1992); Franco Moretti, *Atlas of the European Novel, 1800–1900* (London: Verso, 1998); Marian Rothstein, *Reading in the Renaissance: Amadis de Gaule and the Lessons of Memory* (Newark, Del.: University of Delaware Press, 1999); Paul Giles, *Transatlantic Insurrections: British Culture and the Formation of American Literature, 1730–1860* (Philadelphia: University of Pennsylvania Press, 2001); W. M. Verhoeven, ed., *Revolutionary Histories: Transatlantic Cultural Nationalism, 1775–1815* (Basingstoke: Palgrave, 2002); and Ralph Bauer, *The Cultural Geography of Colonial American Literatures: Empire, Travel, Modernity* (Cambridge: Cambridge University Press, 2003); and A. E. B. Coldiron, "Translation's Challenges to Critical Categories: Verses from French in the Early English Renaissance," *Yale Journal of Criticism* 16.2 (2003): 315–44.

12. For an introduction to and overview of the protean literature on consumption between 1500 and 1800, see John Brewer and Roy Porter, eds., *Consumption and the World of Goods* (London: Routledge, 1993); and esp. Ann Bermingham and John Brewer, eds., *The Consumption of Culture, 1600–1800: Image, Object, Text* (New York: Routledge, 1995). Recent studies have brought new precision to our understanding of the range of institutions that structured women's reading and of women's effect on those institutions. See, for example, Edith Snook, *Women's Reading and the Cultural Politics of Early Modern England* (Aldershot: Ashgate, 2005); Jacqueline Pearson, *Women's Reading in Britain, 1750–1835: A Dangerous Recreation* (Cambridge: Cambridge University Press, 1999); Patricia Howell Michaelson, *Speaking Volumes: Women, Reading, and Speech in the Age of Austen* (Stanford, Calif.: Stanford University Press 2002); and Suellen Diaconoff, *Through the Reading Glass: Women, Books and Sex in the French Enlightenment* (Albany: State University of New York Press, 2005).

13. Juliet Fleming, *Graffiti and the Writing Arts of Early Modern England* (Philadelphia: University of Pennsylvania Press, 2001), 9, 50.

Part I
Pleasures and Prohibitions

The prohibitions that helped define girls' and women's reading between 1500 and 1800 in Europe and America were nearly always founded on cultural attitudes that cast reading as powerful and potentially transformative. Sometimes, particularly in matters of religious controversy, this power was centered on the soul. Two laws enacted a century and an ocean apart reached opposite conclusions about women's appropriate relationship to the Bible, but they depended equally on the assumption that access to the English Bible was a critical matter of the soul. The 1543 Act for the Advancement of True Religion under Henry VIII criminalized the reading of the Tyndale Bible by most Englishwomen, allowing only gentlewomen to read to "themselves alone" but not to anyone else in their household. Conversely, in 1642 New England law required full literacy in English, even for "children & apprentices." More often, however, in prescriptive literature at least if not in law, prohibitions against female literacy and reading were based in the body and its many pleasures. As the essays in this section demonstrate, prescriptions do not, of course, always prevail, but they do usefully locate and describe a set of cultural anxieties and forces. Further, reading, whether it was transgressive or not, for many women constituted pleasure in many forms: sensual and erotic, surely, but also intellectual, material, social, and devotional.

Personal pleasures and cultural prohibitions intersected in the marketplace. Mary Ellen Lamb examines two opposing portraits of female readers—the frivolous consumer of romances and the pious reader of devotionals—that begin to define women's relationships with emergent capitalism. As they link romance reading, luxury goods, and sexual gratification, John Lyly and Philip Stubbes draw the caricatures against which women would define themselves as readers and consumers in a rapidly shifting consumer economy. The heightened attention to the trope of the erotically charged gentlewoman reader, voraciously consuming books and desiring sexual pleasures, posed a marketing challenge for authors and printers, for the sexualized female reader had now to be seduced, not merely satirized. The contrasting stereotype of the pious female reader also had a place in the market of print. Perhaps 40 percent of the increase in book production around 1600 was made up of Bibles and devotional texts. Women's self-defining through book consumption extended beyond the fashion of romances to the rewards of piety, promising the possibility of allowing women to entertain spiritual questions previously reserved for men and to elevate themselves above the commodification of gentlewomen readers at leisure.

Shakespeare may now seem an unlikely subject for anxiety about women's reading given more modern valuations of the cultural capital of his plays and their accessibility for his contemporaries as public performances. Yet, as Sasha Roberts explains, Shakespeare's narrative poems figure prominently in seventeenth-century articulations of the trope of women's reading as merely—and often dangerously—recreational. The records of women's unprecedented engagement with drama in Caroline England, however, show women disrupting these stereotypes and responding to plays much as male readers did. Conduct literature of the time therefore might best be taken, Roberts argues, as reactionary rather than formative. The targets of this prescriptive literature and of misogynist barbs in contemporary drama were often elite or otherwise privileged women. By no coincidence, these women were exercising new independence as consumers in the print marketplace, and by the 1640s printers no longer had any business overlooking women's participation in literary culture and the formation of theatrical taste.

The role of self-fashioning through reading and the participation of women in the formation of literary taste converge in Mary Kelley's study of women's reading in the final years of the eighteenth century and in the early Republic. As the number of books written and printed by Americans increased in these years, a monumental change in readers' sensibility occurred: reading shifted from a trope of eroticism and devotion to a symbol of enterprise. Whereas seventeenth-century women's reading in early America was concentrated on Scripture, eighteenth-century elite culture modeled girls' education on the literary training of their British peers, flooding their libraries with histories and belles lettres. Though the early modern anxieties about romances articulated by Lamb and Roberts persisted and focused on the emergent novel, young women now had regular access to a range of genres in circulating libraries, through literary societies, and at female seminaries. This generation of young women established sustaining connections to books through which they forged identities as readers and began to shape public opinion. While a father was still capable of reprimanding his daughter for reading Shakespeare on a Sunday, that daughter, Kelley shows us, was equally capable in the early Republic of appropriating such a text, playing out its scenes in her head, and fashioning herself through them long after she was sent to bed.

Chapter 1

Inventing the Early Modern Woman Reader through the World of Goods: Lyly's Gentlewoman Reader and Katherine Stubbes

Mary Ellen Lamb

This essay uses two contrasting stereotypes of the woman reader-consumer to explore the intermingling of appetites for romances, for sexual gratification, and for the consumption of luxury goods as described in the late sixteenth century. At opposite extremes as consumers, John Lyly's "gentlewoman reader" and Philip Stubbes's pious Katherine make visible a volatile mixture of cultural prohibitions and personal pleasures gendered as female yet also incorporating issues beyond those of gender. Within the ideologies of emergent capitalism, the reading of romances by women implied not only leisure time and culpable idleness but also the economic wherewithal to buy books of no practical value. Lyly portrays the desires of his gentlewoman reader as participating in her transgressive appetite for other useless luxury goods, such as decorative feathers, spoiled lapdogs, and sweet junkets. No less exaggerated was Stubbes's representation of his wife Katherine, whose devotional reading for the cultivation of her soul represented an implicit critique of bourgeois woman consumers who offered her a world of goods—fine food, prideful apparel, and plays. "Katherine Stubbes's" reading was as subject to her husband's control as was her consumption; and this much-published ideal of the devotional reader also represented a response to the anxieties and exhilarations attending the profusion of goods circulating within a consumerist economy.[1] Through the frivolous woman reader of romance and the sober reader of devout texts, respectively, both Lyly and Stubbes invent women's relationships with emergent capitalism. Displacing early modern anxieties over the increased circulation of goods onto women, both writers represent the dangerous freedom of self-definition possible to women through their reading as a metonym for the similarly dangerous freedom possible through their production of meanings from their modes of consumption. Through and against such stereotypes and the dilemmas they expose within an emergent capitalism, actual women readers would invent their own modes of consumption, of books as well as of goods.

The economist-historian Craig Muldrew has identified the last half of the sixteenth century in England as "the most intensely concentrated period of growth before the late eighteenth century"; in fact, "this process of change . . . was much more intense and problematic than in the eighteenth century."[2] As early as the middle of the sixteenth century, the rise in the accessibility of goods occurred rapidly enough to register a dramatic change within lived experience. This growth of a consumer economy had accelerated to full gear by the late sixteenth and early seventeenth centuries.[3] Aristocrats depleted ancestral wealth to embark on a frenzy of extravagant building projects during this period, and they freely adapted the international style of "paintings, sculpture, fountains, gardens, and triumphal arches" that were, as noted by Linda Levy Peck, so much a part of the "performance of royal and aristocratic power" in Europe.[4] The middling sort also accumulated material possessions within homes of a size and comfort far beyond the financial capacity of their parents.[5] As a contrasting response to this profusion of goods, those who followed Calvinist exhortations to moderate personal luxuries practiced an equally distinctive pattern of consumption as this easy access to goods elevated abstention, whether entirely voluntary or not, from the giddy indulgence in material things to a moral high ground.[6] Thus, for all but the poor this expanding quantity of goods offered, or seemed to offer, unprecedented opportunities for choice: to select not only which goods to consume but, more broadly, also a pattern of consumption. In this way emergent capitalism promised new ways, and a larger choice of ways, for early moderns to form themselves as subjects through the consumption as well as the production of goods.

On every social level, goods—clothing, food, and books—became part of an increasingly complex and inventive language of the self. As T. H. Breen has observed, for colonial America, consumer goods were "woven into a complex cultural conversation about the structure of colonial society" to become "the stuff of claims and counter-claims, of self-representation among people who understood the language of Holland shirts and neat nightcaps."[7] With the power to purchase came, in theory, the power to shape new identities. Breen states that "to make choices from among contending possibilities . . . to rely upon their own reason in making decisions, is in a word, to reconceptualize the entire social order."[8] It is no wonder, then, that conservative contemporaries condemned "sartorial anarchy" as threatening hierarchy, as English persons who chose to dress as "free-floating individuals" disturbed—or even rocked—early modern understandings of clothing ably described by Ann Rosalind Jones and Peter Stallybrass as investing a subject into a system of stable social relations.[9] The destabilizing effects of this power did not go unnoticed. From Philip Stubbes's *Anatomie of Abuses* to the Augustans described by Joyce Appleby, the goods displayed in "haberdashery shops and food stalls" became "dangerous signs of corruption and . . . social disintegration."[10]

Books figured prominently among the goods proliferating over the sixteenth century. Nigel Wheale computes 3,850 titles printed between 1558 and 1578; between 1580 and 1603 the number rose to 7,430. Bibles and other devout literature made up 40 percent of this increase, followed by literature, especially prose fiction and plays published in inexpensive quarto editions.[11] This flood of goods opened up the possibility that persons, including literate women, could be defined and define themselves not only by what they owned but also by what they read. Whether or not a market of women readers was already firmly in place by the late sixteenth century—and Jacqueline Pearson finds little hard evidence for significant recreational reading by women at that time—the book industry vigorously stepped up its appeals to women readers.[12] According to Suzanne Hull, books addressed to women readers reached a peak between 1570 and 1640, when 85 percent of the 163 books in 500 editions addressed to women were published.[13] The profound implications of this change for subject formation is at least as true in the early modern period as for the eighteenth century, as described by Joyce Appleby: "The study of consumption gives us a window on the elaboration of personal identity. This is as true of reading materials as clothes and furnishings—purchasing and enjoying artifacts of material culture involves a constant expression of self."[14] Whether only to herself or also to others, a woman defined herself by what she read—a sermon, a classical translation, or a prose romance—at least as much as by how she dressed, what she ate, or how she furnished her house.

As with other forms of consumption, this apparent freedom of self-definition evoked its own constraints. Even those who stood to profit, such as authors and workers in the print trade, often expressed deep ambivalence through the stereotypes they disseminated for the women reader-consumers of their wares. To address women as active readers was to imagine their ability to respond to texts, to produce interpretations of their reading, and to criticize the texts they read. Like the women playgoers described by Jean Howard, women readers became "licensed to look—and in a larger sense to judge what they saw and to exercise autonomy—in ways that problematised women's status as object within patriarchy."[15] As Helen Hackett notes, the woman reader-consumer also served as a screen for the light or supposedly degraded appetites of male readers.[16] Discourses of consumption categorized males who enjoyed the pleasures of nonpurposive reading as woman-like, or effeminate.[17] Thus, for men as for women, portrayals of the woman reader circulating within the early modern culture became a vehicle for linking discourses of gender to the anxieties—and the pleasures—of consumption.

While the erotic gentlewoman reader was not an early modern invention, she rose to special prominence in the book trade, where her pleasures were imagined as simultaneously sexual and commercial. The emerging genre of fiction in fact required the eroticized gentlewoman reader as a precondition for its writing.[18] Romances collected or written by William Painter, George Pettie, Robert Greene, and Sir Philip Sidney were explicitly dedicated to women, and some of these included direct and often flirtatious addresses to women readers within their texts.[19] Within the book trade anxious projections of unregulated desire onto women became the stuff fiscal dreams were made on. The intoxicating fantasy of the independently wealthy woman consumer, with her (almost) unregulated compulsion to buy the most trivial of goods, became translated into the gentlewoman reader of romance. Serving as a celebrity advertisement, her aristocratic status also offered a flattering subject position for readers of lower ranks. Her fantasized freedom from masculine control of her consumption easily flowed into a fantasy of free sexuality conforming to bourgeois misconceptions of the looser sexual mores of aristocrats. The eroticized gentlewoman reader became a blood relation to the unchaste reader of illicit texts condemned in conduct books. Denouncing chivalric romances, tales of Boccaccio and especially of Ovid, as threats to women's chastity, such texts as Luis Vives' much-published *Instruction of a Christen Woman* offered authors and publishers a thorough education in the promiscuous sexuality of women's textual pleasures.[20] Through the production of romances as a profitable commodity, the prohibitions of conduct books inhabited—took up permanent residence—within the pleasures of prose fiction. All that had changed was their use.

The stereotype of the eroticized gentlewoman reader drew from and also contributed to what Wendy Wall has termed a general "erotics of the commodified book" representing the printed text as a woman's body displayed like a harlot before the eyes of many male voyeur-readers.[21] The widescale displacement of the transgression of social boundaries as a transgression of sexual boundaries becomes even more comprehensible within a capitalist economy that consistently conflates the sexual and the social in the projection of its anxieties and pleasures on the woman consumer. This conflation of consumer and sexual desires, together gendered as female, adapted older classical and Christian discourses ascribing unregulated appetites for sex and for luxury goods as characteristic of those, namely women and effeminate men, lacking the proper masculine control of reason.[22] This continuing association of consumerism and eroticism in almost any modern advertisement—for cigarettes, automobiles, or Coca-Cola, for instance—extends beyond these older discourses to suggest an inherent homology within the experiences of consumption and consummation imagined within a capitalist economy even today.[23] A parallel between sexualized objects and commodities continues to serve as a fundamental trope of capitalism, from Marx's metaphor for commodities as unprotected women deserving rape to Madison Avenue's shameless and stunningly artistic objectification of persons as sexual commodities.[24] The early modern marketing of romances to gentlewomen readers, whether actual or figurative, bears striking similarities to modern ads displaying the evidently sexual pleasure enjoyed, for example, by young models drinking Coca-Cola. Consumers are invited to drink Coca-Cola and to read titillating prose romances, not because they are good for them—they know for a fact that they are bad for them—but because they promise, however absurdly, a superficial erotic fulfillment. Prefatory materials invested early modern books with just such "structures of meaning" as described by Martyn Lee as the function of advertising to create.[25] Yet, as workers in the book trade turned to conduct books to increase profits, powerful cultural discourses condemning those desires remained in place. The often degraded sexuality attributed to gentlewomen readers even in works offered for their purchase may represent an author's ambivalence, not only to the power of the woman consumer but also to the meaninglessness of the exchange, in which an author offers his wares to anonymous consumers he never sees. From this perspective, the simultaneous flattery and self-disgust characterizing the addresses of male authors of prose romances to their gentlewomen readers convey a prescient grasp of capitalism.

These highly gendered contradictions circulating around and within the evolving capitalist ideologies of the early modern period confronted authors of romances with difficult if not impossible marketing challenges. They must reverse a long tradition condemning women's taste for luxury in order to incite a desire to read (and to buy) a book that served little practical or educational purpose. They must present the culturally abhorrent figure of the sexual woman reader not to condemn her but to praise or even seduce her. They must share their awareness of these strategies with potential male readers without alienating women who might buy their books. They must mask their own aversion in the presentation of their work as a desirable commodity to be consumed by anonymous buyers. The curious ambivalence of John Lyly's letter to gentlewomen readers in *Euphues and His England* reveals one writer's struggle with these ideological and moral quandaries. In his much-quoted prefatory letter "To the Ladies and Gentlewoemen of England," Lyly markets this work as women's reading.[26] The extent to which Lyly defines his book as a salable good circulating within a capitalist system of exchange is indicated by the remarkable number of other consumable items listed in this letter: cloth of arras, "sundry silkes," a painting of Venus, sweet water, strawberries, hops, little dogs, junkets, napkins, a lady's casket, cloths and needles, a glass or mirror, a bowl of water serving as a mirror, a sleek stone for smoothing linen, silk ribbon, lawn head coverings, feathers in women's hats, frizzled hair, stomachers and guards, bracelets and bullets. Most of these wares mediate, in one way or another, the relationship between Lyly's book and the woman consumer. She is to read as she plays with her dog; she is to pass the book to her maid as she gives away sweet junkets she is too satiated to eat; she is to read instead of sew so that she will not prick her finger if she becomes sleepy. An implicit critique of aristocratic consumption lies concealed within these activities even as they are used to promote book sales.

The relatively recent rise of the household pet gives point to Lyly's reference to the lady's lapdog. Also referring to spoiled children, the term "pet" raised household animals to a quasi-human status. As Bruce Boehrer has observed, however, these "honorary human beings" were classed only with a "certain kind of human being . . . the pampered darling, the ornamental non-producer who is tolerated precisely because s/he cannot be taken too seriously."[27] Thus, in contrast to a working animal, a lapdog is valued exactly to the extent that it is incapable of performing productive labor. In this respect, the "pampered darling" that is the gentlewoman reader resembles her own lapdog, as does an aristocracy defined by its very freedom from the necessity of labor. Thus, implicit in Lyly's parallel is an acknowledgment of the essential triviality of his book, of the lady who reads it, and of the indolent consumption of goods by those who do not produce them. This critique continues in the gentlewoman reader's literal consumption of sweet junkets, an extravagant food of limited nourishment passed to her maid only after she has eaten her greedy fill. Lyly's advice to replace sewing with reading his book reflects the class-based meanings for aristocratic embroidery created by the expense of silk thread. Lyly's prediction that she will become sleepy, with his possible double entendre that she will then "prick" her finger, shows her distance from a cultural model of virtuous industry. As Jones and Stallybrass have pointed out, this "elite ideal" of feminine behavior obscured the very real labor of poorer women in the cloth trade.[28] This aristocratic ideal took on cultural meanings precisely in its difference from the productive labor of less privileged women. Yet

Lyly levels such distinctions by advertising his book as satisfying a common desire for flattery in women of all social groups. Even the poorest maidens show their "willingness to be pranked" by using a bowl of water to dress their hair and a pebble to smooth their garments.[29]

The consumer-driven form of authorship requiring Lyly to anticipate the unpredictable desires of his readers parallels similar developments in ideas of fashion. Explicitly paralleling the roles of author and woman's tailor, Lyly constructs his authorship in terms of the changing modes of consumption that reached high visibility in the fashions of the clothing trade. In the stable and patriarchal society under considerable pressure by Lyly's time, clothing reified appropriate categories of gender and class status that stressed continuity over time and within social groups. In this system tailors acted as significant purveyors of "the materials of memory" by which investiture signified a socially mediated identity literally put on with specific items of clothing.[30] Similarly, authoritative books of religious and classical learning were to inscribe cultural discourses on the tablets of the minds of docile readers. In pedagogical theory at least, books were to form their readers rather than to cater to their tastes.[31] Just as the decline in livery in favor of an ever-changing fashion allowed more individual choice in apparel, the rapid increase in printed books available across a wider range of social classes enabled individual readers to exert more choice in the books they bought. Authors, like tailors, became subject to the unpredictable whims of consumers, who were gendered as female because of their irrational and unregulated passions to buy.

Lyly's representation of his authorship in terms of the clothing trade becomes most self-deprecating in his parallel of his work to a feather: "There is nothing lyghter then a feather, yet is it sette a loft in a woemans hatte, nothing slighter then haire, yet is it most frisled in a Ladies head, so that I am in good hope, though their be nothing of lesse accounte then *Euphues*, yet shall he be marked with Ladies eyes, and lyked sometimes in their eares."[32] The placement of this feather, such as the one Lyly would have used for writing his text, in a woman's cap reduces the sign of Lyly's authorship to a mere fashion accessory. The woman reader's frizzled hair and feathered cap locate her modes of consumption within an emergent capitalist economy of changing fashion. Lyly's use of a feather, in particular, reveals his underlying critique by drawing into the text an array of vehement social messages. Philip Stubbes inveighed against feathers as a sign of women's mental instability: "These Fethers argue the lightnes of their fond imaginations, and plainly convince them of instabilitie and foly."[33] Jones and Stallybrass gather sources revealing the offense of women's feathers against gender norms: Gascoigne decried the masculine appearance of women who wore "high-copt hattes and fethers" in 1567; a 1619 *Sermon of Apparell* described the "halfe man halfe woman" as "wagging a feather to defie the world"; *Hic Mulier* (1620) defined the "man-woman" as wearing a hat with a "wanton feather."[34] Margaret Ferguson describes the feather as an item of exotica, a "superfluous thing," the kind of luxury item associated with sin and female desire, as mercantilist thinkers displaced their own anxieties about an expanding capitalist market on women.[35] These social meanings implicate Lyly's wish that his book be regarded as "of least account" as a feather in a woman's hat within an unstable, gender-bending, exotic capitalist economy in which a book, like a feather or even an author, is only a commodity for sale.

In another comparison of his book to an item of apparel, Lyly criticizes his readers' preference for luxurious but fragile lawn fabric as an example of bad consumerism characteristic of vain women with plenty of money to waste: "You chuse cloth that will weare whitest, not that will last longest, coulours that looke freshest, not that endure soundest, and I would you woulde read bookes that have more to shewe of pleasure, then ground of profit, then should Euphues be as often in your hands, being but a toy as Lawne on your heads, being but trash, the one will be scarce liked after once reading, and the other is worne out after the first washing."[36] In contemporary television experience, the juxtaposition of "cloth" and "whitest" and "coulours" and "freshest" brings to mind almost daily advertisements for detergents that promise to wash "whiter than white." Yet, if he were sitting in a modern living room, Lyly would disagree. Sound consumerism for early moderns was more concerned with the durability of the fabric. Rather than the refined appearance of an expensive lawn or linen scarf, a wise housewife would consider how *many* washings it can endure. In addition to the substantially higher price of fabrics in Lyly's day, there is another explanation for this difference: at the core of early modern capitalism lay a distrust of what is central to many modern advertisements—the ephemeral, the trivial, the simply pleasurable, in fabrics as in books. Like the insubstantial lawn scarf that dissolves after only one washing, this book cannot serve in its proper function as a bearer of cultural memory. Instead, it merely gives pleasure. Lyly's advertisement presents the pursuit of pleasure for its own sake, with little or no redeeming moral or intellectual value, as the special provenance of idle women with disposable income—in short, female consumers. Visually conflating white pages with a woman's white head covering, Lyly denigrates his book as a "toy," even as "trash" fit only for readers who value pleasure over profit—what would be called a beach book or airport reading in today's throw-away economy, in which the most insubstantial commodities accrue significant profits.

The flirtatious and even erotic pleasure Lyly offers his idle and frivolous women readers anticipates the superficial sexuality characterizing modern advertisements. Lyly's unctuous persona as an author-tailor, a salesman of trivial wares to even more trivial women, merges easily into that of a flattering seducer all too ready to please. To account for unstated material, he employs a risqué comparison between the "backside of the book" and the unseen "back" of a painted Venus. Lyly's invitation to place Euphues "often in your hands, being but a toy" delineates a sordid eroticism of phallic male passivity. The personified *Euphues* attempts to sell himself as a seductive sexual object: "Marked with Ladies eyes, and lyked somtimes in their eares." He is a plaything, a sexual toy, a gigolo. As this self-degradation suggests, beneath this bowing and scraping lurks a barely disguised hostility marking profound sexual anxieties emerging by the end of the letter: "But least I make my Epistle as you do your new found bracelets, endlesse, I wil frame it like a bullet, which is no sooner in the mould but it is made." It is necessary only to remember Gratiano's broad wink as he vows ever to keep safe Nerissa's "ring" at the end of Shakespeare's *Merchant of Venice* to construe the vaginal referentiality of women's bracelets. Lyly's binary between bracelets and purposeful directionality of the male bullet eroticizes linguistic differences by locating them within the genitals. His proposed binary between bullets and bracelets does not hold. Not only do his wandering sentences and elaborate similes resemble bracelets more than bullets but also, in the terms of Lyly's description, even the purposive and masculine bullet is formed by a uteruslike mold.

As understood within this context of emerging capitalism, this pleasure Lyly offers to his gentlewoman reader operates, finally, as a form of prohibition. The conflation of her reading pleasure with eroticized consumer pleasures closes off in advance any serious meanings she might derive from his text. In a mutually constitutive relationship between objects and subjects, the eroticized female reader, with her frizzled hair and feathered hat, has herself become a trivial commodity. As long as she buys the book, what she thinks of it, by definition, can have no significance. This prohibition of any deep or active engagement with his text functions as a defense against the pressure exerted by the growing market of women readers who took their reading seriously and judged books according to the tastes and opinions of their own independent subjectivities.

Lyly's highly ambivalent presentation of the fashionable women consumers of an emergent capitalism prepares for their rejection in "Euphues Glass for Europe," which calls into visibility a very different form of reader. Holding up his book as a "glass" revealing their faults, he urges his supposedly decadent readers of Greece and Rome to reform their reading habits by imitating the pious woman reader of

England. Despite their alleged country of origin, the striking resemblances between these non-English women to the gentlewoman reader of Lyly's preface reveal Lyly's own readers as the objects of criticism: "Imitat the Englysh Damoselles, who have theyr bookes tyed to theyr gyrdles, not fethers, who are as cunning in ye scriptures, as you are in *Ariosto* or *Petrarck* or anye booke that lyketh you best, and becommeth you worst."[37] The substitution of books for feathers is particularly indicative of the pious woman reader's refusal of her power as a consumer and her conformity to a conservative gender ideology. Even more indicative is her substitution of books: she reads Scriptures rather than prose romances by Ariosto, Petrarch, or, as it is implied, by Lyly. Yet even in this image, books are treated as fashion accessories. Englishwomen are imagined as wearing them, not reading them. They are strikingly differentiated from the women consumer-readers of Lyly's preface by their attitude toward clothing: "Yet do they not use theyr apperell so nicelye as you in *Italy*, who thinke scorn to kneele at service, for feare of wrinckles in your silks, who dare not lift up your head to heaven, for feare of rumpling ye rufs in your neck, yet your hands I confess are holden up, rather I thinke to shewe your ringes, then to manifest your righteousnesse."

The contrasts between these women readers are structured not only on what they read—Scripture as opposed to prose romances—but also on their mode of consuming goods. Within a capitalist system, clothing has come to signify differently. Rather than instituting a world of lived relations, rich clothing signifies only itself, deriving its value from its surface appearance rather than from the deeper social relationships it should encode. In this critique Lyly brilliantly adapts Protestant aspersions on Catholics, represented here as Italian women, for an inappropriate attention to the external marks of piety, void of any deep feeling of internal grace. Catholic women provide a screen for the real object of Lyly's critique: reader-consumers as likely to be English as Italian or Protestant as Catholic. Deprived of full interiority of religious devotion, the woman consumer thinks only on her silks, her ruffs, her rings even in the act of prayer. Her expensive clothing brings her anxiety and physical discomfort: she fears that kneeling will crease her dress and she fears that holding her head up will rumple her ruff. Rings, on the other hand, are a different matter, and she holds up her hands to show them off rather than to enact a gesture of religious praise. In both her concern and her vanity she manifests a deep level of ontological anxiety that precludes any felt expression of religious devotion. In Jean Baudrillard's terms, her obsession with physical beauty valorizes an exteriority reducing the body to an object through signs, such as jewelry and cosmetics, that rewrite a cultural order on the body; controlled by capitalism by this means, the body becomes itself a source of alienation for the individual.[38] In early modern terms, she has lost her soul.

The consumer-woman prayer is, of course, as much a caricature as is the consumer-woman reader. Rather than reflecting any actual women, her function is ideological, to co-opt or to shut down the power of the woman consumer. Yet the consumer-woman prayer also expresses some very real issues elicited by capitalism beyond issues of gender. While ontological anxiety expressed by vanity of apparel was scarcely invented by capitalism, the anxieties as well as exhilarations of purchasing and displaying goods were surely intensified as individuals attempted to fashion themselves according to what their money could buy. While there were pious women readers in the medieval period, the early modern book trade offered the opportunities to a larger number of women to enhance their religious interiority by reading devotional texts that provided relief from the disturbing currents and crosscurrents set in motion by capitalist consumption. Prohibition—the refusal to consume luxury goods—came to offer a sense of inner peace, of self-justification, and even its own form of pleasure. Philip Stubbes's *Anatomie of Abuses* describes the peaceful abstention enjoyed by the virtuous Christian woman who, like the Englishwomen in Lyly's "Glass," spurns extravagant clothing in exchange for "ornaments of the mind."[39]

As a tenet of humanist philosophy as well as reformed religion, this dichotomy between an ornate exterior and a profound interior had become commonplace by the late sixteenth century. What sets Stubbes's *Anatomie* apart from other texts is his intimate knowledge of the consumer market. This attack on women's apparel, for example, is notable for its specific information on current fashion, including the prices of cloth: "If the whole gowne be not silke or velvet, then the same shall be layed with lace, two or three fingers broade, all over the gowne or els the most parte. Or if not so . . . then it must be garded with great gardes of velvet, foure or six fingers broad at the least."[40] In his extensive censures of the commonwealth of "Ailgna," or England, Stubbes denounces fashions of both genders, with detailed descriptions of ruffs, hats, doublets, hose, shoes, cloaks, and swords. Meticulous attention to the very objects and practices Stubbes demonizes reveals his barely controlled fascination with goods: the great ruffs smeared in the "devil's liquore" or starch or three or four layers of minor ruffes "placed *gradatim*, step by step beneath another"; doublets made with "wings, welts, and pinions on the shoulder points"; kyrtles bordered with "gards, lace, fringe"; slippers of black, white, green, or yellow velvet, or made of English or Spanish leather, "stitched with silk and imbroidered with Gold, and silver all over the foote."[41] The slightest turn of tone transforms Stubbes's descriptions from censures to advertisements. The sheer intensity of Stubbes's interest complicates Max Weber's delineation of early modern Puritanism. According to Weber, Puritanism fostered capitalism by justifying the accumulation of wealth as the sign of diligence in one's "calling" or vocation. Directions to shun idleness in a life of prayer and productive labor limited amounts of expenditures from this earned affluence in entertainment and self-display. Wealth was not an evil in itself but only as a "temptation to idleness and sinful enjoyment of life."[42]

Among various challenges to Weber's influential theory, Simon Schama's study of the early modern Netherlands argues that, rather than relieving capitalism of its bad conscience, prosperity induced anxieties that the "drowning surfeit" of material success became itself a warning of a spiritual enemy within. According to Schama, "riches seemed to provoke their own discomfort, and affluence cohabited with anxiety."[43] Stubbes's simultaneous fascination with and denunciation of material goods develops further insights into this "enemy within." As the *Anatomie* sets out in loving detail the items of apparel to be despised, the desires to consume that are simultaneously incited and condemned suggest a reversal in the causal relationship between a severe form of Protestantism and capitalism. It was the influx of commercial goods that created an opportunity to increase the watchfulness and self-control at the center of reformed spirituality. Whether elicited by the widespread display of goods in shops or those goods on the persons of urban consumers, Stubbes's detailed knowledge of silvered slippers embroidered with gold suggests an impulse to yield to unregulated consumption familiar to subjects of capitalism in all centuries. The sensation of nonsatiation—of wanting yet more—must have been particularly unsettling when it was still new and strange. It was this very desirability of goods that raised the practice of self-disciplined consumption to a defining virtue. While Jean-Christophe Agnew reminds scholars not to overestimate their numbers or the extent of their conformity,[44] the expanded access to goods provided at least some Puritans with an opportunity to find not only social affiliation but also inner peace. They could use their distinctive pattern of consumption to allay the anxiety accompanying wealth. This pleasure in turning away from an abundant array of goods to find assurance in an identity as God's elect constituted an unexpected dividend provided by a paradoxically beneficent capitalism.

This dividend extended to books. Stubbes concludes his *Anatomie* with an impassioned complaint against the "reading of wicked books," which were "invented . . . by Belzebub, written by Lucifer, licensed by Pluto, printed by Cerberus and set a broche to sale by the infernal furies themselves to the poysning of the whole world."[45] Like other objects of disordered consumption, books enact a pride that destroys not only immortal souls but also the commonwealth. Like Lyly, Stubbes projects issues of consumption onto women readers. If his *Anatomie of Abuses* represents his critique of contemporary society, *A Christall Glasse for Christian Women* provides a positive model for women's behavior modeled on his representation of Katherine, his recently deceased wife. Like Lyly's "Euphues Glass for Europe," *A Christall Glasse* constructs devout reading as an active refusal of the pleasures of consumption, portrayed no doubt accurately as ever-present temptations to this woman of the rising urban bourgeoisie. Signifying her rejection of the worldly "thinges of this life," the act of reading distinguished "Katherine Stubbes" from her more materialistic, worldly women neighbors: "And also little given was shee to this world, that some of her neighbours marvailing why she was no more carefull of it, would aske her sometimes, saying: Mistress Stubbes, why are you no more carefull for the thinges of this life, but sitte alwaies poaring upon a booke, and reading? To whome shee would answere, If I should be a friend unto this world, I should be an enemie unto God: for God and the world are two contraries . . . Christ biddeth me, first seeke the Kingdome of Heaven."[46] "Katherine Stubbes's" reading represents only one of several demonstrations of her antipathy for the world that threatened the integrity of her soul outside her threshold. By enacting an ethic of nonconsumption, "Katherine Stubbes" embodied a silent critique of the new bourgeois woman consumer, here personified as "the dearest friend in the world," tempting her to pleasures: "When her husband was abroad in London, or elsewhere, there was not the dearest friend in the world that could get her abroad to dinner or supper, or to plaies or enterludes, nor to any other pastimes, or disports whosoever: neither was she given to pamper her body with delicate meats, wine or strong drink . . . she utterly abhored all kind of pryde as well of apparell as other wise."[47] In her refusal to consume the worldly pleasures outside her door, "Katherine Stubbes" disciplined the desires so frivolously indulged by her neighbors, constructed by the same discourses of consumption as Lyly's gentlewoman reader. Demonstrating the self-regulation possible to a woman, "Katherine's" virtuous example only confirmed the dangers of the uncontrolled consumption inherent in an emerging capitalist system.

"Katherine Stubbes's" rejection of the world and its commodities reaches extreme form in her desire for death. As the source of her doctrinal knowledge, "Katherine Stubbes's" reading becomes part of this rejection. Displaying the fruits of her pious reading on her deathbed, "Katherine Stubbes" expounds at length and with unswerving accuracy a corpus of intricate doctrines justified, and fixed in some final form, by her death. She enacts the most profound version of anticonsumption as she rejects her husband, her newborn, and her own body as material goods to be despised. Like her neighbors, they are all too much of this world. Kissing her baby, she proclaims to her husband, "I forsake him, you, and all the world, yea, and mine own selfe, and esteeme all things but dung."[48]

While not enough is known of the actual Katherine to assess her husband's accuracy, Philip Stubbes's representation of his wife's brief life and death became a pivotal point in the shaping of the ideology of the Protestant woman reader.[49] The popularity of *A Christall Glasse* points up the deep irony that pious books advocating an ethic of regulated consumption became even more profitable commodities than prose romances. The successful marketing of the devout "Katherine Stubbes" demonstrates the irreverently value-free capacity of the capitalist impulse to appropriate even what would seem to oppose its most basic structure. As Wheale has observed, Bibles and other religious works constituted the largest number of titles published during Elizabeth I's reign.[50] In particular, *A Christall Glasse* went through some twenty-four editions between 1591 and 1635 to become an early modern best-seller.[51] Piety had become big business. The extraordinary popularity of *A Christall Glasse* created the figure of "Katherine Stubbes" not only as a powerful cultural ideal but also as a marketable commodity. Not only through dying but also through buying books and reading them, Protestant women could, like Katherine Stubbes, enact their rejection of a world abundantly and even oppressively present in the floods of goods into urban centers and beyond. Sara Mendelson has described how the piety of devout women of the gentry class came to resemble "a kind of self-imposed career," for, as Diane Willen has aptly noted, "Denied the status of the Puritan divine, women might seek the greater status of Puritan saint."[52] Within their own households women could participate within a spirituality previously reserved for those "set apart": for nuns in a convent and for saints in a desert. The need for guidance in this formidable task of achieving a disciplined and saintly Puritan life created an active market for spiritual how-to books. Translating abstract doctrines into directions for daily life—how much to eat, what to wear, what recreations are lawful—William Perkins' useful *Treatise of Conscience* was one of numerous books that promptly met this new consumer demand for texts of spiritual self-improvement.[53]

The market appeal of this heroics of reading was compelling. The buying of religious works of theology provided not only sanctity but also justification based on the knowledge of doctrine. Their election confirmed by their ability to discern the correct doctrine among many confusing alternatives, Protestant women could, like "Katherine Stubbes," navigate the troubled waters of doctrine with assurance. Even if they were not empowered to preach, they were empowered to know. If only to themselves, ordinary women readers could occupy themselves with matters of abstruse doctrine previously reserved for men. Even if they had not learned Latin or received a university education, ordinary women could educate themselves in the only knowledge that really counted for the survival of their immortal souls. The implications of this form of uncompromising intellectual heroics of reading were obvious, and obviously dangerous. Uncontrolled, the reading of "Katherine Stubbes" threatened to become a radical act, in the same way that the empowerment of other lay readers to read and to interpret Scripture split the Anglican Church and finally the realm. There was a thin line between the education of women readers to be passive recipients of the authority of texts written by men and the authorization of women as active readers empowered by their religious fervor for the correct doctrines necessary for election. Devout reading promised, or threatened, to elevate women above the commodity status to which gentlewomen readers were relegated.

A Christall Glasse negotiates this dangerous potentiality within a women's heroics of reading in various ways. The authority of "Katherine Stubbes" was contained by her imminent death, by her isolation within the household, and especially by her husband's intervention in her reading. In his representation of his wife as the ideal Protestant woman reader, Stubbes succinctly juxtaposes the reformist encouragement to women to read devout texts with the familiar warning to submit to their husbands as their spiritual teachers: "She followed the Commandement of our Saviour Christ, who biddeth us search the scriptures, for in them you hope to have eternall life. She obeyed the commandement of the Apostle, who biddeth women to be silent, and to learne of their husbands at home."[54]

A Christall Glasse pushes the submission of "Katherine Stubbes" to her husband beyond this Pauline directive. Rather than drawing her own conclusions from her reading, "Katherine Stubbes" repeatedly refers questions of interpretation to the judgment of her husband: "She would spend her time in conferring, talking and reasoning with her Husband of the Word of God, and of Religion, asking him what is the sense of this place, and what is the sense of that? How expound you this place, and how expound you that? What observe you of this place, and what observe you of that?"[55] The very number of these questions she asks betrays a nervous exaggeration concerning the possibility of bringing her reading into complete conformity with her husband's.

Even confined within the household, women's reading of devotional tracts posed a potential threat to the gendered hierarchy of the Protestant marriage. In the early seventeenth century William Heale delineated a stereotype of religious women readers as domineering or even shrewish in their relationships with their husbands. Reading religious works had empowered rather than contained these women, whom Heale criticizes as "too too holy women-gospellers, who weare their testament at their apron-strings" for catechizing and even preaching to their husbands.[56] William Gouge's usually conservative conduct book *Of Domesticall Duties* allowed a wife's noncompliance with her husband's demands because of "scruples" for religious or moral reasons, at least in matters of "no great consequence." Gouge advises that if the husband cannot convince her, then when possible he "ought . . . to forbeare to presse her conscience."[57] Yet, Gouge also stresses repeatedly the subordination of wives even to unworthy husbands, and R. Valerie Lucas argues that this emphasis on women's willing subjection describes a culture disturbed by the presence of nonconforming wives.[58] Akiko Kusunoke has claimed that disobedience, at least in religious matters, may have been in fact a direct result of the Puritan emphasis on the individual conscience, which encouraged women to develop "a sense of self in relation to God."[59] This development of an individual self was reinforced by the practice of private reading. According to Roger Chartier, the privatization of reading was "undeniably one of the major cultural developments of the early modern era," for in liberating readers "from the control of the group," silent reading made it possible "to cultivate an inner life."[60] Thus, women who read religious texts silently at home were perhaps more, rather than less, likely to disagree with their husbands, especially about matters concerning their souls. Whatever the piety of these women readers or the writers who wrote for them, the commercial values of the book trade treated them as an increasingly lucrative market.

Lyly's frivolous readers decked out in feathers and frizzled hair and Philip Stubbes's unworldly "Katherine" who wished only for death—both caricatures express powerful and formative cultural discourses. The consumption of these discourses, like individual readings of books, yet allowed considerable personal agency. Michel de Certeau's insistence on the agency of the consumer informs his eloquent description of reading as a form of "silent production," with the "drift across the page," the "improvisation and expectation of meanings," the inventions of memory.[61] This silent production of personal meaning applies to the act as well as the content of reading. From airport reading to reading to a young child to studying for an exam, the meaning of each act of reading determines the speed, concentration, and significance of the process. De Certeau has represented reading as poaching, the free appropriation of an author's ideas for a reader's own purposes. However, readers are also poached, not through the tyrannous imposition of authorial agendas but through the customary modes of a reader's use of the books her mind inhabits. Books number importantly among the myriad of tools through which persons form themselves; and like any familiar tool, books also form people, not as transcendent containers of abstract thought but as material objects that are picked up and put down, forgotten on dusty shelves, and lovingly tucked within oversized chairs.[62]

What, then, might an early modern woman have been communicating to others as she picked up a particular book? What cultural categories of gender or class might she have been challenging? Alone in their closets or in their gardens, what did their act of reading mean to these women? How did they define themselves to themselves as they read? Did an old and much-read book take on deeper significances for an early modern woman than a new book did? Or did a new sermon or romance take on value in its novelty? Did the act of reading also change over a woman's lifetime?[63] Consumers use goods in unpredictably inventive ways as aspects of their own self-invention. These ways are not entirely divorced from the consumers' culture, but neither are they entirely determined by any one cultural discourse. In the early modern period, the figures of fashionable women readers and pious women readers alike were designed to shut down the individual and serious meanings the women could derive from texts. However, the creative uses of these figures, and the discourses that inform them, by such women readers as Isabella Whitney, Aemilia Lanyer, and Anne Clifford to create meanings—from their texts and from their lives—were undoubtedly as impressive as they were varied.[64]

Notes

I wish to thank Heidi Brayman Hackel, who organized the conference "Emergence of the Female Reader, 1500–1800," and the other speakers whose ideas were so useful to my own. I also thank Jean Howard for providing me a copy of her then unpublished paper, now appearing as "The Evidence of Fiction: Women's Relationship to Goods in London City Drama," in *Culture and Change: Attending to Early Modern Women,* ed. Margaret Mikesell and Adele Seeff (Newark: University of Delaware Press, 2003), 161–76.

1. I use quotation marks around "Katherine Stubbes" to indicate a probable difference between this stereotype and the actual wife of Philip Stubbes.

2. Craig Muldrew, *The Economy of Obligation: The Culture of Credit and Social Relations in Early Modern England* (Houndsmills: Macmillan, 1998), 20–21.

3. For early modern increases and other valuable insights into early modern consumption, see Linda Levy Peck, *Consuming Splendor* (Cambridge: Cambridge University Press, 2005); Ann Rosalind Jones and Peter Stallybrass, *Renaissance Clothing and the Materials of Memory* (Cambridge: Cambridge University Press, 2000), 17–23; introduction and essays in Lena Cowen Orlin, ed., *Material London, ca. 1600* (Philadelphia: University of Pennsylvania Press, 2000); John Brewer and Roy Porter, eds., *Consumption and the World of Goods* (New York and London:

Routledge, 1993), esp. Peter Burke, "*Res et verba:* Conspicuous Consumption in the Early Modern World," 148–81, and Carole Shammas, "Changes in English and Anglo-American Consumption from 1550 to 1880," 177–205. See also Lisa Jardine, *Worldly Goods: A New History of the Renaissance* (New York: Doubleday, 1996); Fernand Braudel, *Civilization and Capitalism, 15th to 18th Century,* vol. 1, *The Structures of Everyday Life,* trans. S. Reynolds (Berkeley and Los Angeles: University of California Press, 1992), 183–265 (food and drink), 266–333 (houses, clothes, fashion); Karen Newman, *Fashioning Femininity and English Renaissance Drama* (Chicago: University of Chicago Press, 1991), 111–27; Chandra Mukerji, *From Graven Images: Patterns of Modern Materialism* (New York: Columbia University Press, 1983); Keith Wrightson, *English Society, 1580–1680* (New Brunswick, N.J.: Rutgers University Press, 1982), 171–81; Lawrence Stone, *Crisis of the Aristocracy, 1558–1641 (Abridged)* (Oxford: Oxford University Press, 1967), 86–95, 249–67; Joan Thirsk, *Economic Policy and Projects: The Development of a Consumer Society in Early Modern England* (Oxford: Clarendon Press, 1978). Thomas Smith, *Discourse of the Commonweal* (London, 1549), 64, represents the sudden growth of shops.

4. Linda Levy Peck, "Building, Buying, and Collecting in London 1600–1625," in *Material London, ca. 1600,* 284.

5. Lena Cowen Orlin, *Private Matters and Public Culture in Post-Reformation England* (Ithaca, N.Y.: Cornell University Press, 1994), 255; Thirsk, *Economic Policy and Projects,* 106–32.

6. Philip Stubbes, *The Anatomie of Abuses* (London, 1583).

7. T. H. Breen, "The Meanings of Things: Interpreting Consumer Economy in the Eighteenth Century," in *Consumption and the World of Goods,* 250.

8. Ibid., 257.

9. Jones and Stallybrass, *Renaissance Clothing,* 5.

10. Joyce Appleby, "Consumption in Early Modern Social Thought," in *Consumption and the World of Goods,* 163.

11. Nigel Wheale, *Writing and Society: Literacy, Print and Politics in Britain, 1590–1660* (London: Routledge, 1999), 56.

12. Jacqueline Pearson, "Women Reading, Reading Women," in *Women and Literature in Britain, 1500–1700,* ed. Helen Wilcox (Cambridge: Cambridge University Press, 1996), 83; Helen Hackett, *Women and Romance Fiction in the English Renaissance* (Cambridge: Cambridge University Press, 2000), 7–9; Wheale, *Writing and Society,* 56. Suzanne W. Hull, *Chaste, Silent, and Obedient: English Books for Women, 1475–1640* (San Marino, Calif.: Huntington Library, 1982), 1. Low estimates of women's literacy by David Cressy, *Literacy and the Social Order* (Cambridge: Cambridge University Press, 1980), 145, have been challenged by Margaret Spufford, *Small Books and Pleasant Histories* (Athens: University of Georgia Press, 1982), 22.

13. Hull, *Chaste, Silent, and Obedient,* 1.

14. Appleby, "Consumption," 172.

15. Jean Howard, *The Stage and Social Struggle in Early Modern England* (New York and London: Routledge, 1994), 79.

16. Hackett, *Women and Romance Fiction,* 11.

17. John Sekora, *Luxury: The Concept in Western Thought, Eden to Smollett* (Baltimore: Johns Hopkins University Press, 1977), 40–44, discusses a seminal classical tradition associating excessive consumption and effeminacy. For men's reading of "ladies' texts," see Juliet Fleming, "The Ladies' Man and the Age of Elizabeth," in *Sexuality and Gender in Early Modern Europe,* ed. James Grantham Turner (Cambridge: Cambridge University Press, 1993), 158–81.

18. Fleming, "Ladies' Man," 158. See also Helen Hackett, "'Yet Tell Me Some Such Fiction': Lady Mary Wroth's *Urania* and the 'Femininity' of Romance," in *Women, Texts, and Histories, 1575–1760*, ed. Clare Brant and Diane Purkiss (London and New York: Routledge, 1992), 40. The eroticized woman reader is ably discussed by Sasha Roberts, "Reading Not in a Room of Her Own: The Trope of the Eroticized Woman Reader," in *Renaissance Configurations: Voices/Bodies/Spaces, 1580–1690*, ed. Gordon McMullan (New York: St. Martins Press, 1998), 30–63; and Eve Rachele Sanders, "Interiority and the Letter in *Cymbeline*," *Critical Survey* 12.2 (2000): 49–70.

19. Addresses to imagined women readers are discussed by Caroline Lucas, *Writing for Women: The Example of Woman as Reader in Elizabethan Romance* (Philadelphia: Open University Press, 1989); Fleming, "Ladies' Man"; Hackett, *Women and Romance*; and Mary Ellen Lamb, *Gender and Authorship in the Sidney Circle* (Madison: University of Wisconsin Press, 1990), 72–115.

20. Luis Juan Vives, *Instruction of a Christen Woman*, trans. Richard Hyrde (London, 1585), E1v. See Pearson, "Women Reading, Reading Women," 91; Hackett, *Women and Romance*, 10; and Linda Woodbridge, *Women and the English Renaissance: Literature and the Nature of Womankind, 1540–1620* (Brighton: Harvester, 1984), 117.

21. Wendy Wall, *The Imprint of Gender: Authorship and Publication in the English Renaissance* (Ithaca, N.Y.: Cornell University Press, 1993), 202.

22. Sekora, *Luxury*, 40–44. See also Michel Foucault, *The Use of Pleasure*, vol. 2 of *The History of Sexuality*, trans. Robert Hurley (New York: Vintage Books, 1986), 84–85, for an influential classical technique of the self. This suspicious view of luxury is one extreme; a somewhat more moderate view also present in the early modern period has been discussed by Peck, *Consuming Splendor*, 6–11.

23. Ian Archer, "Material Londoners?," in *Material London, ca. 1600*, 186, notes that for early moderns "the desire for goods was linked with sexual desire" in the Christian tradition. For postmoderns, Jean-Francois Lyotard, *The Libidinal Economy*, trans. Iain Hamilton Grant (London: Athlone Press, 1993), invents a more abstract model in the libidinal fragment served by money in the *jouissance* of capital.

24. Karl Marx, *Das Kapital: A Critique of Political Economy*, ed. Frederich Engels and condensed by Serge Levitsky (Washington, D.C.: Regnery Publ., 2000), 196.

25. Martyn Lee, *Consumer Culture Reborn: The Cultural Politics of Consumption* (New York and London: Routledge, 1993), 17.

26. See, for example, Hackett, *Women and Romance*, 76–83; Lori Humphrey Newcomb, *Reading Popular Romance in Early Modern England* (New York: Columbia University Press, 2001), 45; Lucas, *Writing for Women*, 47. Quotations from Lyly's work are from *Euphues and His England*, in *The Complete Works of John Lyly*, ed. R. Warwick Bond (1902; Oxford: Clarendon Press, 1967), 2:1–230; quotations from the prefatory letter "To the Ladies and Gentlewoemen of England" are from 2:8–10.

27. Bruce Boehrer, "Shylock and the Rise of the Household Pet: Thinking Social Exclusion in *The Merchant of Venice*," *Shakespeare Quarterly* 50.2 (1999): 154.

28. Jones and Stallybrass, *Renaissance Clothing*, 103.

29. The ideological functions of the poor woman or the maid-reader, emerging soon after this time, are ably discussed by Newcomb, *Reading Popular Romance*, 1–5, 89–90.

30. Jones and Stallybrass, *Renaissance Clothing*, title and intro., 1–15.

31. Mary Thomas Crane, *Framing Authority: Sayings, Self, and Society in Sixteenth-Century England* (Princeton, N.J.: Princeton University Press, 1993), 8, 53–76.

32. Hackett, *Women and Romance,* 77, ably discusses "linked concepts of idleness, fashion, folly and flightiness" personified as female in these passages; the quotation is from Lyly, *Euphues and His England,* 10.

33. Stubbes, *Anatomie,* D8^{r}.

34. Jones and Stallybrass, *Renaissance Clothing,* 79.

35. Margaret Ferguson, "Feathers and Flies: Aphra Behn and the Seventeenth Century Trade in Exotica," in *Subject and Object in Renaissance Culture,* ed. Margreta de Grazia, Maureen Quilligan, and Peter Stallybrass, Cambridge Studies in Renaissance Literature and Culture, 8 (Cambridge: Cambridge University Press, 1996), 242.

36. Lyly, *Complete Works,* 2:9–10. In the following discussion, all quotations from this prefatory letter will be taken from 8–10.

37. Ibid., 2:199. In the following discussion, quotations are taken from this page.

38. Jean Baudrillard, *For a Critique of the Political Economy of the Sign,* trans. Charles Levin (St. Louis: Telos Press, 1981), 94–101.

39. Stubbes, *Anatomie,* G4^{r}.

40. Ibid., F6^{r}.

41. Ibid., F4^{v}–F5^{v}, F8^{r}.

42. Max Weber, *The Protestant Ethic and the Spirit of Capitalism,* trans. Talcott Parsons (1930; London: Routledge, 1992), 163.

43. Simon Schama, *The Embarrassment of Riches* (New York: Knopf, 1987), 124, 326. For other criticisms of Weber's influential theory, see Fernand Braudel, *Civilization and Capitalism, 15th to 18th Century,* vol. 2, *Wheels of Commerce,* trans. S. Reynolds (New York: HarperCollins, 1983), 570, which locates the rise of capitalism in material factors in a Protestant northern Europe. Jean-Christophe Agnew, *Worlds Apart: The Market and the Theater in Anglo-American Thought, 1550–1750* (Cambridge: Cambridge University Press, 1986), 23, questions widespread conformity to ascetic principles as early modern capitalists "saved *and* spent, and in doing so, ushered in modernity."

44. Agnew, *Worlds Apart,* 23.

45. Stubbes, *Anatomie,* P7^{r-v}.

46. Philip Stubbes, *A Christall Glasse* (London, 1591), A3^{r}-A3^{v}.

47. Ibid., A3^{r}.

48. Ibid., B1^{r}.

49. See Suzanne Trill, "Religion and the Construction of Femininity," in *Women and Literature in Britain, 1500–1700,* 35.

50. Wheale, *Writing and Society,* 56.

51. A. W. Pollard and G. R. Redgrave, *A Short Title Catalogue of Books Printed in England, Scotland, and Ireland, 1475–1640,* 2d ed. (London: Bibliographical Society, 1976), 370–71.

52. Sara Mendelson, "Stuart Women's Diaries and Occasional Memoirs," in *Women in English Society, 1500–1800,* ed. Mary Prior (London: Methuen, 1985), 189; Diane Willen, "Godly Women in Early Modern England: Puritanism and Gender," *Journal of Ecclesiastical History* 43 (1992): 563.

53. William Perkins, *Treatise of Conscience* (London, 1606), 551, 579, 583.

54. Stubbes, *Christall Glasse,* A2^{v}.

55. Ibid.

56. William Heale, *Apologie for Women* (Oxford, 1609), 35–36. Akiko Kusu-

noke, " 'Their Testament at Their Apron-strings': The Representation of Puritan Women in Early Seventeenth-Century England," in *Gloriana's Face: Women, Public and Private in the English Renaissance,* ed. S. P. Cerasano and Marion Wynne-Davies (Detroit: Wayne State University Press, 1992), 185–204, ably discusses this passage.

57. William Gouge, *Of Domesticall Duties* (London, 1620), 376–77.

58. R. Valerie Lucas, "Puritan Preaching and the Politics of the Family," in *The Renaissance Englishwoman in Print: Counterbalancing the Canon,* ed. Anne M. Haselkorn and Betty S. Travitsky (Amherst: University of Massachusetts Press, 1990), 232.

59. Kusunoke, "Their Testament," 188.

60. Roger Chartier, "Reading Practices," in *A History of a Private Life,* vol. 3, *Passions of the Renaissance* (Cambridge: Harvard University Press, 1989), 116, 125.

61. Michel de Certeau, *The Practice of Everyday Life* (Berkeley and Los Angeles: University of California Press, 1984), xxi.

62. For an important interrogation of the primacy of the subject over the object, see the introduction and essays in *Subject and Object in Renaissance Culture.*

63. These questions reflect insights by Mary Douglas and Baron Isherwood, *The World of Goods: Towards an Anthropology of Consumption* (1979; London: Routledge, 1996), ix, 38–45, for whom goods form a means of constituting an intelligible universe to confirm or challenge categories of culture; by Colin Campbell, "Understanding Traditional and Modern Patterns of Consumption in 18th-Century England: A Character-Action Approach," in *Consumption and the World of Goods,* 40–57, who stresses the subjective use of goods for self-definition as opposed to communication; and by Arjun Appadurai, "Introduction: Commodities and the Politics of Value," in *The Social Life of Things: Commodities in a Cultural Perspective,* ed. Arjun Appadurai (Cambridge: Cambridge University Press, 1986), who traces the lives of goods changing over time. Janice Radway, *Reading the Romance: Women, Patriarchy, and Popular Tradition* (Chapel Hill: University of North Carolina Press, 1982), led the way for the study of the act of reading, as opposed to the focus on the content of books, in her study of women readers of Harlequin romances.

64. I am exploring these and other women readers in terms of discourses of consumption in my current book project, with the working title "Early Modern Women Readers and the Consumption of Goods."

Chapter 2

Engendering the Female Reader: Women's Recreational Reading of Shakespeare in Early Modern England

SASHA ROBERTS

Shifting Grounds of Gender and Genre

In the context of early modern women's reading, gender is a surprisingly problematic category of critical analysis—both definitive and reductive, enabling and restricting. The example of women reading Shakespeare in Caroline England (1625–49) is a pertinent example: if on the one hand we can observe practices of "engendering" in rhetorical constructions of women's reading of Shakespeare, on the other hand the scattered traces of early modern women's reading not only counter such practices but, crucially, also prompt questions about what it means to understand their reading under the organizing rubric of gender. This is not to ignore or slight fundamental gender discrimination in the early modern period, especially in terms of *access* to literary culture and texts. To be sure, men far outnumber women as named owners or autographers of Shakespeare volumes in the seventeenth century.[1] However, the devil lies in the details, and what so often remains undetailed in the historical record of women's reading is the extent to which gender makes a difference *at the level of interpretation.* As David McKitterick puts it, "the question insistently poses itself: how was women's reading distinctive?"[2]

In this essay I want to pursue McKitterick's question by exploring two key arguments: first, since rhetorical constructions of early modern women's reading are confounded at every turn by historical practice, the prohibitions against and stereotypes of women readers promulgated in conduct literature can best be understood as reactionary, not formative; second, the formation of women's reading is intimately—indeed, fundamentally—mediated by genre. In turn, issues of genre are mediated by chronology; thus, a finely calibrated history of women's reading—

including its distinctiveness or otherwise—will pay careful attention to how specific genres developed, consolidated, and declined in specific periods.

Of course, at the level of rhetorical representation women's reading was insistently figured as profoundly distinct from men's. When in the 1640s Richard Brome playfully remarked that "Ladies . . . never look / But in a Poem or in a Play-book," and then only "scrible down / When such a Lord or fashion came to Town" in the volume's margins, he was reiterating an already worn trope of women's reading as merely recreational, directed at pleasure, not intellectual or spiritual profit.[3] In fact, men were also voracious readers of recreational literature in early modern England; indeed, the most extensive libraries of recreational literature belonged to men in the period: Sir Robert Gordon of Gordonstoun (1580–1656), for instance, owned more than 60 French romances, while Edward, the second viscount of Conway (1594–1665), held some 343 romances and 350 English plays in his library.[4] Yet, the trivialization of women's recreational reading was, and remains still, a remarkably enduring trope, marking a continuum from the prohibitions of sixteenth-century humanist educators to the parodies of eighteenth-century women's reading of gothic fiction to the dismissal of sensationalist novellas reputedly read by breathless Victorian women.

Behind these continuities lie more complex questions of chronology that the case study can illuminate. My particular concern is with the chronological conjunction of the emergence of the woman reader of Shakespeare and the consolidation of English "dramatic poesy" (drama) as a genre in Caroline England. In the broad sweep of early modern England, the period of the 1620s–40s represents a turning point for the woman reader of drama, and of "recreational" literature (especially plays, poetry, and romances) more widely. By the 1630s women had gained unprecedented visibility as producers and consumers in print culture. Maureen Bell's analysis of the emergence in 1510–1640 of "female literature" in print (recreational literature, practical guides, and devotional works addressed to women, and titles on the "woman" controversy) demonstrates that the 1630s saw the highest increase in publication of first editions of "female literature."[5] This was followed in the 1640s by a surge in women's published writings (especially religious prophecies), while by 1641 no fewer than 773 women had dedications addressed to them in published British books.[6] In keeping with this wider picture, not only are there more records relating to women reading Shakespeare from the 1630s than for any other decade before the late seventeenth century but also they encompass a more extensive range of sources than for any previous decade—from conduct literature to marginal traces of gentlewomen readers to passing commentaries by women. Further, these records not only disrupt conventional stereotypes (both early modern and modern) of women's literary activity; they also reveal women working in ways analogous to male readers and sometimes alongside them, and they point to the possibilities of women's engagement with mainstream literary culture. As such they prompt me to rethink the question of what exactly it means to read as a woman.

Disrupting the Rhetoric of Conduct Literature

Before the civil wars *Venus and Adonis* was more closely associated with women readers than any other Shakespearean work. This was not simply on account of the narrative poem's popularity in the period (it was Shakespeare's "best-selling" work before the civil wars, reaching sixteen editions by 1638); the poem's Ovidian origins, repeated use of bawdy innuendo, and salacious subject matter—an older woman lusting after and dominating a young man—swiftly earned *Venus and Adonis* a reputation as a wanton work. Hence, early allusions to male readers of *Venus and Adonis* frequently stressed the use of the poem by young men either for titillation or as a seduction manual.[7] Women, however, were predictably characterized as vulnerable to the erotic temptations of *Venus and Adonis*, unable to impose self-restraint when reading the poem, especially in private beyond the supervision of their husbands and fathers.[8]

In Jacobean comedy and satire the trope of the eroticized woman reader of *Venus and Adonis* was deployed largely for comic or satirical effect—as in Thomas Middleton's *A Mad World My Masters* (1608), in which the cuckold Master Harebrain ridiculously attempts to regulate his wife's reading of the poem and other "wanton pamphlets," or John Davies of Hereford's titillating account of "the coyest Dames" reading the poem's "bawdy Geare" for their "Closset-games," included in satirical verses against the print trade pandering to the lowest common denominator.[9] However, in the 1630s the trope took a new turn when conduct writers deployed *Venus and Adonis* as a troubling exemplum of women's illicit reading habits. Thus, Richard Brathwaite in *The English Gentlewoman* (1631) warns his gentlewomen readers that "*Venus* and *Adonis* are unfitting Conforts [*sic*] for a Ladies bosome," and in *The English Gentleman* (1630) laments that women carry about "(even in their naked Bosomes, where chastest desires should only lodge) the amorous toyes of *Venus* and *Adonis*," while in *Amanda or the Reformed Whore* (1635 and 1639) Thomas Cranley's fictional prostitute Amanda keeps a copy of *Venus and Adonis* alongside other "amorous Pamphlets" on a shelf "close underneath" her bed.[10]

With John Johnson's publication of his *Academy of Love Describing ye*

Folly of Younge Men and ye Fallacy of Women (1641), the temperature was raised still higher on the trope of the eroticized woman reader of Shakespeare. The vice chancellor Cupid takes Johnson on a tour of "Loves Library," where his female, sexually "liberall arts" students (13) read romantic and erotic works for "recreation"—including Philip Sidney's *Arcadia*, the works of the 1630s dramatists Philip Massinger and "shaving" James Shirley, and "*Shakespeere*, who (as *Cupid* informed me) creepes into the womens closets about bedtime, and if it were not for some of the old out-of-date Grandames (who are set over the rest as their tutoresses) the young sparkish Girles would read *Shakespeere* day and night, so that they would open the Booke or Tome, and the men with a Fescue [bookmark] in their hands should point to the Verse" (99). Johnson's dream narrative extends the titillating potential of Brathwaite's anxious vision of women holding Shakespeare to their "naked Bosomes"; here tonal control cannot be sustained within the discourse of conduct literature. However, Johnson was also working with an established and eroticized trope of the collegiate woman who was both intellectually and sexually forward. Hence the collegiate ladies in Ben Jonson's *Epicoene* (1609) not only manipulate their sexual favors (especially to their own husbands) but also "censure poets and authors and styles, and compare 'em, Daniel with Spenser, Jonson with tother youth [Shakespeare], and so forth"; as such, argues John Pitcher, they become "disturbing hybrids, women with too much male in them."[11]

The woman reader of Shakespeare was not simply co-opted as a key player in ostensibly scandalous scenes of sexual and textual intimacy. She was repeatedly figured as elite: Johnson's female students of Massinger, Shirley, and Shakespeare have sufficient "lands [to be] mortgaged" and "annuities consumed" (16); Wenceslaus Hollar's frontispiece to *The Academy of Love* depicts a throng of gentlemen and gentlewomen in the elegant environs of a classically styled banqueting hall; Richard Brathwaite addresses himself to "gentlewomen" readers; even the prostitute Amanda parades as a gentlewoman. However, policing the lifestyles of the gentry and the aristocracy was never going to be easy. Indeed, like so much conduct literature, Brathwaite's views may best be regarded not as formative of behavioral norms but as *reactionary* in mode—hence his lament in *The English Gentlewoman* that it is precisely "*this latter age* [my italics] in mine opinion, [that] deserved just reproofe. Education is a second Nature, and this hath given that freedome to women, as they may . . . pass a whole afternoone in a Bay-window, in Congies, Courtsies, and other useless *Compliments*" (63–64).

Of course, it is not only educational but also economic freedom at stake here. The rhetorical prohibitions against privileged women reading Shakespeare for pleasure could not turn the tide of women's increasing independence within an expanding literary marketplace. And thus, for all its withering reductiveness, the trope of the eroticized woman reader of Shakespeare assumes that gentlewomen were independent consumers of books. Indeed, it could be argued that the inexorable logic of the marketplace superceded that of patriarchal control over women's reading—at least in the case of *Venus and Adonis*. Hence by 1640 we witness precisely the commodification of *Venus and Adonis* for the female reader, with lines from the poem culled as suitable "complements" for use by "Ladyes, Gentlewomen, Schollers, and Strangers" in the printed commonplace book *The Academy of Complements* (1640). As Mary Ellen Lamb suggests, when the publishing industry expanded into new markets and audiences, it "attempted to rehabilitate the promiscuous reader into a 'fair lady,' an elite and discerning gentlewoman reader."[12] Turning to the scattered traces of women reading Shakespeare in Caroline England is to confront precisely what conduct literature habitually denies women: literary discernment and judgment.

Women and Literary Discernment: The Counterexamples of Gentlewomen Readers

If *Epicoene*'s equation of women's literary discrimination with sexual manipulation was controversial in 1609, it was quite out of step by the 1630s. John Pitcher suggests that *Epicoene*'s "disturbing hybrids" speak to Jonson's "real unhappiness [with] women voicing any opinions at all (a silent woman would be a miracle), and most men in Elizabethan and Jacobean society would have concurred," but this generalization cannot be sustained; as Pitcher concedes, "there was not much chance that intelligent women who had read English poetry and drama would take Venus or Cressida or Cleopatra as their role models, but they might well come to expect the men in their lives, particularly their suitors in marriage, to have read Shakespeare or Chaucer."[13] We can take this argument further: instead of serving only to *differentiate* between men's and women's reading, in certain contexts playbooks and poetry may be regarded precisely as a point of *connection* between men and women readers—think of Dorothy Osborne debating the merits of Ovid, Calprenède, and Madeleine de Scudery, among others, with Sir William Temple in the 1650s.[14] We get a sense of this in the c. 1626 account by Richard James, a Fellow of Christ Church College Oxford, that a "young Gentle Lady" who "read ye works of Shakespeare made me this question. how Sr. John Oldcastel Faslstaffe or Fastalf, as he is written in ye Statute book of Maudlin Colledge in Oxford . . . could be dead in ye time of Harrie ye fift, and agin live in ye time of Harrie ye Sixt to be banished for cowardize." The allusion suggests a discerning woman reader with a keen attention to Shakespeare's anachronistic chronology (and a possible familiarity with Magdalen College, Oxford) whose reading of Shakespeare becomes the occasion for the exchange of ideas.[15] Indeed, Jonson engaged in the exchange of literary and theatrical ideas with women when working on masques at the courts of Anna of Denmark and Henrietta Maria, closet drama for the Newcastle-Cavendish family, and occasional lyric poems. As is so often the case, the workings of literary culture complicate the work of literary tropes.

In stark contrast to the limiting assumptions of the long-established genre of conduct literature, the nascent genre of English literary criticism that emerged from the later sixteenth century conceived gentlewomen as, not least, able and discerning readers of vernacular literature: George Puttenham's *Arte of English Poesie* (1589), for instance, was not only dedicated to Elizabeth I but also directly addressed the literary ambitions of gentlewomen readers; while Dudley North's *A Forest of Varieties* (1645) rightly assumed the sustained literary engagement of his dedicatee, Lady Mary Wroth.[16] In addition, literary discernment is precisely what exercised Anne, Lady Southwell, in a rare piece of women's literary criticism before the civil wars: her epistolary defense of poetry addressed as a letter "To my worthy Muse, the Ladye Ridgway" (Cicely, Lady Ridgway, a maid of honor to Elizabeth I and later countess of Londonderry), transcribed in a folio manuscript miscellany of "The workes of the Lady Ann Sothwell Decem: 2 1626."[17] Southwell speculates that Lady Ridgway's hostility to poetry can be blamed in part on the erotic verse of Shakespeare and Marlowe: "I will take vppon mee to knowe, what hath soe distasted your palate against this banquett of soules, devine Poesye. Some wanton Venus or Adonis hath bene cast before your chast eares, whose euill attyre, disgracing this beautiful nimph, hath unworthyd her in your opinion. . . . To heare a Hero & Leander or some such other busy nothing, might bee a meanes to skandalize this art. But can a cloud disgrace the summer? will you behold Poesye in perfect beautye."[18] While Southwell concurs with the likes of Brathwaite that *Venus and Adonis* makes unsuitable reading for chaste women, the site of anxiety in Southwell's "letter" is not the chastity of the woman reader but the status of divine poesy itself; further, Southwell does not let a man speak for her but trusts in her own authority as a discerning judge of literature. In fact, given Southwell's familiarity with the work of John Donne, the urbane humor of her likely contributions to the rhetorical game of "Newes" played out in Thomas Overbury's *A Wife, now a Widow* (1614), and her dexterous command of rhetorical tropes in her own literary writing, her rejection here of amorous poetry may well be tinged with irony.[19] Even so, her *professed* distaste for Shakespeare's poem was not apparently shared by another mid-seventeenth-century gentlewoman,

Frances Wolfreston, and the differences between these two women's approaches to *Venus and Adonis* are instructive—a pertinent reminder of how early modern women readers from the same social class might bring contrasting interests and agendas to their reading.

The unusually extensive library of Frances Wolfreston (1607–77) at Statfold Hall, Staffordshire, both conforms to and denies contemporary stereotypes of women's reading matter. On the one hand, it is noted for its sheer volume of so-called recreational reading matter—plays by the likes of George Chapman, Thomas Dekker, Thomas Heywood, Marlowe, Massinger, and Shirley; poetry by Donne, Michael Drayton, Robert Greene, George Gascoigne, and George Wither; and no fewer than ten Shakespeare quartos. On the other hand, over half of Wolfreston's library was devoted to works of history, politics, theology, medicine, and languages.[20] Among her Shakespeare quartos was the only surviving copy of the first quarto of *Venus and Adonis*, now in the Bodleian Library (Bodleian Arch. G.e.31), which Wolfreston clearly claimed for herself in her autograph on its title page: "frances wolf hor bouk." There is no evidence that Wolfreston's piety or respectability was compromised by her ownership of *Venus and Adonis*; rather, her autograph in the volume, the pains she took in her will to preserve her book collection, and the very fact of the volume's survival indicate otherwise.

In fact, there is good reason to suggest that Wolfreston took an active interest in precisely the most notorious bawdy passage of Shakespeare's poem: Venus's description of her body as an erotic landscape (ll. 229–40). Wolfreston rarely annotated her books, but in her copy of *Venus and Adonis* are faded vertical lines in the margin (not visible in facsimile) marking passages of the printed text; although we cannot be sure that Wolfreston was the annotator, she remains the most compelling candidate since no other readers have autographed the volume and the annotations are written in an ink similar to Wolfreston's autograph and appear to date from the same period. One of the annotations is a line running the length of lines 221–34 in the poem, culminating in Venus's blazon of her body as a park to be explored by the roving Adonis: "Graze on my lips, and if those hills be dry, / Stray lower, where the pleasant fountaines lie" (ll. 231–34; sig. C1^{v}). On this and the facing page there are also several ink blots (sigs. C1^{v}–C2^{r}); clearly this bawdy passage in the poem that so intrigued contemporary commentators also caught the annotator's interest. Significantly, it is not unique among annotations to Wolfreston's books: in her copy of the printed commonplace book *Englands Helicon* (1600) she wrote "[sa]me tune" against "The Shepheards Song of *Venus* and *Adonis*" attributed to Henry Constable—a reference to the "tune of crimson ueluet," which she had recorded against the previous lyric (I. G.'s "Faire *Phillis* and her Shepheard").[21] Like Shakespeare's poem, Constable's "Song" features an assertive, sexually controlling Venus and a coy Adonis; indeed, with its close verbal echoes, Constable's "Song" has been suggested as a possible source for Shakespeare's poem.[22] Aside from "Faire *Phillis*," Wolfreston did not appear to annotate any other poem in her copy of *Englands Helicon*; evidently Constable's "Song" had particular appeal for her. If, on the one hand, it may be simply a matter of coincidence that Wolfreston owned and perhaps marked both Shakespeare's and Constable's poems on Venus and Adonis, on the other hand, her possible engagement with two poems so resolutely focused on Venus's sexual assertiveness goes to show how early modern women were as intrigued as men by the literary portrayal of rampant, lustful women. Images of women that we might assume appealed to a male readership or audience nonetheless found female consumers.

Wolfreston's annotations are unusual: as Heidi Brayman Hackel points out, "the scarcity of women's marginalia"—perhaps because of the combined ideological pressures on and trivialization of women's reading, the practice of aural reading, or the habit of reading away from a desk or table—"poses an obstacle in the recovery of women's reading practices."[23] Even so, Wolfreston's marginalia counters Brome's image of women's marginalia as mere gossip-and-fashion scribbling, for in her annotations Wolfreston emerges as a careful, active, and critical reader interested in the workings of character and plot—a reader with her own creative responses to the texts in front of her. Thus, she wrote an approving note on Thomas Heywood's *Second Part of the Iron Age* (1632), remarked on R. Mead's *Combat of Love and Friendship* (1654) "a very prity one, all of love & copells of lovers," and wrote out a detailed plot summary of John Ford's *Love's Sacrifice* (1633).[24] She evidently took an interest in the debate on women, owning reprints of Joseph Swetnam's *The Arraignment of Lewd, Idle, Froward and Unconstant Women* (1645), Philip Stubbes's *A Christall Glasse for Christian Women* (1646), and I. A.'s *The Good Womans Champion; or, A Defence for the Weaker Vessell* (1650?), on which she wrote "frances wolfreston her book / in prais of wemen a good one"—suggesting her endorsement of the tract's criticism of antifeminist literature and, more speculatively, pointing to the possibility of her resistant or oppositional reading of other works in her library, such as Swetnam's *Arraignment* or John Taylor's *Divers Crab-Tree Lectures* (sig. A3^r).[25]

On the one hand, this profile of annotations conforms to the notion that women's reading was distinctive in being centered on "female literature" and recreational reading matter: Wolfreston, after all, appears to respond to the representation of a woman (Venus), to the debate on women, and to plays and poems on men and women in love. Indeed, we might posit for Wolfreston what Richard Levin advances for early modern women at the theater: "what might be called the gender-concern or even gender-loyalty of women spectators."[26] However, this is not the whole story, for the verses she added on "caine and dauid" to the back flyleaf to Charles Hammond's apocalyptic *The World's Timely Warning Piece* (1660)—a Fifth Monarchist chapbook lamenting the recent "Wars . . . the brother betraying the brother" (9)—address the unequal dispensation of political justice: "Was justes equall? Was her ballens even / When Cain was punished, David was forgiven . . . ?"[27] Given Royalist attempts to claim Charles as another King David, Wolfreston's verses attacking David's "giltt" and "plott" of "homicide" take on an anti-Royalist edge. Wolfreston concludes by drawing a personal moral: "if I lament my sins: thou wilt forbeare / to punish Lord." As Gerald MacLean has argued, Wolfreston applies "national politics to herself by reading against the grain of Stuart propaganda"; in so doing she authorizes herself as "a political subject in her own right"—an instance perhaps of how sectarian discourse of the 1640s and 1650s enabled women to construct themselves as social and historical agents.[28] Here spiritual concerns and political loyalties dominate; it seems less helpful to speak of Wolfreston reading as a woman than reading as an anti-Royalist or as a Christian. As Maureen Bell points out for women's writing, "so great is the variety of kinds of writing produced by women that it is reasonable to question the extent to which women writers can be seen as a 'group' at all: arguably their primary identifications and alliances were to do with class or religious/political positions, rather than gender."[29] We need also to admit that variety—and its methodological consequences—in the field of women's reading.

If, through the exercise of literary judgment, Southwell and Wolfreston variously disrupt contemporary notions about the indiscriminancy of women's recreational reading, Lady Anne Merrick's allusion to Shakespeare further complicates the gendered dynamics of recreational reading. In her letter of January 21, 1638, to Mrs. Lydall, written from Wrest Park near Silsoe in Bedfordshire, Merrick laments "howe lonelie and solitarie the countrie at this tyme is, soe tedious indeede to me" and wishes that she could join Mrs. Lydall in London "to see the Alchymist, which I heare this tearme is reviv'd, and the new playe a friend of mine sent to Sr John Sucklyng and Tom Carew (the best witts of the time) to correct. But for want of these gentile recreations, I must content my selfe here with the studie of Shackspeare, and the historie of woemen, all my countrie librarie."[30] Since the noun "*study*" denoted attentive reading and reflection directed at learning or literary composition (*Oxford English Dictionary* [hereafter *OED*]), it seems reasonable to suppose Anne Merrick's *intensive* reading of "Shackspeare"—perhaps finding pragmatic or moral sententiae, attending to matters of style, or analyzing the organizing structure(s) of a work.

We do not know what copy of "Shackspeare" Merrick was reading (although "studie" is arguably suggestive of a Folio edition), but the "historie of woemen" she alludes to is probably a reference to Heywood's *Gunaikeion: Or, Nine Bookes of Various History Concerninge Women* (1624), which inaugurated a significant niche for Heywood as a writer on women's history, long after the first publication of his earlier drama. Heywood's *Gunaikeion* assumes a readership interested in women's cultural agency and literary production, with examples of women "famous either for Valour or Beautie," for "masculine Vertue" or learning—including one of the earliest citations of a canon of (aristocratic) women's writing, "Of women excellent in Poetrie" (which includes the "ingenious" Mary Wroth and the "learned" Mary Sidney).[31] *Gunaikeion* would make for fascinating intertextual "studie" alongside "Shackspeare," but Shakespeare and Heywood cannot compass the world: Merrick's emphasis here is on the limitations of "my countrie librarie" and the "tedious" restrictions her environment placed on her literary and theatrical "recreations." In this respect reading Shakespeare in the country becomes emblematic of restriction—and perhaps, given Merrick's keen assessment of current writers, of old-fashioned taste.

Yet, this narrative of limitation needs rethinking. Merrick demonstrates her engagement with urbane literary culture in the letter—as a reader, a playgoer, and a critic of literature confident in her own judgment of who are "the best witts of the time." As with the "young Gentle lady" intrigued by Shakespeare's chronology, Anne, Lady Southwell's judgment of divine poesy, and Frances Wolfreston's annotations to her books, it is hard to press for a conclusive narrative of gender distinctiveness out of Merrick's act of literary discernment. Further, Merrick's "recreations" suggest not only gentility ("gentile recreations") but also theatrical exchange between men and women ("the new playe a friend of mine sent" to Suckling and Carew). Indeed, Wrest Park offered the opportunity to develop that engagement: in 1638 it was the property of Henry, Lord Grey de Ruthin and Earl of Kent, husband to Elizabeth Grey, née Lady Elizabeth Talbot (1582–1651), a significant literary patron in the period. By the 1620s Elizabeth and her husband spent much of their time at Wrest Park, where Elizabeth successfully cultivated a circle that included John Selden (to whom she eventually left her fortune), Robert Cotton, and Thomas Carew. Indeed, Sir John Suckling wrote that "in my Lady *Kents* well-being much of ours consists," while Carew's "To My Friend G.N. from Wrest" celebrates the lack of pretension, hospitality, and sociability at Wrest Park: "Nor think [that] Wrest of narrowness complains / Or straitened walls; for she more numerous trains / Of noble guests daily receives . . . Than prouder piles" (ll. 47–53).[32] The coincidence of Merrick's engagement with Suckling and Carew alongside Elizabeth Grey's in the same period in the same house strongly suggests that Merrick may have had access to Elizabeth's literary circle; consequently, we should pay more attention to the operations of irony in Merrick's letter and, perhaps, to the modifier "howe lonelie and solitarie the countrie *at this tyme is*" (late January was, after all, out of season). By the 1640s the wily stationer could no longer afford to ignore what Merrick's letter registers: the *participation* of women in literary and theatrical culture.

Engendering the Woman Reader of Drama in Caroline England

Historical narratives of early modern women's reading are often shaped by exclusion, not participation. This is far from surprising in the context of the humanist curriculum and institutional centers of learning and reading—although even here women's axiomatic exclusion as readers is punctuated by counterexamples of (for instance) early modern women writing and exchanging Latin verse.[33] The shifting ground of women and drama in the Caroline period—of gender and genre—constitutes something more than counterexample, however; it marks a turning point, a wider change, albeit for the privileged few. In addition, since change so often muddies the waters, the positioning of women and drama in the 1620s–40s is fraught with complex conjunctions and disjunctions of exclusion and participation—complexities that also figure the woman reader of Shakespeare in the period.

What Maureen Bell observes for print culture at large Sophie Tomlinson also finds for theatrical culture: "the increasing cultural visibility of women, specifically in the domain of theatrical performance," by the 1630s. As a consequence, Caroline drama demonstrates "a new attitude towards female theatricality, hitherto a focus of ambivalence in Renaissance drama and English culture in general."[34] Such "theatricality" was centered on the court of Henrietta Maria, whose sponsored masques all date to the 1630s (*Chloridia*, 1631; *Tempe Restored*, 1632; *The Temple of Love*, 1635): as Julie Sanders notes, while Anne of Denmark and her court women participated in court masques and entertainments, Henrietta Maria "shifted the parameters of female performance in the late 1620s [by] importing French courtly conventions to Whitehall," speaking and dancing in court drama and performing, with her ladies-in-waiting, both male and female roles. "These were consciously transgressive, consciously ground-breaking actions and performances," argues Sanders, making "gender and performance [a] topic of high cultural currency"—witnessed in a cluster of plays from the period that addressed the issue of women and performance (Jonson, *The New Inn*, 1629; Massinger, *The City Madam*, 1632; Shirley, *The Bird in a Cage*, 1633) and William Prynne's mammoth antitheatrical tract *Histriomastix* (1633), which both struck out against the monstrous pile of paper wasted by the proliferation of books and famously equated women actresses with "Notorious Whores" in the index (for which, assumed to be a slur against the queen, Prynne's ears were consequently cut off).[35]

Moreover, the role of women as *consumers* of drama intensified in the Caroline period, entailing an unprecedented investment in women's literary taste and wit. Michael Neill argues that "the emergence of women, especially as an important constituent of the courtly audience, was probably a more important factor in shaping Caroline taste" than the influence of Inns of Court men was, and he credits that constituency of women with "the emergence of a distinctive kind of Caroline heroine, remarkable for her constancy, courage, and lofty dignity" (as in Massinger's Pulcheria from his 1631 *The Emperor of the East* and the line of Ford heroines from his 1630s plays). Similarly, Richard Levin argues for "the increasing importance of upper-class women as arbiters of taste" in the Caroline theater: hence prologues and epilogues in plays of the period make direct appeals to women, such as the prologue to James Shirley's *The Coronation* (1635) celebrating "noble Gentlewomen" as "first within my thoughts. . . . As free, and high Commissioners of wit"—a sentiment Shirley repeats in the prologue to *The Imposture* (1640) assuring the "Ladies" that "In all his Poems, you have been his care"—or the epilogue to Richard Brome's *The Court Beggar* (c. 1639), appealing to the "Ladyes" for their "suffrages [For] th'humble Poet. Tis in you to save / Him, from the rigorous censure of the rest."[36]

Within the space of a few decades, print culture responded to such shifts in theatrical culture. Despite the implied range of its readership, the prefatory matter to the 1623 Shakespeare First Folio makes no reference to women readers: instead the Folio is presented, as was the 1616 Jonson Folio before it, in terms of an exchange of work between men. By 1647 with the publication of the Beaumont and Fletcher Folio this all changes: a neat marker of the emergence of the woman reader of drama in the Caroline period, and as such a useful counterpoint by which to read allusions to women reading Shakespeare in the period. Thus, in his address from "The Stationer to the Readers" Humphrey Moseley indicates the importance of a female readership for drama, explaining that he limited the Folio to previously unpublished plays because to include reprints "would have rendred the Booke so Voluminous, that *Ladies* and *Gentlewomen* would have found it scarce manageable, who in Workes of this nature must first be remembred." For Peter Blayney, "an unqualified 'must be remembred' might have been simple gallantry, but 'must *first* be remembred' suggests that Moseley envisaged a readership in which women outnumbered men."[37]

Certainly there are examples of women reading large numbers of playbooks from the mid-seventeenth century: as David McKitterick notes, for instance, in the 1650s Elizabeth Puckering paid "particular attention to printed drama, as Humphrey Moseley pursued his policy of issuing new as well as old plays" and amassed a considerable collection of printed drama (which probably included the Second Folio of Shakespeare).[38] Even so, as Marta Straznicky points out, Moseley's address remains addressed to "Gentlemen," whom he characterizes as more intellectually discerning, widely read, and commercially empowered than ladies: "besides," he continues, "I considered those Former pieces had been so long printed and re-printed, that many Gentlemen were already furnished; and I would have none say, they pay twice for the same Booke" (sig. A3^{r}).[39] Moreover, the relentless series of dedicatory poems and addresses that prefaces the actual plays—forty items by almost as many "*Gentlemen*" (sig. g2^{r})—arguably constructs a forum of homosocial literary exchange whose competitive dynamics Richard Brome, for one, was keenly alert to: "You, that are here before me Gentlemen. . . . where you versifie [I'll] write. . . . I can guess / Who has a greater share of Wit, who lesse" (sig. g1^{r}).

Yet, in the prefatory matter to the Beaumont and Fletcher Folio the appeal of (especially) Fletcher's work to women readers is insisted on in ways quite unimaginable to the Shakespeare First Folio. Women's responses to the plays are repeatedly referenced—from being moved, like men, to tears or smiles (Thomas Stanley, sig. b4^{v}; compare George Lisle, sig. b1^{r}, and Levin in "Women in the Renaissance Theatre Audience," 171); from proving "amorous" (Henry Harington, sig. f4^{v}) to practicing caution (Roger L'Estrange, sig. c1^{v}); from encouraging in "Lady's eyes a power more bright" (Stanley, sig. b4^{v}) to discouraging women from the vain pursuit of "*Pleasure* and *Inconstancie*" (Roger L'Estrange, sig. c1^{v}). A recurring trope is the assumed "gender-concern or gender-loyalty" (to quote Levin) of women readers and spectators toward those plays that explicitly address women as a topic and/or the "woman question" (such as *Womans Prize, or the Tamer Tamed, Women Pleas'd*, and *The Faire Maid of the Inne*). Thus, Edmund Waller writes, "Our greatest Ladyes love to see their scorne / Out done by Thine, in what themselves have worne" (sig. b2^{r}), while Robert Gardiner and G. Hill both play on play titles: "Here's that makes *Women Pleas'd*, and *Tamer tam'd*"; "Hee taught (so subtly were their fancies seiz'd) / *To Rule a Wife, and yet the Women pleas'd*" (sigs. c2^{v} and f1^{v}).

The most marked conjunction and disjunction between the figuring of the woman reader of Beaumont and Fletcher and that of Shakespeare comes in Thomas Peyton's "On Mr Fletcher's Works," which develops at length the scene of women reading "that Huge Tome of wit" in "Ladies Closets." While the "Laick sister" will "straight flie to thee," the nun or "Novice" will slowly "steale a gentle smile," "Breath on thy Lines a whisper, and then set / Her voyce up to the measures," before dismissing "all her pretty Bookes" (sig. a3r). Whereas for Shakespeare in John Davies of Hereford's satirical poem of 1611 or Johnson's dream narrative of 1641 the scene of women reading in their closets is a marker of illicit activity or mere titillation—doing Shakespeare's reputation little good in the process—here the act of play reading in "Ladies Closets" is transposed to the service of critical "prayse" (sig. a3r). Nonetheless, the "holy" sister's reverence for Fletcher's "Tome" is cast in terms of seduction: the stealing of a "smile," the breath of a "whisper," a newfound devotion. Yet, Peyton also characterizes women's engagement with the work of Fletcher at the level of ingenuity and form: here it is his "wit," "Lines," and "measures"—the stuff of literary form—rather than his sympathetic portrayal of women, that form the basis of his appeal to the woman reader.

This speaks to the larger project of the prefatory matter of the 1647 Beaumont and Fletcher Folio, anticipated in the 1623 Shakespeare Folio: the investment of poetic and critical respectability in the genre of vernacular drama. The rules of engagement were different for closet drama; as Marta Straznicky has shown, the private and scholarly associations of "closet" drama allowed it to be figured as fit material for an intellectual elite comprised of both men and women.[40] By contrast, the critical reputation of vernacular drama for the public stage and print trade was more tenuous; dramatic canonization was still in process. Hence, John Earle's concerted effort to rein the Beaumont and Fletcher canon into the remit of "serious" literature. Dismissing the view that Beaumont's plays constitute recreational reading—"I will not yeeld thy Workes so meane a Prayse . . . Nor with that dull supinenesse to be read / To passe a fire, or laugh an houre in bed"—Earle calls for "a more serious houre on [Beaumont] bestow / Why should not *Beaumont* in the Morning please, / As well as *Plautus, Aristophanes*? . . . these our Learned of severest brow / Will deigne to looke on" (sig. C4r). What we witness, then, in the Beaumont and Fletcher Folio is the convergence of women's increasing visibility as readers of drama with the project to invest vernacular drama with critical respectability a project that became centered on the canonization, particularly in print, of the so-called "triumvirate of wit"—Shakespeare, Jonson, and Beaumont and Fletcher.

In the end, of course, Shakespeare was to supercede Fletcher as the early modern woman reader's and writer's dramatist of choice. By the late seventeenth century Shakespeare's female readers were increasingly visible as part of an urbane, metropolitan elite—no longer an amorphous group that could be readily dismissed in narratives of seedy goings-on behind closed doors—a reflection of the increasing opportunities for women as producers and participants within the literary marketplace after the Restoration. In addition, although women writers such as Margaret Cavendish, Aphra Behn, Delarivier Manley, and Mary Pix repeatedly drew attention to the difficulties of publishing as a woman, when they came to deploy Shakespeare their concern was less with gender as an issue than the operations of literary (especially neoclassical) taste or the passing of literary judgment. Changing tastes assured Shakespeare's centrality in the early to mid-eighteenth century: by 1726 Lewis Theobald was able to remark that Shakespeare had grown to be so "universal" a writer that "very few Studies, or Collections of Books" were without his works, and "there is scarce a Poet, that our *English* tongue boasts of, who is more the Subject of the Ladies Reading"; ten years later the Shakespeare Ladies Club was founded to petition theater managers to put on revivals of Shakespeare's plays, paving the way for Garrick's revival of Shakespeare in the 1740s.[41] The rhetoric of trivialization and the operations of exclusion that characterized women's reading of Shakespeare in the early seventeenth century—and which took a turning point in the 1620s-30s—had receded so far into the background as to be scarcely visible. Hierarchies of rank, in fact, emerge as more visible and divisive than those of gender: records relating to the history of early modern women reading Shakespeare remain overwhelmingly focused on the elite and the educated. Inequalities of class often cut deeper than those of gender.

This is one reason why if we were to follow the trajectory of a different genre—the prose romance, the psalter, the prophecy, the primer, the herbal, the jest book, the chapbook, ancient philosophy, or the rhetorical treatise in Latin—the terrain for the history of early modern women's reading would look quite different. It may be a truism that different genres enjoyed different readerships (which, of course, overlapped in sometimes surprising ways); nonetheless, an understanding of the impact and specificities of genre should inflect the methods and claims that we may propose for the history of women's reading. Genre is as vital—as mediating—as the more familiar litany of categories of critical analysis in the history of literature and women's reading: gender, class, race, religion, politics, history, region.

This returns me to engendering. In early modern England the term to "engender" meant to "beget," to "make," to "generate"; the pun on "gender," so obvious to a twenty-first-century reading public, was not so readily available. Although the use of "gender" to discriminate between the biological sexes of masculine, feminine, and neuter was current beginning in the fourteenth century, the use of "gender" to emphasize the social and cultural as opposed to biological distinctions between the sexes came into being only as late as 1963 (*OED*, gender n. 2a and 3b). What I think remains useful about the early modern definition of "engender" in the context of women's reading in the seventeenth century is its emphasis on *creation* and *multiplicity* rather than division and limitation. Even as early modern women's reading and access to literary culture were fundamentally different from men's at many levels, the interests, operations, and agency of early modern women readers cannot be reduced to gender alone; even as it remains foundational, gender cannot always be the central category of critical analysis in the history of women's reading. Rather, the complexity and variety of women's literary engagement—not only in terms of gender but also at the level of wit and form, politics and spirituality, class and age, region and locality—bring us closer to the early modern sense of "engendering" precisely as generation.

Notes

1. I discuss patterns of ownership of Shakespeare volumes among early modern women and the position of women as resistant readers of Shakespeare in *Reading Shakespeare's Poems in Early Modern England* (Houndmills: Palgrave Macmillan, 2003), ch. 1.

2. David McKitterick, "Women and Their Books in Seventeenth-Century England: The Case of Elizabeth Puckering," *Library*, 7th series, 1 (2000): 359–80, 365.

3. Richard Brome, "Upon *Aglaura* Printed in Folio," in *Parnassus Biceps: Or Severall Choice Pieces of Poetry, Composed by the best Wits that were in both the Universities before their Dissolution*, comp. Abraham Wright (London, 1656), sig. E5r.

4. T. A. Birrell, "Reading as Pastime: The Place of Light Literature in Some Gentlemen's Libraries of the 17th Century," in *The Property of a Gentleman: The Formation, Organisation and Dispersal of the Private Library, 1620–1920*, ed. Robin Myers and Michael Harris (Winchester: St. Paul's Bibliographies, 1991), 113–31, 119–20, 122–25.

5. Maureen Bell, "Women Writing and Women Written," in *The Cambridge History of the Book in Britain*, volume 4, *1557–1695*, ed. John Barnard and D. F. McKenzie with Maureen Bell (Cambridge: Cambridge University Press, 2002), 431–51, 437, and figures 20.2–3.

6. Franklin B. Williams, Jr., "The Literary Patronesses of Renaissance England," *Notes and Queries*, new series, 9 (1962): 364–66, 365.

7. I examine the transmission of and early modern responses to *Venus and Adonis*, by both men and women, in Roberts, *Reading Shakespeare's Poems*, 2, 20–61, 62–101.

8. John Pitcher, "Literature, the Playhouse and the Public" in *The Cambridge History of the Book in Britain*, volume 4, *1557–1695*, ed. John Barnard and D. F. McKenzie with Maureen Bell (Cambridge: Cambridge University Press, 2002), 351–75, 369.

9. Thomas Middleton, *A Mad World My Masters* (London, 1608), ed. Standish Henning (London: Edward Arnold Ltd, 1965), 1.2.43–47; John Davies of Hereford, *The Scourge of Folly* (London, c. 1611), 231. See Roberts, *Reading Shakespeare's Poems*, 31–34.

10. Richard Brathwaite, *The English Gentlewoman* (London, 1631), 139, and *The English Gentleman* (London, 1630), 28; Thomas Cranley, *Amanda or The Reformed Whore* (London, 1635), 32.

11. Pitcher, "Literature, the Playhouse and the Public," 4:368.

12. Mary Ellen Lamb, "Constructions of Women Readers," in *Teaching Tudor and Stuart Women Writers*, ed. Susanne Woods and Margaret P. Hannay (New York: Modern Language Association, 2000), 23–34, 30. For *The Academy of Complements*, see Roberts, *Reading Shakespeare's Poems*, 11, 59–60, 100, 214n94.

13. Pitcher, "Literature, the Playhouse and the Public," 4:368–69.

14. See Dorothy Osborne, *Letters to Sir William Temple*, ed. Kenneth Parker (Harmondsworth: Penguin, 1987), esp. 59–60, 79–80, 128, 131, 145–46, 164–65, 180. Indeed, we see the interchange of work between men and women readers even in their consumption of erotic literature in early modern England; for instance, Stephen Powle's manuscript miscellany includes bawdy verses ascribed to "a learned wooman" and transcribed "at the request of a fine Lady" (Bodleian MS Tanner 169). See Ian Frederick Moulton, *Before Pornography: Erotic Writing in Early Modern England* (Oxford: Oxford University Press, 2000), 55.

15. British Library Additional MS 33785, sig. 2r. The allusion comes in the context of the dedication of an "edition of Ocleve" on "The Legend and defence [of] Sr. John Oldcastel" to Sir Henry Bourchier, and the "young Gentle Lady" in question is "of your [i.e., Bourchier's] acquaintance"; as such, there is no compelling reason to presume that James fabricated the episode.

16. I discuss women's literary engagement in the field of early modern literary criticism in "Feminist Criticism and the New Formalism: Early Modern Women and Literary Engagement," in *The Impact of Feminism in Renaissance Studies*, ed. Dympna Callaghan (Houndmills: Palgrave Macmillan, 2007), 67–92.

17. Folger Shakespeare Library MS V.b.198, fols. 3r–3v. For a transcript of the complete miscellany, see *The Southwell-Sibthorpe Commonplace Book: Folger Ms. V.b.198*, ed. Jean Klene (Tempe, Ariz.: Medieval & Renaissance Texts & Studies, 1997); on the volume's scribes, see xxxvi–xxxviii.

18. Folger MS V.b.198, fols. 3r–3v. Klene transcribes "attyre" as "affyre" (*Southwell-Sibthorpe Commonplace Book*, 5).

19. Anne Southwell's possible responses to Donne's "Newes from the very Country" and Sir Thomas Overbury's "Newes from Court" were both published without attribution in *A wife now the Widdow of Sir Thomas Ouerburye* in 1614.

20. For Wolfreston, see Paul Morgan, "Frances Wolfreston and 'Hor Bouks,'" *Library*, 6th series, 11.3 (September 1989): 197–219, 204, 211–19; and J. Gerritsen, "*Venus* Preserved: Some Notes on Frances Wolfreston," *English Studies Presented to R. W. Zandvoort*, supplement to *English Studies* 45 (1964): 271–74. For her collection of chapbooks, see Tessa Watt, *Cheap Print and Popular Piety, 1550–1640* (Cambridge: Cambridge University Press, 1991), 315–17.

21. *Englands Helicon* (London, 1600), British Library C.39.e.48, sigs. Z2r, Y4r.

22. Hyder Edward Rollins, ed., *A New Variorum Edition of Shakespeare: The Poems* (Philadelphia: J. B. Lippincott, 1938), 391–92.

23. Heidi Brayman Hackel, "'Boasting of Silence': Women Readers in a Patriarchal State," in *Reading, Society and Politics in Early Modern England*, ed. Kevin Sharpe and Steven N. Zwicker (Cambridge: Cambridge University Press, 2003),

101–21, 106–7. On marginalia in a scholarly context, see William Sherman, *John Dee: The Politics of Reading and Writing in the English Renaissance* (Amherst: University of Massachusetts Press, 1995), 65–75.

24. Morgan, "Frances Wolfreston and 'Hor Bouks,' " 204, 215.

25. I. A., *The Good Womans Champion* (London, [1650?]), British Library 12330.a.21, 3. See also Morgan, "Frances Wolfreston and 'Hor Bouks,' " 211, 216, 218.

26. Richard Levin, "Women in the Renaissance Theatre Audience," *Shakespeare Quarterly* 40 (1989): 171.

27. Charles Hammond, *The World's Timely Warning Piece* (London, 1660), British Library Cup.408.d.8/4, back flyleaf. See also Morgan, "Frances Wolfreston and 'Hor Bouks,'" 205, 207, 217. In addition to *The World's Timely Warning Piece,* Wolfreston autographed Hammond's *ENGLNADS ALARUM-BELL* [sic]. *To be rung in the eares of all true Christians* (London, 1652) alongside a clutch of religious pamphlets published during the civil war and Interregnum, including the work of John Andrewes and Andrew Jones (now in the British Library).

28. Gerald MacLean, "Print Culture on the Eve of the Restoration" (paper presented at Folger Shakespeare Library seminar "Partisan Culture in an Age of Revolution," directed by Derek Hirst and Steven Zwicker, Washington, D.C., fall 1991), 1–2.

29. Bell, "Women Writing and Women Written," 434.

30. Lady Anne Merrick to Mrs. Lydall, January 21, 1638, *Calendar of State Papers,* Conway Papers, 142. For an abridged copy, see *Calendar of State Papers, Domestic Series, of the Reign of Charles I. 1638–1639,* ed. John Bruce and W. D. Hamilton (London: Longman, 1871), 342. As Heidi Brayman Hackel notes, Merrick's letter "supports the possibility of a gentlewoman's multiple, distinct collections housed at her various residences" ("The Countess of Bridgewater's London Library," in *Books and Readers in Early Modern England: Material Studies,* ed. Jennifer Andersen and Elizabeth Sauer [Philadelphia: University of Pennsylvania Press, 2002], 144).

31. *Gunaikeion: Or Nine Bookes of Various History Concerninge Women* (London, 1624), sigs. A6^r–A6^v, 398.

32. Sir John Suckling quoted in John Aubrey, *Brief Lives, Chiefly of Contemporaries, Set Down by John Aubrey, between the Years 1669 and 1696,* ed. Andrew Clark, 2 vols. (Oxford: Clarendon Press, 1898), 2:220–22; Thomas Carew, "To My Friend G.N. from Wrest," repr. in *The Country House Poem,* ed. Alastair Fowler (Edinburgh: Edinburgh University Press, 1994), 89–95. For Elizabeth Grey, see H. C. G. Matthew and Brian Harrison, eds., *Oxford Dictionary of National Biography,* vol. 23 (Oxford: Oxford University Press, 2004), 833–34. In the 1650s Dorothy Osborne (living some six miles away at Chicksands) was on intimate terms with Lady Susanna Grey de Ruthin, who teasingly produced poems from one of Osborne's admirers "to abuse mee withall, & has putt a tune to them that I may hear them all manner of way's" (letter 56, January 28/29, 1654, in *Letters to Sir William Temple,* ed. Kenneth Parker [Harmondsworth: Penguin, 1987], 167–68). See also Osborne's meeting "at Wrest again" in letter 57, February 4/5, 1654, in ibid., 172.

33. See Jane Stevenson, *Women Latin Poets* (Oxford: Oxford University Press, 2005).

34. Sophie Eliza Tomlinson, "Too Theatrical? Female Subjectivity in Caroline and Interregnum Drama," *Women's Writing* 6.1 (1999): 65–79, 66. See also Tomlinson's " 'She that plays the King': Henrietta Maria and the Threat of the

Actress in Caroline Culture," in *The Politics of Tragicomedy*, ed. Gordon McMullan and Jonathan Hope (London: Routledge, 1992), 189–207.

35. Julie Sanders, "Caroline Salon Culture and Female Agency: The Countess of Carlisle, Henrietta Maria, and Public Theatre," *Theatre Journal* 52 (2000): 449–64, 450; Julie Sanders, *Caroline Drama: The Plays of Massinger, Ford, Shirley and Brome* (Plymouth: Northcote House, 1999), 33, 41.

36. Michael Neill, " 'Wits Most Accomplished Senate': The Audience of Caroline Private Theaters," *Studies in English Literature, 1500–1900* 18 (1978): 342–60, 343; Levin, "Women in the Renaissance Theatre Audience," 169, 173.

37. Peter Blayney, "The Publication of Playbooks," in *A New History of Early English Drama*, ed. John D. Cox and David Scott Kastan (New York: Columbia University Press, 1997), 383–422, 415.

38. McKitterick, "Women and Their Books," 380, 377. For an astute analysis of Moseley's publication of drama, see Paulina Kewes, "'Give Me the Social Pocket-books . . .': Humphrey Moseley's Serial Publication of Octavo Play Collections," *Publishing History* 38 (1995): 5–21.

39. Marta Straznicky, "Reading through the Body: Women and Printed Drama in Early Modern England" (paper delivered at the Annual Meeting of the Renaissance Society of America, New York, April 2004).

40. Marta Straznicky, "Closet Drama," in *The Blackwell Companion to Renaissance Drama*, ed. Arthur F. Kinney (Oxford: Blackwell, 2004), 416–30.

41. Lewis Theobald, *Shakespeare Restored: or, a specimen of the many errors, as well committed, as unamended, by Mr Pope in his late edition of this poet* (1726; repr. New York: AMS Press, 1970), v–vi. On the Shakespeare Ladies Club and the growth of women's reading of Shakespeare in the eighteenth and nineteenth centuries, see Ann Thompson and Sasha Roberts, eds., *Women Reading Shakespeare, 1660–1900* (Manchester: Manchester University Press, 1997), 2–7.

Chapter 3

Crafting Subjectivities: Women, Reading, and Self-Imagining

Mary Kelley

> *It is only by attention that as our eyes pass over a book, we transfer its knowledge into our own minds. No book will improve you which does not make you think; which does not make your own mind work.*
>
> —*Catharine Maria Sedgwick,* Means and Ends, of Self-Training

"I read constantly and find it teaching," Hannah Heaton confided in a diary that spanned the last forty years of the eighteenth century. Heaton most assuredly did as she claimed, keeping a daily schedule that took this resident of rural Connecticut from the Bible to the meditations of John Bunyan to the treatises of Thomas Shepard, Solomon Stoddard, and Michael Wigglesworth. Born in 1788 and an ardent reader from an early age, Sarah Josepha Hale read with the same constancy. However, Hale devoted herself to secular literature, which she embraced with the passion that Heaton reserved for Bibles, psalm books, and devotional works. Immersing herself in Shakespeare, Hale made his plays and poems daily companions. The future essayist and editor took pleasure in Addison and Pope, the future poet in Cowper and Burns. Hale, whose career as a woman of letters began with the publication of the novel *Northwood* in 1827, registered the appeal of fiction in her enthusiastic response to Ann Radcliffe's *The Mystery of Udolpho*, a novel that Hale recalled had instilled a determination to "promote the reputation of my own sex, and to do something for my country."[1]

In the books they selected, Heaton and Hale illustrate fundamental changes in taste and sensibility that were well under way in the final decades of the eighteenth century. Hannah Heaton would have been surprised (and almost certainly dismayed) to learn that she was the more idiosyncratic of the two readers. The godly books to which Heaton remained unswervingly loyal still constituted an important share of the reading done by post-Revolutionary Americans. Now, however, these readers were equally drawn to the belles lettres that Hale embraced. At least initially, Hale and the readers with whom she kept company relied on the literature of the former mother country, which was either imported from Great Britain or reprinted in the United States. The number and the variety of reprints increased rapidly in the 1790s, the same decade in which Hale, who was already apprenticing for her career, devoted herself to secular literature. Books authored by Americans and printed in the United States entered the literary marketplace in increasing numbers during the first two decades of the nineteenth century.[2]

A Relish for Substantial Intellectual Food

Herself a reader of many books, Maria Drayton Gibbes took care to tell readers of *her* book why it was important to keep a volume of commonplaces. In a passage that testified to the formation of a self-identity as a woman of reading, she explained that such a book "is not only useful, but *Necessary* to a man of reading, or man of letters." In claiming this privileged status in the second decade of the nineteenth century, Gibbes fashioned herself as an equal partner with men, who had been the traditional custodians of literary culture. Embracing this self-representation was no small matter. Whether distinguishing between rhetorical strategies, discerning implications, or rendering judgments, women such as Gibbes were taking license to act on and to generate meaning from a broad spectrum of reading.[3]

That Gibbes identified herself as a woman of reading, or a woman of letters, highlights the degree to which representations of female readers intersected with gender conventions in the early Republic. Post-Revolutionary textual and visual portrayals limned a woman whose virtue was manifest in and generated by the cultivation of books. This representation stood in contrast to seventeenth-century proscriptions that had sharply limited a woman's act of reading. The founder of Massachusetts Bay and the colony's first governor, John Winthrop, recorded the plight of one Ann Hopkins. This young woman had "fallen into a sad infirmity, the loss of her understanding and reason," as he noted in his journal in April 1645. The cause was easily discernible, at least to Winthrop—Hopkins had given "herself wholly to reading and writing, and had written many books." Her fate would have been entirely different had she "not gone out of her way and calling to meddle in such things as are proper for men, whose minds are stronger." Winthrop granted that a little reading and writing were permissible amid "household affairs, and such things as belong to women." However, any more intense engagement, any more expansive venture into the world of books, risked damage to if not destruction of minds of lesser strength than men's.[4]

The Scriptures were exempted from the restrictions imposed by Winthrop and his successors in the early eighteenth century, as were Hannah Heaton's sermons, Psalters, and devotional works, which were entered into the lists in the battle to save sinners and set them on the road to virtue. In addition to the Bible, these were the books that British Americans, regardless of sex, were expected to read on a daily basis. The books of learned culture and the pens inscribing learnedness were still considered the possessions of men, however. When members of the eighteenth-century elite introduced their daughters to the course of study that their British counterparts were pursuing, the force of earlier restrictions lessened, and volumes of history, biography, and belles lettres were introduced into a lady's library. Custodians of this library celebrated the "moral improvement" that derived from the study of history—"it will give you the richest knowledge of men and things," the Reverend John Bennett told women in his "Letters to a Young Lady." Originally published as *Letters to a Young Lady on a Variety of Useful and Interesting Subjects* in 1789, Bennett's essays were excerpted by the *American Museum* two years later. Bennett designated biography as history's companion, presenting the increasingly popular genre as "most useful and interesting to a woman." He also commended the *Tatler*, the *Spectator*, and the *Guardian* for the many "lessons in morality contained in their pages." Hannah More did the same in 1799, telling readers of *Strictures on the Modern System of Female Education* that women, in addition to studying history, ought to discipline their minds with Isaac Watts's *Logic*, Joseph Butler's *Analogy*, and John Locke's *Essay on Human Understanding*.[5]

The same Reverend Bennett was deeply concerned about the role played by fiction in the critically important project of moral formation. In declaring himself against novels, he insisted that they "corrupt all principle." Less apocalyptic but nonetheless serious reservations were manifest in the essay that an anonymous "gentleman" published in the *Columbian* magazine in 1787. Characterizing fiction as "a dangerous sort of reading," he insisted that novels "tend to raise false ideas in the mind, and to destroy the taste for history, philosophy, and other branches of useful science." The aversion to novels notwithstanding, the "gentleman" did acknowledge the currency of the genre that he disdained: "if a young lady will not entirely give them up, those [novels] of Richardson, and the Amelia and Tom Jones of Fielding, are the least exceptionable." Resistance seemed to be yielding to resignation, at least in terms of two of the century's most popular novelists. Other critics remained adamant, however. Nearly a quarter of a century after the "gentleman's" lament about the impact of fiction, James Madison, bishop of the Episcopal Church and president of William and Mary, warned his daughter Susan that novels tended "to vitiate the taste and to produce a disrelish for substantial intellectual food." Women ought instead to relish the history, biography, and belles lettres that had constituted the informal education offered elite daughters in the colonies, that the Bennetts and the Mores had welcomed into a lady's library, and that had been introduced into the curricula at the female academies.[6]

In the early decades of the nineteenth century, readers with the same devotion to books as Hannah Heaton and Sarah Josepha Hale added to the canon Hale had forged in the last decades of the previous century. Mary Howell, Maria DeReiux, Elizabeth Phillips Payson, and Maria Drayton Gibbes read as widely as did Hale in British literature. Increasingly as well, they were attracted to the literature written and published in the United States. Residents of Rhode Island, Virginia, Massachusetts, and South Carolina, these readers illustrate the broad geographical reach of print in post-Revolutionary America. The fact that Howell, DeReiux, Payson, and Gibbes lived in towns or cities is significant. Like Hale a decade or two before them, they had access to bookstores, social and circulating libraries, and literary societies—all of which were stocking the history, travel literature, poetry, moral philosophy, biography, natural history, and fiction that had become regular fare for such women.[7]

Whatever the title chosen or the time taken with a book, Howell, DeReiux, Payson, and Gibbes made reading a constant in their lives. In the spring of 1801 Howell testified to her engagement with Pope, Milton, and Cowper, poets with whom she had "always been *familiar,* tho' never *intimate.*" In the winter of 1802 this resident of Providence, Rhode Island, recorded the forty-three volumes she had read in the previous six months. William Godwin's *Memoirs of Mary Wollstonecraft,* Charles Rollin's *Ancient History,* James Cook's *Voyages,* Oliver Goldsmith's *History of Rome,* and a volume of Shakespeare's plays were included, as were two recently published American novels, Charles Brockden Brown's *Ormond* and Tabitha Tenney's *Female Quixotism.* The fifty-five-page record of "Books Read by M. M. DeReiux" lists the 381 books that this Virginian engaged between 1806 and 1823. Maria Margaret DeReiux's reading, which she listed alphabetically for each year, was similar to the record left by Howell, with one notable exception—more than half of DeReiux's entries were novels. Elizabeth Phillips Payson indexed the same preferences. In the commonplace book that she kept between 1806 and 1825, Payson recorded 341 titles along with "extracts from and remarks upon some of the books I have read." Payson attended to Pope, Milton, and Cowper. She delved into Rollin and Goldsmith. She journeyed with writers of travel literature. Still, as she acknowledged, fiction appealed to her the most. She relished the British novelists Hannah More, Daniel Defoe, Jane Austen, and Sir Walter Scott. She took to Americans with equal enthusiasm, noting and commenting on Tenney's *Female Quixotism*, Hannah Webster Foster's *The Boarding School*, and Washington Irving's *Sketchbook*. The commonplace book that Maria Drayton Gibbes kept in the same decades highlighted biography, another genre that was attracting a large number of readers. Beginning with a preface in which Gibbes noted that commonplace books were designed "especially [to] note capital points in [one's] reading," this South Carolinian filled 118 pages with observations on and quotations from scores of books, including Plutarch's *Lives*, Boswell's *Life of Samuel Johnson*, Lady Fanshawe's *Memoirs*, and William Roscoe's *Life of Lorenzo De'Medici*.[8]

Entering the World of Reading: The Many Uses of Books

The records left by women who attended academies and seminaries index the role these schools played in forging connections between the books students were reading and the subjectivities they were fashioning. The letters, commonplace books, journals, and diaries constitute an archive that illuminates not only the process through which an individual subjectivity was crafted but also the importance of books as sources of cultural capital that would be used for a host of purposes, including the making of public opinion. These women embraced books, literally and figuratively. Selecting them as companions on voyages of discovery, they relished the play of ideas, delighted in unexpected insights, and pondered the implications of newly found knowledge. Perhaps most notably, they constituted books as sites for meditations on and experiments with individual subjectivities they were fashioning. Sixteen-year-old Caroline Chester, a student at Sarah Pierce's Litchfield Female Academy in Litchfield, Connecticut, spoke to the significance that women attached to reading in this regard, whatever their ages or the circumstances of their lives. Books, she declared in the commonplace book she kept during her tenure at Litchfield, were the means by which "we learn how to live." These readers explored ideas and personae, sampling perspectives and measuring relevance for their lives. And then, still using books as a primary resource, they set about making and remaking subjectivities.[9]

"We learn by example," New Hampton Female Seminary's Sarah Sleeper declared in the opening sentence of a memoir honoring Martha Hazeltine, the woman who had taught her at the seminary that Sleeper now headed. The testimonial was more than rhetorical. Many students at female academies and seminaries shared in Sleeper's formative experience—interacting with and adopting as a personal ideal a teacher who had already made books the vehicle for pursuing knowledge. Sarah Porter, the founder of Miss Porter's School in Farmington, Connecticut, was one such teacher. A woman who looked to books as "fountains of knowledge," Porter integrated reading into the rhythm of daily life, spending a morning with Euripides' *Alcestis*, turning a few days later to Richard Hildreth's *History of the United States*, setting aside an hour here and there for Wordsworth's *Excursion*, and devoting an afternoon to *Novalis's Journal*. Porter spent evenings reading to students, introducing them to James Hamilton, Harriet Beecher Stowe, and Susan Warner. She stocked her school's library with recently published history, biography, and fiction. "Reading," as one M.S.R. titled a composition she wrote while enrolled at the school, was an imperative for Sarah Porter. Already instructed by Porter in the tenet that nineteenth-century Americans had inherited from colonial readers of the *Tatler*, M.S.R. opened her composition with a paraphrase from Richard Steele's Isaac Bickerstaff, related to readers nearly 150 years earlier: "reading is to the mind what exercise is to the body as it is strengthened and invigorated by it." M.S.R. was hardly alone in rifling the pages of the *Tatler*. Students at other academies and seminaries did the same. Recording maxims such as Steele's in journals, in compositions, and in debates that took place in the literary societies housed at their schools, they testified to the persistence of reading in polite letters. M.S.R. and her counterparts had been taught the corollary maxim, that reading was more than a matter of matching mental to physical fitness. Books, as Porter's student had learned, were endowed with the same foundational purpose they had served in colonial America—"improving their morals or regulating their conduct."[10]

In giving books to reward accomplishment, in sharing personal libraries, in sponsoring literary societies, and in using reading to strengthen bonds with students, the Sarah Porters of female schooling engaged in a host of practices that defined reading as a *woman's* enterprise. Like other teachers in post-Revolutionary America, Jane Barnham Marks rewarded excellence with tokens of achievement. Some instructors presented students with elaborately inscribed certificates. Others gave them autograph albums. Marks, a teacher at the South Carolina Female Collegiate Institute, chose Priscilla Wakefield's aptly titled *Mental Improvement* as a gift for one of her students. On the flyleaf of Harriet Hayne's copy, an inscription dated June 4, 1821, tells us that Hayne had achieved the highest status in third class in geography. Years later Harriet Hayne, following Marks's precedent, presented the volume to her sister Sarah, who carefully inscribed her name on the title page. Bessie Lacy reversed this pattern, giving the *Personal Recollections* of English author Charlotte Elizabeth Tonna to her most valued teacher at Greensboro, North Carolina's Edgeworth Seminary. Describing the gift as a "testimonial of gratitude" in a letter written in 1848, Lacy told her father why a book was appropriate and Julia St. John an equally appropriate recipient. At St. John's invitation, teacher and student had spent their evenings reading together. Lacy informed her father that St. John had been "highly gratified and surprised—said she would prize it as a gift from Bessie and also as completing the set of Charlotte Elizabeth's works." In Lacy's selection of Tonna's *Recollections* and in St. John's response, the attachment to reading was manifest, as was the identification with an exemplar of female learning who was widely read on both sides of the Atlantic.[11]

The teachers who served as personal models and the pedagogy they practiced instilled the habit of reading in women who attended academies or seminaries. The experience of Martha Hauser, a student at Greensboro Female College in Greensboro, North Carolina, in the early 1850s, highlights the degree to which they learned the lesson. In a letter she sent to Julia Conrad Jones, a graduate of Salem Academy, Hauser said she was taking "American Geography, Smellie's Philosophy of Natural History, Algebra, and modern Geography." She was doing her best to command the art of composition, a task she lamented as "the pest of my life." Conversely, she was delighting in mathematics, "the only thing I have any talent for." All these academic subjects duly recorded in the letter, Hauser told Jones, "I intend to employ all my spare time reading something that will prove beneficial to me." The reason was obvious, at least to this student and, she presumed, to her correspondent: "I think it one of the essentials of female education that she be well read."[12]

The learning that students made their own through reading and the more formal education they received in classrooms intersected, supplementing and reinforcing each other. This intersection and its significance in preparing students for lives as makers of public opinion are readily evident in the journal of Charlotte Forten. An African American who had been sent from her home in Philadelphia to complete her schooling, Forten attended two public schools in Salem, Massachusetts, both of which were coeducational. Racism, which limited the educational opportunities available to African Americans, had a decisive impact on Forten. Philadelphia's public schools remained segregated throughout the years in which Forten was being educated, and the city's private academies and seminaries denied admission to African Americans. Before Charlotte's Salem education, Robert Forten, a nationally famous antislavery leader, had chosen to tutor his daughter at home rather than send her to one of Philadelphia's segregated schools. The instruction he provided was no more important than the principle he and his sisters, Harriet, Margarretta, and Sarah Forten, projected in their daily lives. For Robert Forten and his sisters, intellectual achievement and social influence had no color. In dedicating her journal to marking "the growth and improvement of my mind from year to year," the younger Forten laid claim to the same principle.[13]

Dated May 24, 1854, the initial entry in Forten's journal narrated a day shortly after her arrival in Salem. The student had applied herself to arithmetic, recited lessons, and practiced music. She had also "commenced reading 'Hard Times,' a new story by Dickens." The day concluded, Forten had "spent the evening in writing." In the month that followed, she was schooled in English grammar, modern geography, and American history, in addition to arithmetic. The course of reading marked in the daily entries spoke to larger ambitions. Deliberately preparing herself for the life her father and aunts modeled for her, Forten engaged a broad spectrum of texts. Impressed by those whom she read, Forten exclaimed: "Oh! that I could become suddenly inspired and write as only great poets can write, or that I might write a beautiful poem of two hundred lines in my sleep as Coleridge did." Forten discovered one poet who embodied those aspirations. Elizabeth Barrett Browning had succeeded in creating the beautiful and in dedicating her achievement to larger social purposes. Forten's exemplar "increased our love for the good and the beautiful," as she said in her journal. In addition to the Bible, Forten took up Thomas Macaulay's *History of England*, the sermons of Theodore Parker, and Lydia Maria Child's biography of Germaine de Staël. Macaulay and Parker were important sources for fashioning a subjectivity that envisioned both secular and sacred history as progressive. DeStaël was still more important. Not only did this woman of letters embody female learning at its most dazzling, but she also applied her formidable intellect to a host of genres, ranging from fiction to literary criticism to poetry to political essays to history. The local antislavery newspapers provided timely information on the most divisive issue that antebellum Americans faced—informing Forten about the calls for abolition and the deepening sectional crisis that culminated in the Civil War. All these authors were makers of public opinion. In addition, all provided Forten with ideas and strategies from which she selected as she apprenticed herself for engagement with the nation's civic discourse.[14]

During the nearly three years that Forten was enrolled at a local school in Salem and, following her graduation with distinction, began to attend the town's normal school, the subjects she studied changed, as did the books in which she immersed herself. The pattern, which had been recorded in the journal's initial entry, remained the same, however. Forten applied herself to astronomy, natural philosophy, and English literature. She read with no little discernment the poems of

Cowper, Tennyson, Wordsworth, and Byron; the histories of William Hickling Prescott; the novels of Maria Edgeworth, Scott, Brontë, and Hawthorne; and the memoirs of Hannah More. She took pleasure in Milton's *Paradise Lost*, Emerson's *English Traits*, Plutarch's *Lives*, and Margaret Fuller's *Woman in the Nineteenth Century*. These were also the years of Forten's apprenticeship. A regular participant in the local and regional antislavery societies, she took lessons from the masters of rhetoric Charles Remond, Wendell Phillips, and William Lloyd Garrison. Forten began to publish poetry in the *Liberator* and the *National Antislavery Standard*. In her journal, as in her life as a student, Forten made little if any distinction between the formally constituted instruction of the classroom and the reading she did on her own. In equal measure, both served the same purpose in Forten's adult life as a teacher on South Carolina's Sea Islands during the Civil War and as a writer for periodicals, including the *Liberator*, the *Atlantic Monthly*, and the *Christian Register*.[15]

Readers who had completed their schooling and had embarked on adulthood testified to the influential role that books continued to play in their lives. Letters, commonplace books, journals, and diaries show that the engagement, the purposes, and the identification with learned women that had informed their reading as students continued unabated. They also show that books began to serve still other uses. For many of these women, reading opened outward, initiating lives as makers of public opinion in communities throughout the United States. Reading propelled Bessie Lacy into leadership of benevolent associations, literary societies, and public libraries in Charlotte, North Carolina. It had the same impact on the Bostonian Susan Huntington, whose childhood had been "marked by sensibility, sobriety, tenderness of conscience, and a taste for reading," as the compiler of her memoirs noted. In measuring the relative weight of her obligations, this wife of a minister and mother of three children spoke in the language of a gendered republicanism that called women to engagement in their nation's civil society. "One's own family has the first claim to the attention and active exertions of a married lady," she declared. Having acknowledged that the household was her primary responsibility, Huntington looked outward. Convinced that "industrious women," whatever their marital standing, were able to take their place in public life, she called herself and all who read her to meet the obligations of female citizenship. Women ought to "redeem as much [time] as possible for the duties of public charity," she wrote to a friend in January 1815. Huntington proved to be a most industrious woman. A leader of Boston's Female Education Society, Female Tract Society, and Female Bible Society, all of which relied on print to further their causes, Huntington set about schooling Boston's poor in evangelical Protestantism. In a similar dedication of print to the shaping of public opinion, members of Hopkinton, New Hampshire's Chesterfield Benevolent Society founded the town's library and stocked its shelves with volumes they had selected as appropriate for the town's residents. African American women, who turned books they read as members of literary societies into resources for challenges to the institution of slavery, were the most striking example. Reading together at the meetings of their societies, members began authoring poetry and prose that insisted African Americans be secured in the freedoms already accorded whites. Published in antislavery newspapers and performed in exhibitions, these literary and rhetorical productions persuaded an ever-widening circle of readers to work on behalf of emancipation.[16]

Books served equally important private purposes, turning an individual reader inward and inviting communion with a fully realized world set apart from life's external circumstances. They provided the occasion for a solitary commingling of the shifting subjectivities of reader and text that could kindle the imagination and lead to unexpected outcomes. The spontaneous idea, the fleeting connection, the pleasure of recognition, the discovery of an unanticipated dimension of self—all were generated through intense encounters that were given their shape by affect. Reading could spark flights of fancy as individuals played with a limitless number of subjectivities. The laughter, the drollery, the whimsical experiments with language and perspective sprinkled through the diaries and journals partake in this playfulness. The reactions were spontaneous, the ends unanticipated. When Caroline Howard Gilman remarked on "the privilege of reading," she spoke to these dimensions—"a privilege, which not only gives a spring to the happiest thoughts, but peoples solitude, softens care, and beguiles anxiety."[17]

The intense yearning for books manifest in the letters, commonplace books, journals, and diaries registers the sustained and sustaining role that reading played in the lives of these women. The desire to take a volume in hand and converse with its author is expressed with a powerful intensity in the journal of Julia Parker, a graduate of one of New England's seminaries and a teacher at academies in Germantown, Pennsylvania and Clarendon, South Carolina. In the entry she made in July 1838, this reader recorded a "morning at home *alone.* I love to be much *alone.*" Yet, Parker had hardly been alone. She had spent that morning "with those glorious minds with which *I*, even *I*, may hold sweet communion through the works they have left, as rich legacies." Sarah Alden Ripley spoke to this connection with a similar resonance in a letter she sent to George Simmons, the associate pastor who presided with her husband Samuel at the Independent Congregational Society in Concord, Massachusetts. Instead of attending services one Sunday, Ripley had slipped away and spent the morning reading Saint Augustine. Seated at a window, she had left the world behind and had walked with Augustine along "the pathway to virtue and Heaven."[18]

The library that was Margaret Bayard Smith's "supreme delight" was filled with minds who engaged Smith's "reason" and "affections." "My Books," as Smith titled an essay she published in 1831, were the companions who remained at her side "when forsaken by other friends." Books, she told readers of the *Ladies' Magazine*, "were with me still—when happy, they made me happier—when sad, they enlivened—when sick, they amused—when troubled, they soothed me." In these moments of sympathetic affiliation, a reader might well experience repair and regeneration of a life that had gone awry. "Come then, my Books," Eliza Sweet commanded as this resident of Savannah, Georgia, took refuge with "companions safe / Soothers of pain, and antidote to care." The books that in solitary retreat consoled were also sources of inspiration. From the poems, philosophical musings, and religious commentary with which she filled her commonplace book, Sweet assembled the compass with which she reckoned the course of her life. A distillation of all the reading that she had done, Sweet's book within a book was "friendly to wisdom, virtue, and to truth."[19]

Whether placed on a shelf, held in a hand, or tucked away in a workbasket, the material artifact served still another purpose: anchoring a reader's identity no matter the circumstances in which she found herself. Never was this recourse to books more meaningful than when women left households and communities with which they were familiar and embarked on journeys into the unknown. Serving as tangible symbols of the world from which they had been separated, books sustained these readers. They reduced the sense of dislocation that many experienced and grounded their lives in unfamiliar settings. When books were inadvertently left behind, their significance as cherished objects was soon evident. In the fall of 1839 Mary Early left her home in Lynchburg, Virginia, to attend the recently established Female Collegiate Institute in Buckingham County. She wrote to her family immediately after her arrival at the school. Could her mother send Early her most valued possession—my "Book," she declared, adding in parentheses "Home by Miss Sedgwick," a tale of social mobility achieved less through competition and capitalist acquisition than through the practice of the republican values in which Early was being schooled. More than two decades earlier Abigail Bradley had received a similar letter from a daughter being schooled at Sarah Pierce's Litchfield Female Academy. Abby's book of "sacred history" had to be sent immediately. The mother dispatched the volume along with copies of a Latin dictionary and Hugh Blair's *Lectures,* both of which Bradley needed for her courses. Alice Aldrich Lees had not a book but a library to anchor her as she set about replicating the world that had surrounded her. Shortly after she and her husband moved from Smithfield, Rhode Island, to Holden, Massachusetts, in the spring of 1830, Lees asked her sister Lucy to send "the Marseilles spread, all the articles in the garret cupboard belonging to me, my box of patches and remnants standing on a shelf in the upper closet, my comb box, pattern box, round work basket, piece book, gingham frock with cape and belt, [and] all my books." Preceded by a list of goods associated with a woman's household responsibilities, "all my books" stood alone and alone was underlined. Her insistence that the books be sent spoke to the degree to which Lees's sense of self had been shaped by her engagement with reading. Equally telling was the fact that she had not left all her books behind—Lees mentioned at the end of her letter that she was taking pleasure in Sir Walter Scott's *Anne of Geierstein.*[20]

"The Best Company You Can Have"

In a letter to his daughter Isabella, Kentuckian John Price counseled the ten-year-old about the relationship between readers and books. "Books," he told her in 1853, "are the best company you can have—they never tell tales upon you, and you always have them at command." Price's comment, which captured an important truth about these women's engagement with books, spoke to the larger dimensions of reading. Because books "never tell tales upon you," the exchange between readers and texts could be as private or as public as individuals desired. And because readers could "always have them at command," individuals could shape texts to their purposes, using them for private pleasures and public acts. Women could exercise agency in many ways. Employed to achieve a variety of interlinked objectives, reading could be a vehicle for education, a source for identification with learned women, and a basis for an apprenticeship as a woman of letters. Equally notably, women could take them as manuals of instruction in forming their own opinions and in making public opinion. A student at Sarah Pierce's Litchfield Female Academy, Mary Bacon spoke to all of these ends. "From books," she told her brother, "we learn the situations, manners, customs, virtues and vices of our own and distant countr[ies]." Together, she added, Bacon and her brother could use reading to "press forward in the road of improvement." That was exactly the road women were asked by Sarah Josepha Hale to travel. Hale, one of antebellum America's most influential makers of public opinion, called women to the task of the nation's improvement. Beginning with the familiar disclaimer that "wealth, scientific knowledge, political power—we have none of these aids," Hale nonetheless authorized women to chart America's course. In reading books, and particularly in reading "the books most appropriate for our sex," she encouraged women always to bear in mind that "the development of the human mind and the direction of public opinion are both committed to women."[21]

However they struck the balance between the public and the private, between the book as instrumental and the book as pleasure, these readers played a central role in the making of a text. Margaret Fuller provides a telling if singular example. Determined to make his eldest daughter "the heir of all he knew," Timothy Fuller took responsibility for drilling Margaret in Latin and guiding her reading in classical literature. He welcomed her into his library, where she immersed herself in Shakespeare, Cervantes, Molière, Fielding, Smollett, and Scott. Reading Shakespeare on a Sunday led to an emotionally charged conflict between father and daughter. When told by Timothy, "Shakespeare, that won't do; that's no book for Sunday; go put it away and take another," the eight-year-old did and did not. Initially she placed the volume on the shelf, albeit without selecting a substitute for "Romeo and Juliet," the play she had been reading. Then she yielded to desire, retrieved the volume, and opened its pages again. Margaret managed to read nearly half the play before Timothy asked the same question and received the same answer. Incensed that she had disobeyed him, he ordered his daughter directly to bed. The fact that she no longer had the text at hand mattered little if at all—"alone in the dark, I thought only of the scene placed by the poet before my eye, where the free flow of life, sudden and graceful dialogue, and forms, whether grotesque or fair, seen in the broad lustre of his imagination, gave just what I wanted. My fancies swarmed like bees, as I contrived the rest of the story;—what all would do, what say, where go." Other readers may not have appropriated a text to the degree that Fuller did on this occasion, but they read with the same eye to self-defined needs and desires. Acting with the agency that Fuller's response illustrates, they interrogated, intervened, and revised to create meanings beyond those intended by either authors or publishers. These readers were "poachers," as Michel de Certeau has labeled them. In the space between reader and text, they produced pluralities of meanings. Day in and day out, month in and month out, year in and year out they relied on those meanings as they fashioned subjectivities as autonomous and communicative thinking women.[22]

Notes

"Crafting Subjectivities: Women, Reading, and Self-Imagining" is drawn from Mary Kelley, *Learning to Stand and Speak: Women, Education, and Public Life in America's Republic* (Chapel Hill: University of North Carolina Press, 2006).

1. Hannah Heaton, "Experiences of Spiritual Exercises," in *The World of Hannah Heaton: The Diary of an Eighteenth-Century New England Farm Woman,* ed. Barbara E. Lacey (DeKalb, Ill.: Northern Illinois University Press, 2003), 155 (see also Lacey's introduction, xi–xxx); Sarah Josepha Hale, *Woman's Record: Sketches of All Distinguished Women from "The Beginning" till A.D. 1850* (New York: Harper and Brothers, 1853), 687.

2. In her research on colonial women's reading, Mary Alice Baldwin found that some seventeenth- and eighteenth-century women read Shakespeare, Congreve, Pope, Fielding, and Dryden. Baldwin also found citations to the *Spectator,* Giovanni Marana's *Turkish Spy,* the *Tatler,* Burton's *Anatomy of Melancholy,* and Richardson's *Pamela.* Kevin Hayes confirmed Baldwin's findings. Analyses of inventories in post-Revolutionary Vermont and Virginia reveal patterns similar to the reading in which Sarah Hale engaged. See Mary Alice Baldwin, "The Reading of Women in the Colonies before 1750," "Unpublished Essay," n.d., Alice Baldwin Papers, Duke University Archives, Duke University, Durham, N.C.; Kevin Hayes, *The Colonial Woman's Bookshelf* (Knoxville: University of Tennessee Press, 1996); William Gilmore, *Reading Becomes a Necessity of Life: Material and Cultural Life in Rural New England, 1780–1835* (Knoxville: University of Tennessee Press, 1989), 254–82; and Joseph Kett and Patricia McClung, "Book Culture in Post-Revolutionary Virginia," *Proceedings of the American Antiquarian Society* 94 (1984): 97–148. On the importance of reprinting, see James Green, "The Rise of Book Publishing in the United States, 1785–1840," in *An Extensive Republic: Print, Culture and Society in the New Nation,* ed. Robert Gross and Mary Kelley, vol. 2 of *History of the Book in America* (Chapel Hill: University of North Carolina Press, forthcoming 2008).

3. Commonplace Book of Maria Drayton Gibbes, Gibbes-Gilchrist Papers, South Carolina Historical Society, Charleston.

4. John Winthrop, *The Journal of John Winthrop, 1630–1649,* ed. Richard S. Dunn, James Savage, and Laetitia Yeandle (Cambridge, Mass.: Belknap Press of Harvard University Press, 1996), 570. The other female presence in Winthrop's journal was the intellectually inclined Anne Hutchinson, who experienced an equally disastrous fate. On reading practices in British America, see David Hall, "Readers and Writers in Early New England," David Hall, "The Chesapeake in the Seventeenth Century," and David Hall and Elizabeth Carroll Reilly, "Practices of Reading" in *The Colonial Book in the Atlantic World,* ed. David Hall and Hugh Amory (New York: Cambridge University Press, 2000), 117–51, 5–82, 377–410; David Hall, "Readers and Reading in America: Historical and Critical Practices" and "The Uses of Literacy in New England, 1600–1850," in David Hall, *Cultures of Print: Essays in the History of the Book* (Amherst: University of Massachusetts Press, 1996), 169–87, 36–78; and Linda J. Doherty, "Women as Readers: Visual Representations," *Proceedings of the American Antiquarian Society* 107 (1998): 335–88.

5. John Bennett, "Letters to a Young Lady," *American Museum* 10 (September–October 1791): 146; Hannah More, *Strictures on the Modern System of Female Education,* vol. 1 (Charleston, Mass.: Samuel Etheridge, 1800), 94. Bennett's "Letters" were reprinted from *Letters to a Young Lady on a Variety of Useful and Interesting Subjects, Calculated to Improve the Heart, to Form the Manners, and Enlighten the Understanding,* which was published in London in 1789. More's *Strictures* appeared in London in 1799. Sarah Eleanor Fatherly identified the importance of the British curricular model in "Gentlewomen and Learned Ladies: Gender and the Creation of an Urban Elite in Colonial Philadelphia" (Ph.D.

diss., University of Wisconsin, Madison, 2000). See also Sarah Eleanor Fatherly, "'The Sweet Recourse of Reason': Elite Women's Education in Colonial Philadelphia," *Pennsylvania Magazine of History and Biography* 128 (2004): 229–56.

6. Bennett, "Letters to a Young Lady," 202; Anonymous, "To the Editor of the Columbian Magazine," *Columbian* 1 (September 1787): 645; James Madison to Susan Randolph Madison, [1811], in Thomas E. Buckley, ed., *Virginia Magazine of History and Biography* 91 (1983): 98–104. On these censures, see Carla Mulford's introduction to two early American novels, William Hill Brown's *The Power of Sympathy* and Hannah Webster Foster's *The Coquette* (New York: Penguin Classics, 1996), ix–li.

7. Journal of Mary Howell, Manuscripts, Connecticut Historical Society, Hartford; Commonplace Book of Maria Margaret DeReiux, Virginia Historical Society, Richmond; Commonplace Book of Elizabeth Phillips Payson, Arthur and Elizabeth Schlesinger Library on the History of Women in America, Radcliffe College, Cambridge, Mass.; Commonplace Book of Maria Drayton Gibbes, Gibbes-Gilchrist Papers, South Carolina Historical Society, Charleston.

8. Journal of Mary Howell, April 21, 1801, February 7, 1802; Commonplace Book of Maria Margaret DeReiux (n.p.); Commonplace Book of Elizabeth Phillips Payson (n.p.); Commonplace Book of Maria Drayton Gibbes (n.p.). If the records of the American Whig Society, a literary society at Princeton, are a reliable indicator, fiction was an equally popular choice among male readers. Fiction and poetry constituted 32.5 percent of the volumes taken from the society's library between 1813 and 1817. The second largest category was history. Students attended to Goldsmith and Rollin along with Gibbon. Members also left their Latin and Greek grammars at the door of the library, reading instead Pope's *Homer* and Dryden's *Virgil*. See James McLachlan, "*The Choice of Hercules*: American Student Societies in the Early 19th Century," in *The University in Society: Europe, Scotland, and the United States from the 16th to the 20th Century*, ed. Lawrence Stone (Princeton, N.J.: Princeton University Press, 1974), 449–94.

9. Journal of Caroline Chester in Lynne Templeton Brickley, "Sarah Pierce's Litchfield Female Academy," in *To Ornament Their Minds: Sarah Pierce's Litchfield Academy, 1792–1833*, ed. Theodore Sizer et al. (Litchfield, Conn.: The Litchfield Historical Society, 1993), 45.

10. Sarah Sleeper, *Memoir of the Late Martha Hazeltine Smith* (Boston: Freeman and Bollen, 1843), 1; diary of Sarah Porter, December 29, 1853; M.S.R., "Reading," in *Miss Porter's School: A History in Documents, 1847–1948*, ed. Louise Stevenson, 2 vols. (New York: Garland, 1987), 1: 43, 130–31, also 40–43, 164, 166–68. The quotation from Isaac Bickerstaff that M.S.R. paraphrased is as follows: "Reading is to the mind what exercise is to the body, as by one, health is preserved, strengthened, by the other virtue which is the health of the mind is kept alive, strengthened and confirmed." See "The Lucubrations of Isaac Bickerstaff Esq.," *Tatler* 147 (March 18, 1710).

11. Harriet Hayne's *Mental Improvement* is deposited in the South Carolina Female Collegiate Institute Collection, South Caroliniana Library, University of South Carolina, Columbia. See Bessie Lacy to Drury Lacy, January 27, March 2, 1848, Drury Lacy Papers, Southern Historical Collection, University of North Carolina, Chapel Hill.

12. Martha Hauser to Julia Conrad Jones, March 9, 1853, Jones Family Papers, Southern Historical Collection, University of North Carolina, Chapel Hill.

13. Brenda Stevenson, ed., *The Journals of Charlotte Forten Grimke* (New York:

Oxford University Press, 1988), 58, 59, 156. Charlotte Forten's father was the son of James Forten, who had founded with Sarah Douglass's mother the school that Sarah attended and later headed as an adult. Forten's aunt Harriet Forten married Robert Purvis, another nationally famous antislavery leader. See also Nellie McKay, "The Journals of Charlotte Forten-Grimke: *Les Lieux de Memoire* in African American Women's Autobiography," in *History and Memory in African-American Culture,* ed. Genevieve Fabre and Robert O'Meally (New York: Oxford University Press, 1994), 261–71; Carla Peterson, *"Doers of the Word": African-American Women Speakers and Writers in the North, 1830–1860* (New York: Oxford University Press, 1995), esp. 176–95; Carla Peterson, "Reconstructing the Nation: Frances Harper, Charlotte Forten, and the Racial Politics of Periodical Publication," *Proceedings of the American Antiquarian Society* 107 (1998): 301–34; and Susan M. Ryan, *The Grammar of Good Intentions: Race and the Antebellum Culture of Benevolence* (Ithaca, N.Y.: Cornell University Press, 2003), esp. 131–42.

14. Stevenson, *Journals of Charlotte Forten Grimke,* 59, 156, 105.

15. Ibid., 60, 123, 86, 71, 81, 145, 84, 94, 95, 144, 143, 154, 108, 93, 84.

16. Drury Lacy Papers, Southern Historical Collection, University of North Carolina, Chapel Hill; Susan Huntington, "To a Friend," January 3, 1815, in *Memoirs of the Late Mrs. Susan Huntington of Boston Mass. Consisting Principally of Extracts from Her Journal and Letters,* ed. Benjamin B. Wisner (Boston, 1826), 119; Minutes of the Chesterfield Benevolent Society, Arthur and Elizabeth Schlesinger Library for the History of Women in America, Radcliffe College, Cambridge, Mass.; Dorothy B. Porter, "The Organized Educational Activities of Negro Literary Societies, 1828–1846," *Journal of Negro Education* 5 (October 1936): 555–76; Julie Winch, " 'You Have Talents—Only Cultivate Them': Philadelphia's Black Female Literary Societies and the Abolitionist Crusade," in *The Abolitionist Sisterhood: Women's Political Culture in Antebellum America,* ed. Jean Fagan Yellin and John C. Van Horne (Ithaca, N.Y.: Cornell University Press, 1994), 101–18; Elizabeth McHenry, " 'Dreaded Eloquence': The Origins and Rise of African American Literary Societies and Libraries," *Harvard Library Bulletin* 6.2 (1995): 32–56; Elizabeth McHenry, *Forgotten Readers: Recovering the Lost History of African American Literary Societies* (Durham, N.C.: Duke University Press, 2002), esp. 38–68.

17. Caroline Howard Gilman to Caroline Howard White, [n.d.], Caroline Howard Gilman Papers, South Carolina Historical Society, Charleston.

18. Julia Parker, *Life and Thought: Or, Cherished Memorials of the Late Julia A. Parker Dyson,* ed. E. Latimer (Boston, 1871), 63; Sarah Alden Ripley to George Simmons, [n.d.], Sarah Alden Bradford Ripley Papers, Arthur and Elizabeth Schlesinger Library for the History of Women in America, Radcliffe College, Cambridge, Mass.

19. Margaret Bayard Smith, "My Books," *Ladies' Magazine* 4 (September 1831): 404–05; Mary Eliza Sweet, [1820s], Georgia Historical Society, Savannah. I am grateful to Frederika Teute for sharing Smith's essay with me.

20. Mary Virginia Early to Elizabeth Early, October 26, 1839, Early Brown Family Papers, Virginia Historical Society, Richmond; Abigail Bradley to Abigail Bradley, July 4, [1814], Bradley-Hyde Papers, Arthur and Elizabeth Schlesinger Library for the History of Women in America, Radcliffe College, Cambridge, Mass.; Alice Aldrich Lees to Lucy Aldrich, March 8, 1830, Rhode Island Historical Society, Providence. On books as physical embodiments of memory, see Susan M. Stabile, *Memory's Daughters: The Material Culture of Remembrance in Eighteenth-Century America* (Ithaca, N.Y.: Cornell University Press, 2004), esp. 1–16.

21. John Price to Isabella Downing Price, May 29, 1853, Charles Barrington Simrall Papers, Southern Historical Collection, University of North Carolina, Chapel Hill; Mary Bacon, "Composition Written at Litchfield," in *Chronicles of a Pioneer School from 1792–1833*, ed. Emily Noyes Vanderpoel (Cambridge, Mass.: Harvard University Press, 1910), 72; Sarah Josepha Hale, in *Godeys Lady's Book* 34 (January 1847): 51. See also Catherine Belsey, "Constructing the Subject, Deconstructing the Text" in *Feminisms: An Anthology of Literary Theory and Criticism*, ed. Robyn R. Warhol and Diane Price Herndl (New Brunswick, N.J.: Rutgers University Press, 1993), 593–609.

22. Margaret Fuller, in Mary Kelley, ed., *The Portable Margaret Fuller* (New York: Viking Penguin, 1994), 12; Michel de Certeau, *The Practice of Everyday Life*, trans. Steven Rendall (Berkeley: University of California Press, 1984), 165–76. There is now a considerable body of scholarship on the practice and performance of reading. See Janice Radway, *Reading the Romance: Women, Patriarchy, and Popular Literature* (Chapel Hill: University of North Carolina Press, 1984), esp. 47–118; Radway, *A Feeling for Books: The Book-of-the-Month Club, Literary Taste, and Middle-Class Desire* (Chapel Hill: University of North Carolina Press, 1997), esp. 305–51; Radway, "On the Sociability of Reading: Books, Self Fashioning, and the Creation of Communities," keynote address delivered at the conference "The Emergence of the Female Reader, 1500–1800," Oregon State University, Corvallis, May 18, 2001; Cathy N. Davidson, *Revolution and the Word: The Rise of the Novel in America* (New York: Oxford University Press, 1986), esp. 55–79; Barbara Sicherman, "Sense and Sensibility: A Case Study of Women's Reading in Late-Victorian America," in *Reading in America: Literature and Social History*, ed. Cathy Davidson (Baltimore: Johns Hopkins University Press, 1989), 201–25; Sicherman, "Reading and Ambition: M. Carey Thomas and Female Heroism," *American Quarterly* 35 (March 1993): 73–103; Sicherman, "Reading *Little Women*: The Many Lives of a Text," in *U.S. History as Women's History: New Feminist Essays*, ed. Linda K. Kerber, Alice Kessler-Harris, and Kathryn Kish Sklar (Chapel Hill: University of North Carolina Press, 1995), 245–66; Roger Chartier, *The Order of Books: Readers, Authors, and Libraries in Europe between the Fourteenth and Eighteenth Centuries*, trans. Lydia G. Cochrane (Cambridge: Polity Press, 1994), esp. 1–23; William H. Pease and Jane H. Pease, "Traditional Belles or Borderline Bluestockings? The Petigru Women," *South Carolina Historical Magazine* 102 (2001): 292–308.

Part II
Practices and Accomplishment

In countless literary and pictorial representations, the woman who reads reads alone. Poring over books, engrossed in letters, these solitary readers embody the seamless fusion of subject and text; they seem to have escaped into some unreachable, interior imaginative space. Despite the potency of these images, much of women's reading, like men's reading, was neither solitary nor private. Instead, as scholars have discovered, reading regularly took place in explicitly social, even sociable, contexts. Just as important, even when women read silently and privately, they often did so with social aims in mind. Reading was surely intended to inculcate virtues that signaled a particular sort of feminine selfhood, be it pious or polite, domestic or learned, or (most frequently) a selfhood that encompassed all of these qualities to one extent or another. But these qualities—like the selves they helped constitute—were enacted, observed, and judged by a larger public, encompassing family and community. Women looked to texts of all kinds not only to craft subjectivity but also to display it before others. These displays ranged from the performative to the material. Women read aloud, and they not only talked about their reading; they talked in ways that revealed their immersion in a world of elevated print. In addition, they created a rich material world, including samplers, needlework pictures, and watercolor paintings, which insistently connected feminine "accomplishments" not only to the mastery of a particular skill but also to the mastery of literary culture.

It should not surprise us that women's reading so often culminated in practices that placed them—and the fruits of their accomplishment—on display. How could it not, given that it so often indexed the virtues and vices of women in general and individual readers in particular? In other words, the performative and artifactual worlds created by female readers validated a distinctly feminized engagement with a textual world and certified certain women as exemplars of their sex and of a larger community of letters. Yet it would be a mistake to cast the practices and accomplishments that accompanied women's reading simply as evidence of their subordination, as signposts in a Whiggish trajectory that starts with women's outright exclusion from the world of books and culminates in their unfettered, ungendered access to that world. Display cut in multiple directions. If it marked women as *female* readers, situated within historically specific gendered constraints, it also marked them as *readers.* More to the point, the gendered conventions that governed literacies simultaneously located female and male readers and writers along a continuum and in opposition to one another. As the essays in this section demonstrate, these continuums and oppositions worked in tandem. Women (and men, for that matter) read not only as gendered subjects but also as members of families, classes, and nations.

The practices and accomplishments that structured Anglo-American women's reading between 1500 and 1800 reflect these multiple roles and identities. Early modern samplers and reading employed similar alphabetization. This was more than superficial similarity. Sewing and reading were linked in a variety of early modern texts. As Bianca F.-C. Calabresi observes, writers who applauded women's reading and those who disdained it pointed to the ways in which it was complemented by their needlework. However, samplers did more than recapitulate the literacies of books and hornbooks; they initiated their own, employing both romanized and nordic letterforms. Moreover, the majuscule letterforms common to samplers were in turn reproduced in a variety of other media. Taking a well-known hand-copied giftbook presented by Princess Elizabeth Tudor to her stepmother Katherine Parr as a case in point, Calabresi reveals a canny princess deploying needlework letterforms, rendered in ink, and feigning ignorance of roman and italic capitals to pass herself off as an unthreatening subordinate. Elizabeth's mastery of embroidered and written letterforms alerts us to the multiple literacies available to some Renaissance women and suggests the ways in which those literacies might have been manipulated.

Long regarded as the special preserve of men, classical learning became a necessity for women with the rise of a transatlantic, heterosocial culture of politeness. Because the graceful conversation of gentlemen regularly touched on the classics, gentlewomen needed to be knowledgeable auditors who could also provide complementary, if not precisely comparable, conversational gambits of their own. This was no mean feat, not least because the vast majority of women lacked the linguistic skills to read classical texts in the original Greek and Latin. As Caroline Winterer demonstrates, Anglo-American women's classicism depended on the modern vernacular, on books that were about the ancient world but not of it. These books sanitized myth and history to render them compatible with feminine propriety and piety. At the same time, they spawned a rich material world, including not only the books but also artifacts ranging from wallpaper to illustrative paintings and embroideries that figured the classical world as part of the contemporary one. Significantly, this textual, performative, and material entrée into the classical world did not propel women down the paths forged by Catharine Macaulay or Mercy Otis Warren, whose learning took on a distinctly politicized, overtly republican edge. As Winterer observes, classicism spoke to most ladies in the dialect of genteel decorum rather than political commitment.

Catherine E. Kelly traces the relationship between reading and accomplishment in the first decades of the American Republic, raising questions about women in the public sphere. Like Calabresi and Winterer, she emphasizes the connections between reading and accomplishment. They were similarly problematized by an expansive periodical press, which pondered the precise quantities and varieties signaling virtue and decadence, questions made more pressing by the consumer revolution. The connections between reading and accomplishment were not discursive only. Early national academies and seminaries offered increasing numbers of female students a curriculum that connected literary culture, including the emerging canon on taste, with training in dancing, music, painting, and especially ornamental needlework. The cultivated minds, graceful bodies, and material objects that resulted from this training entitled women to a measure of publicity; this publicity was ritualized in annual academy exhibitions that placed students and the fruits of their learning (including commonplace books, essays, paintings, and needlework) on display. Women's cosmopolitan learning not only made them visible exemplars of republican taste but also helped enforce the class-based exclusivity of that taste. Yet, as Kelly observes, women's presence in the public sphere, secured through reading and accomplishments alike, was inherently ambiguous for it exposed the connections between consumption and luxury on the one hand and the self-fashioning necessary for republican refinement on the other.

Taken together, the following essays alert us to the interpenetration of the textual and the material—to the samplers, wallpapers, and watercolors that documented, validated, and publicized women's reading. They also foreground the social ends of reading, documenting how women's reading advanced their places within and well beyond their families. By locating reading more precisely in a constellation of practices that were derived from and reinforced multiple and competing hierarchies, these essays remind us that women's reading served not only to set them apart from society, fixing them as subordinates or transgressors; often enough, it also allowed them to operate and advance in society.

Chapter 4

"you sow, Ile read": Letters and Literacies in Early Modern Samplers

Bianca F.-C. Calabresi

Midway through Thomas Heywood's 1608 play, *The Rape of Lucrece: A True Roman Tragedie,* the drama's antagonist, Sextus Tarquin, describes the challenges to wives' chastity while their husbands are at war:

> . . . ist possible thinke you, that women of young spirit and full age
> Of fluent wit, that can both sing and dance,
> Reade, write, such as feede well and taste choice cates,
> . . . .
> Can such as these their husbands being away
> Emploid in forreine sieges or elsewhere,
> Deny such as importune them at home?[1]

While Sextus seems most encouraged by a feminine desire for sweets "[t]hat keep the veines full, and enflame the appetite" (E4v), he also includes women's literacy as one of the female activities that threaten sexual sobriety. To counter this accusation, Heywood's next scene shows a chaste Lucrece dutifully reading when surprised by her husband, Colatine, and his friends.[2] Staying up to supervise the household in Colatine's absence, she has instructed her maid, "Here take your worke againe, a while proceede, / And then to bed, for whilst you sow, Ile read" (F2r).

This essay explores the link between these two feminized activities, specifically the potential place of sewn letters in the development of women's literacy during the early modern period. This connection might at first appear counterintuitive: indeed, Colatine's fellow soldiers miss the role of the book as an instrument of probity altogether, exclaiming at the sight of Lucrece reading, "By Ioue Ile buy my wife a wheele and make her spin" and "If I make not mine learn to liue by the prick of her needle for this, Ime no *Roman*" (F2r). However, the rhetorical pairing of proper reading and sewing, particularly when those activities are differentiated by status, increasingly emerges as a counterpoint to the conventional early modern opposition of needle and text. The frontispiece of Giovanni Ostaus's manual for *The True Perfection of Drawing Various Sorts of Embroidery etc.*, printed in Venice in 1561, likewise shows Lucretia discovered with a book, surrounded by female servants spinning and sewing, even as the caption similarly conflates the two textual activities as equivalent female labor, describing Lucretia as "found amongst them at work" ("trouata in mezzo d'esse à lauorare").[3]

This elision of praiseworthy literacy and needlework draws reinforcement from the early modern period's multiple uses of the verb "to sow."[4] For the early modern auditor or reader of English in particular, *sowing*—planting in one's own or another's mind, disseminating, distributing abroad—and *sewing*—needlework, including cross-stitch, cutwork, stump work, and a range of other practices—were not only homophonic and orthographically identical but also conceptually similar. The 1594 printed quarto of Shakespeare's *Titus Andronicus* plays on this interchangeability when Marcus describes Philomel as having "in a tedious Sampler, sowed her minde."[5]

Marcus hardly means that Philomel reveals her rape in what is now thought of typically as a sampler, a rectangular piece of needlework displaying a range of practice stitches. In the sixteenth and seventeenth centuries a sampler, like Philomel herself, was a paradigm, a model: on the one hand, "an archetype"; on the other hand, an "illustrative or typical instance." John Palgrave defines "sampler" (with tautological etymology) as "an exampler of a woman to work by."[6] Early sewn samplers provided women with prototypes for their own pieces, as an alternative to expensive pattern books and as fuel for artistic competition. From the late sixteenth century on, about the time when it began to display alphabets, the sampler grew increasingly associated with individual handiwork and proficiency—it became more and more the "exampler of" the woman who worked it.[7] At the same time, however, developing ideologies of gender meant that such sewn works were seen as the material manifestations of exemplary women: those praiseworthy dames who, in John Taylor's words, "vse their tongues lesse, and their Needles more."[8]

Such prescriptions made for tedious samplers indeed. Yet this essay argues that precisely because these set pieces were considered to be "sown" in the sense of "published" as well as "sewn" with a needle, they interacted in significant ways with questions of female literacy in the period.[9] More specifically, because these pieces are frequently lettered, and because those letters participate in and differentiate themselves from the systems that organize handwritten and printed characters in the period, we need to consider them as alternative sites where literacies might originate, be registered, or be contested.[10] In the pages that follow, I examine several instances where sewn and written literacies coincide, in order to propose that needlework be understood as a Renaissance writing technology in its own right. I argue that these additional letter forms too have important repercussions for readings of gender and status difference in the early modern period and moreover for changing notions of textuality then and now—that they should be seen less as *alternatives* to written or typographical letters than as part of a continuum of reading and writing practices. In short, I will suggest the improbable notion that *sewn* letters—that is, letters formed by a needle on or with fabric—could be seen as a source and form of reading and writing.

* * *

Given the growing prevalence of letters in early modern samplers, might Renaissance girls have learned to read and make the alphabet through looking at and making needlework in the absence of or in addition to books? For boys and girls alike, the first step in reading-only literacy was "alphabetization," most basically the memorization and repetition of the series of letters known then as now as the ABCs. Although knowledge of the alphabet was habitually inculcated through exposure to a rudimentary printed text, there seems in principle no reason why the same pedagogy might not occur through looking at or creating needlework letters, a form of production that many scholars have argued was becoming increasingly gender-specific in the sixteenth and early seventeenth centuries.[11]

Many early modern samplers from Europe and the American colonies do contain lines or rows of alphabets as an integral and recognizable feature of the genre. Such lines of letters have been taken as primarily useful for teaching girls how to initial household linens or sewn "movables."[12] In their position and construction, however, these letters closely resemble the beginning lines of hornbooks—the wooden palettes inscribed or pasted with alphabets that were used for the most basic reading instruction.[13] The frequent placing of the majuscule letters before the miniscule (the reverse of the didactic sequence for learning to *write* letters) was one distinctive marker of a primary text. Another was the appearance at the head of the alphabet of the "crisscross row" or "crossrow," so called for the "christ cross" mark that functioned as an apotropaeic guarantor of proper reading and as an invocation to memory.[14] (See Figure 4.1.)

For example, Jane Bostocke's English sampler of 1598, in the Victoria and Albert Museum, shows a sequence of capital letters set off by just such a crossrow, most likely for the use of the Alice Lee whose birth is

Figure 4.1. The Jane Bostocke sampler. Linen embroidered with silk and metal threads, with pearls and beads. English, 1589. V & A Images/Victoria and Albert Museum, London; Museum Number: CT58353.

commemorated in the piece. At two years old, while younger than most early modern school-goers, Lee would have been approaching the age at which children of both genders could begin to learn the alphabet. The seventeenth-century essayist Thomas Tryon urged women, "At a Year and a Half or Two Years Old, shew them [children] their Letters, . . . make frequent Repetitions in their hearing, putting the Letters in their Sight." Through rote listening and viewing, "in a little time, they will easily and familiarly learn to distinguish the Twenty Four Letters, . . . and by this method, your Children, un-accountably to themselves, will attain to Read and Write at Three, Four, or Five years old."[15]

Bostocke's alphabet similarly fosters learning "familiarly" through "frequent Repetitions." The shapes of the alphabet's letters on the upper line closely resemble the larger letters below that form Alice Lee's name and commemorate her birth, encouraging a transfer of rudimentary reading skills from the first line to the second. The similarities between the *A* of the alphabet and that which begins the word "Alice" underneath it, in particular, suggest that once Lee has mastered the letters of the crossrow, she will be able to decipher her own beginnings—her name and the incidents of her birth—and thus to recognize herself as one of the subjects of the piece.

Yet, the inclusion of the crossrow does more than interpellate its young reader into literacy and the social order by demonstrating the effects of the study of letters. Through its use of such a common visual symbol, the sampler also advertises for a wider audience than Alice Lee its status as a reading *text*, calling attention with the crossrow to its own participation in the pedagogy of early instruction and its engagement with the standards of the genre—invoking an intertextuality that emphasizes for additional readers the sewn sampler's similarity and equivalency to its print fellows and the role of female domestic labor and female communities in the production of literacies.

Despite their lower literacy rates in the sixteenth and seventeenth centuries, women were frequently represented in print and manuscript as the source of initial literacy instruction. Margaret Spufford cites several seventeenth-century accounts of young children being taught by women to read, whether by their mothers at home or at the houses of neighbor women and "schooldames"—widows and "wives of day-labourers and of small craftsmen"—who supplemented their incomes by such instruction.[16] However, in Great Britain, at least, sites of commercial needlework also seem to have been strongly associated with early literacy pedagogy. Edmund Coote's 1596 writing manual, the *English Schoole-Master,* addresses itself to both "Men and Women" (A2[r]), including "Taylors, Weavers, Shop-keepers, Seamsters, and such other, as have undertaken the charge of teaching others" (A3[r]).[17] Similarly, Francis Clement enjoins "the litle Children" at the begining of his *Petie Schole* to find further instruction with local textile makers: "Frequent ye now the Taylers shop, / and eeke the Weavers lombe; Ther's neither these, but can with skill / Them teach that thither come."[18] He singles out female fabric workers in particular as new sources of reading instruction:

The Semstresse she (a Mistresse now) hath lore as much to reade,
As erst she had in many yeares
compast by silke and threede
I can not all by name rehearse,
For many moe you see:
Come make your choyce, let toies alone,
and trifles: Learne A.B.

Clement's upwardly mobile seamstress, "a Mistresse now," moves easily from one didactic position to another thanks to the commensurability of her reading and sewing knowledge, her "lore"—that is, information and erudition—in both domains.[19] Indeed, her credentials as a reading teacher increase in Clement's eyes specifically because of the material she has already "compast" in "silke and threede": here "compast" indicates not only her circumscription of a body of learning but also her ability to invent or "artfully contrive" in those media as well.

A more pejorative linking of rudimentary reading to women's sewing appears in William Hawkins's play *Apollo Shroving*, written for the 1626 Shrove Tuesday celebrations of the schoolboys of the Free-School of Hadleigh in Suffolk and published by Robert Mylbourne in London the following year. In a common misogynist device, the prologue is interrupted by a female audience member who demands proof that the play will answer her desires as a spectator. To reassure her, the exasperated schoolboy invites her to peruse the title page (the "Rowle"), leading to a parody of remedial reading practices in which the housewife sounds out syllables haltingly:

PROL. Take out thy fescue, and spell here, in this one-leau'd booke. Tell the stitches in this sampler of blacke and white.
LALA. A. P. ap.
PROL. A. P. ap? Thou fumbling Ape, A, per se, A. P. O. L. pol
LALA. A. per se, A. P. O. L. pol, L. O. lo. *Apollo.* On my maidenhead this is Latine. We shall bee choaked with a dogrell Latine Play for all this.[20]

The humor depends on the play's assumption that the female spectator can read only phonetically; yet, the conceit also conflates hornbook and sampler as sites of initial reading instruction, relying on the audience's recognition that samplers regularly contained letters and that those letters could be "read" as rudimentary texts produced for female readers. Significantly, Hawkins's trope differentiates printed and sewn texts by their particular physical features—multiple or single pages (leaves), mono- or polychrome letters—not by their inherent textuality or legibility per se, even for beginners. Both forms of text can be deciphered with the aid of a fescue or pointer for indicating letters; both can be "spelled" or "told," to use early modern pedagogical parlance.

Recent literacy studies have begun to distinguish the ability to read letters from the ability to form letters with the hand, and these more traditional definitions of literacy from the ability to recognize the cultural meanings and implications of different letters—as apart from the other two skills. Armando Petrucci, the paleographer and historian of the book, writes of the "absolute figurative" value that classical letters held in the early modern period.[21] A capacity to identify the symbolic associations of letters, despite the inability to make out the words that they formed, in Latin or the vernacular, constitutes what one might call—for want of a better term—*graphic* literacy. To give just one example of such a capability, Renaissance women illiterate in Latin are represented frequently as nonetheless recognizing what the seventeenth-century printer Joseph Moxon identified as the elevating effect of the roman majuscule, or capital letter: "When he [the Compositor] meets with proper Names of Persons or Places," Joseph Moxon explains, "he Sets the . . . first Letter with a Capital or—as the Person or Place he finds the purpose of the Author to dignifie—all Capitals; but then, if conveniently he can, he will set a space between every Letter, and two or three before and after that Name, to make it show more Graceful and Stately. . . . For Capitals express Dignity where-ever they are Set, and Space and Distance also implies stateliness."[22]

Hawkins's play evokes, and relies on its audience's recognition of, such multiple definitions of literacy for the early modern period. These literacies are marked as strongly gendered at this moment, defining its female spectator as "illiterate" equally through her halting perusal and her resistance to foreign tongues and letterforms, particularly to Latin and the dignifying effect of the roman capital. Yet, while *Apollo Shroving* places the ideology of English xenophobia in female mouths, printed sewing guides assumed that feminine needlework could function as a site for international artistic display and economic exchange, not least in the formation and recognition of alphabetical letters, and that its female practitioners were able to decipher printed and sewn texts on several levels.

The 1596 *Booke of Curious and strange Inuentions, called the first part of Needleworkes* advertises itself on the title page as a product and producer of *translatio*, having been "first imprinted in *Venice*" but now "newly printed in more exquisite sort for the profit and delight of the Gentlewomen of England." In Taylor's *Needles Excellency* it is the stitches themselves that are imported, in a list that invokes and resembles parallel descriptions of alternative sign systems coming into European view in this same period: they hail, according to Taylor, "[f]rom the remotest parts of Christendome," and throughout the globe, for "some of these rare Patternes have beene set / Beyond the bounds of faithlesse *Mahomet*: / From spacious *China*, and those Kingdomes East,/ And from great *Mexico*, the Indies West" (A2[r]). Both books are set in roman type, an increasingly international face and one thought appropriate only for advanced texts, thus implying that their female readers are pedagogically sophisticated enough to appreciate Taylor's distinction between "cunning workes . . . /(Too hard for meane capacities to reach)" and others "As plaine and easie as are A B C" (A1[v]). At the same time, such alphabetical analogies indicate the degree to which such texts, even—or especially—pattern books for female "work," actively participate in the formation of hierarchies of literacy.

Taylor's work is paradoxical in this sense. As Jones and Stallybrass have noted, he praises authors such as Mary Sidney and Elizabeth I for their needlework rather than for their writing. Yet, he also invokes circumstances in which sewing might constitute writing as well: "There's nothing neare at hand, or farthest sought, / But with the Needle may be shap'd and wrought" (A1[v]). The capacious past tense of "work," "wrought" in the sixteenth century had a specific connotation of needlework within its broader sense of "made or constructed by means of labour or art; fashioned, formed."[23] However, "wrought" equally could mean fashioned in a verbal sense—as "composed" or "written"—and be spelled alternately "wrought, wroght, wrout, or wrote." Taylor's invocation of the "True History, or various pleasant fiction" (A1[v]) that needlework can convey, then, sidesteps whether such narratives are depicted verbally or visually; indeed, his other references to texts within needlework suggest the simultaneous presence of both forms of representation (see below). Likewise, seventeenth-century Anglo-American school samplers use the verb "wrought" or "rout" to describe the production of the needlework as a whole. A 1691 sampler worked by Hannah Canting, now in the Fitzwilliam Museum, contains three alphabets, all in majuscules, and four versions of the maker's name—the last with a description of the piece's origin as a school assignment made for Mistress Judah Hayle: "HANNAH CANTING / IS MY NAME AND WI / TH MY NEDEL I ROV / T THe SAMe & IVDA / HAYLe IS MY DAMe."[24] A 1537 epitaph for the Londoner Elizabeth Lucar uses "wrote" in a similarly indefinite fashion, saying of the merchant's wife admiringly:

> She wrote all Needle-workes that women exercise,
> With Pen, Frame, or Stoole, all Pictures artificiall.
> Curious Knots, or Trailes, what fancie could devise,
> Beasts, Birds, or Flowers, even as things natural:

Three manner Hands could she write them faire all.[25] (See Figure 4.2.)

There is more to say about Jane Bostocke's sampler in this context, both as a source for fostering visual and verbal literacies in their broadest sense and in its narrower construction as a lettered document. Remaining for the moment on the question of reading-only literacy, however, it becomes clear that Bostocke's text differs in its teachings from the standard hornbook even as it resembles it. While the hornbook's letters are in gothic type, reflecting the belief that such black or "English" letters were the simplest to read and therefore the most appropriate for beginners, the sampler's letters appear by and large in a more romanized form. Yet there are significant exceptions to such Continental parallels in the piece: the barred *A*'s and *I*'s that appear both in the alphabet and in the names and inscription are sewn letterforms common to northern Europe throughout the sixteenth and seventeenth centuries but rarely seen in manuscript or printed texts.[26] Conversely, Italian needlework, even that as theatrically intimate as a pair of sixteenth-century woman's breeches now in the Prato Museum of Textiles, uses classical roman *I*'s for names and inscriptions (in this case the repeated stitched demand "VOGLIO IL COR".)[27] A 1603 sewn pillow cover by Mary Hulton, celebrating the ascendancy of James I to the throne, further suggests that sewn capitals in England often had their own form: Hulton, who uses a barred *A* in her first name, eschews the classicizing roman capital for the new monarch, instead creating a characteristically English gallimaufry of barred initials for the Latin abbreviation, *IR*, to flank the shield of newly united Britain.[28] Nearly a century later Hannah Canting uses barred *I*'s in all her sewn inscriptions, save those inscribing roman numerals. These continuing graphic phenomena suggest that rather than simply *duplicating* the visual literacies of the book, and the international styles of the border-crossing pattern guides, samplers also initiate and inculcate their own literacies, which, as I will discuss in the following section, might then be replicated or alluded to in other media and other hands.

* * *

In their chapter on "The Needle and the Pen," Ann Jones and Peter Stallybrass identify the transmission of female visual knowledge made possible by samplers such as Bostocke's, and they acknowledge such pieces as material dramatizations of "connections between women."[29] As with reading and writing literacies, the role of sewn copying and *copia* in early modern subject formation should not be underestimated. One might go further to suggest that the working of multiple hands in the sampler, including the filling in of Bostocke's name in seed pearls, pro-

Figure 4.2. Hannah Canting, linen band sampler embroidered in polychrome silks in cross, hem, double running, Algerian eye, satin, chain, whipped stem, and trellis stitch. English, 1691. Fitzwilliam Museum, University of Cambridge. Dr. J. W. L. Glaisher Bequest, P.83-1928.

vides an additional mode of copying and the production of *copia* accessible primarily to women, one that might have provided an alternative, if similar, mode of inscription to that used by writing pedagogy for boys.[30] Accordingly I want to turn now to another site of multiple hands, in which copying also demonstrates an affective relationship and posits differing modes of literacy: the not-yet-queen Elizabeth Tudor's 1544 New Year's gift to her stepmother Katherine Parr.

Recent scholars have examined how this hand-copied and embroidery-bound translation of Marguerite d'Anguoulême's *Le Miroir de l'âme pécheresse* (1531) constructed a relationship between the eleven-year-old daughter and the wife of the English king.[31] Using anthropological theories of gift exchange and the traffic in women, critics have found in the work a strong degree of self-promotion and self-mastery on the part of the young princess.[32] However, by not attending closely to the forms of capitalization displayed in the sewn and written letters of the work as a whole, such readings overstate the power that the text ascribes to its maker in the presence of its ideal reader, misconstruing the subject position that the object constructs for the giver and for the recipient.[33] (See Figure 4.3.)

Turning to the book, we see how those familial relationships are reinforced by its frequent material representations of union, sewn and written, that include the use of joined classicized capitals. The manuscript offers an equally powerful example of majuscules demanding to be read, an example which contrasts significantly with its cover, however.[34] Inside, the roman capitals that begin the dedication suggest a further connection between giver and recipient, one that suggests a strategic use of precisely the lesser position of power implied by the inability to "freely copy" the great letter. Katherine's name is written in classical majuscules as "KATHERIN." The final *E* that would conclude her name forms the first initial of the otherwise minuscule "Eliza-beth" that follows, thus linking the two together. Indeed, enchaining or linking hand in hand the letters of proper names is one of the functions of such ciphers, according to the writing instructor Giovambattista Palatino.[35] (See Figure 4.4.)

The elision of the *E* is the more noticeable given the relative lack of capital letters throughout the book. Titles and "Dignities" such as "your highness," "quene," and "princes" all appear in minuscule. All references to religious figures also are written in "small" letters—"god," "virgin mary," "switte iesus"—as are proper names—"salomon," "adam," "luke."[36] Moreover, except when it follows an end point, the pronoun *I* always appears as *i*, not only in the body of the translation but also in the introduction where Elizabeth addresses Parr ostensibly in her own voice. Given the intermittent, but regularized, presence of conventional capitalization, one cannot conclude simply that Elizabeth did not

Figure 4.3. Elizabeth Tudor's 1544 New Year's gift to her stepmother Katherine Parr. Bodleian Library, University of Oxford, MS. Cherry 36, front cover and spine.

know how to write majuscules at this age. Nonetheless, the text creates the strong impression that she has only partially acquired that ability.

To become a proper humanist and civic subject in the Renaissance one had to copy letters properly. Printed models for characters became widely available in the sixteenth and seventeenth centuries through

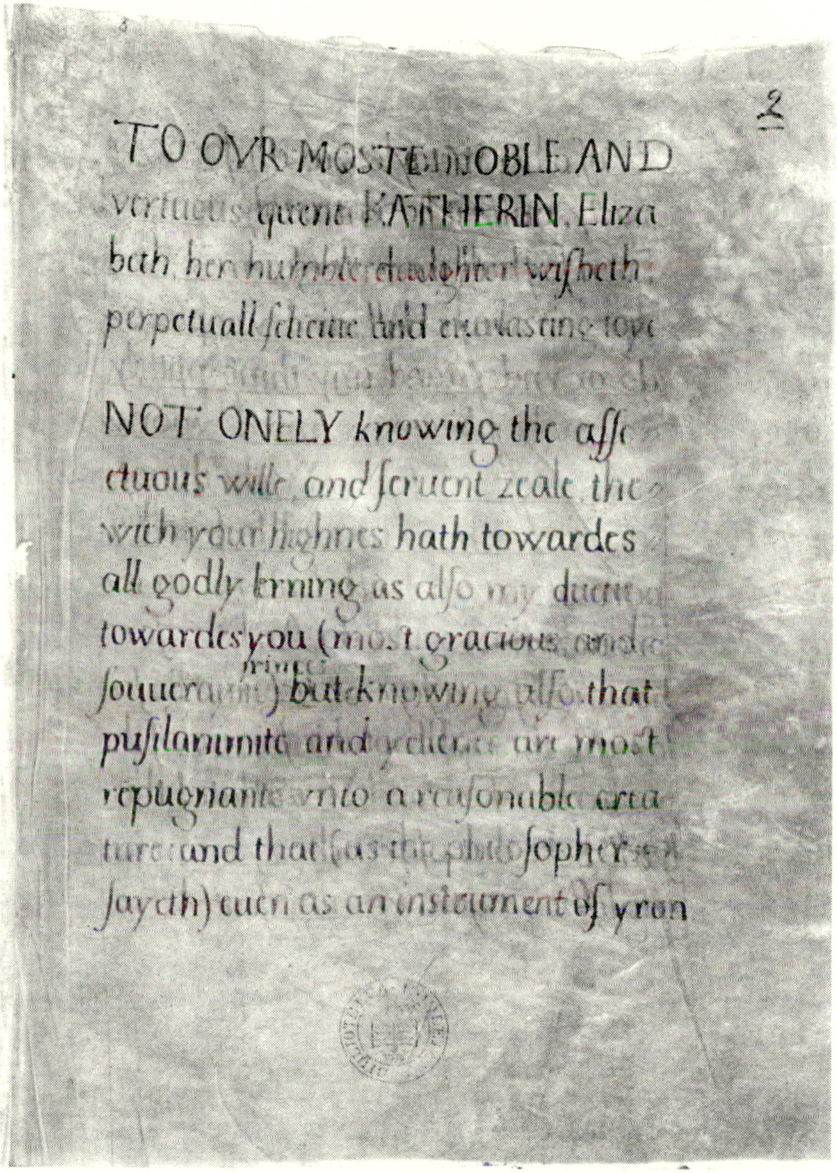

2

TO OVR MOSTE NOBLE AND
vertuous quene KATHERIN, Eliza
beth her humble daughter wisheth
perpetuall felicitie and everlasting ioye

NOT ONELY knowing the affe
ctuous wille, and feruent zeale, the
which your highnes hath towardes
all godly lerning, as also my duetie
towardes you (most gracious and
soueraigne princes) but knowing also that
pusilanimite and ydlenes are most
repugnante vnto a reasonable crea
ture and that (as the philosopher
sayeth) euen as an instrument of yron

Figure 4.4. Dedication inscribed by Elizabeth Tudor in the 1544 gift book.
Bodleian Library, University of Oxford, MS. Cherry 36, fol. 24v.

engraved handbooks and writing manuals. However, the mastery of majuscules implied an advanced level of pedagogic engagement, one where the student's hand had already in some sense been inscribed in the alphabetical order of the letter.[37] Almost exclusively, handwriting manuals leave the great letter until the end of the discussion, not simply for the propriety of moving from smaller to large but because most instructions for majuscules require a knowledge of the basic strokes used in making minuscules.[38]

Hence, while some celebrated treatises on writing contain detailed descriptions for how to form the capital letter, the majority, like Palatino's and Arrighi's, leave the reader relatively free from overt direction, at most suggesting, "exert yourself to learn to make your Majuscules as you find them here in the inscribed examples."[39] To the writer who has successfully passed the initial stage, the texts now hold out the promise of an individuated subjectivity as the reward for interpellation into the dominant ideologies of the hand.

Conversely, Elizabeth's copy presents her as an intermediate student in need of correction. Introducing the work to Parr, she states, "i knowe that as for my parte, wich i haue wrought in it: the (as well spirituall, as manuall) there is nothinge done as it shulde be nor els worthy to come in youre graces handes, but rather all vnperfyte and vncorecte."[40] The double mention of manual labor and receptive hands serves to call attention to the handcrafted nature of the gift; yet, the language speaks as much of writing as of needlework. The dedication employs an extended trope of textual emendation and erasure to articulate Elizabeth's desired didactic relationship with Parr: "yet do i truste * also that oubeit it is like a worke wich is but begonne, and shapen: that the syle [*sic*] of youre excellent witte and godly lerninge in the redinge of it . . . shall rubbe out, polishe, and mende (or els cause to mende) the wordes (or rather the order of my writting) the wich i knowe in many places to be rude, and nothinge done as it shuld be." The conflation of the giver with the manuscript, as for example in the line "But i hope, that after to haue ben in youre graces handes: there shall be nothinge [in it] worthy of reprehension," links her "rude" writing and its unpolished order to an "vncorecte" self. The partial capitalization of the italics similarly shows Elizabeth as "newe begonne and shapen." Rather than advertising the writer's mastery, the form of the manuscript (like its rhetoric) demonstrates her continued need to be "taken in hand," as an incomplete being whose mastery of subjecthood "(as well spirituall, as manuall)" is "vnperfyte."

However, if the young Elizabeth employs the roman capital selectively in her opening dedication to make visible the interdependency she hopes to invoke between herself and the queen through this gift, she uses yet another capital form, one whose signification Katherine Parr was equally likely to recognize, in her translation of Marguerite de Navarre's preface to the work. Elizabeth renders the French fairly literally, while making adjustments for the change from verse to prose. She follows Navarre's choices in syntactical structure and vocabulary, translating

> Si vous lisez ceste oeuvre toute entiere,
> Arrestez vous, sans plus, à la matiere,
> En excusant la rhyme et le languaige,
> Voyant que c'est d'une femme l'ouvraige,
> Qui n'a en soy science, ne sçavoir

as "IF thou doest rede thys whole ~~w~~ worke: beholde rather the matter and excuse the speche, consydering it is the worke of a woman: wiche hath in her neyther science or knowledge." Even while maintaining characteristic verbal fidelity to her source, however, Elizabeth's text unusually reinforces and emphasizes this claim to be "d'une femme l'ouvraige"—"the work of a woman"—through a visual strategy.[41] A darkened *I*, larger than the following roman capital or the italics of the body text, initiates the manuscript—a letterform that derives its meaning not from other scripted or typographical hands but from the mastery of sewn letters in which Elizabeth has already demonstrated her abilities. Recognizable as one of the two forms of capital *I* used later by Jane Bostocke, Mary Hulton, and Hannah Canting, the "barred I" here appears in a similarly mixed lettering but in an unusual medium—ink rather than thread. Nonetheless, the letter continues to bear traces of its originary context. By inscribing her uncial *I* in this other, northern letter form, Elizabeth both makes a partisan appeal to Katherine Parr's own nonitalic mixed hand and taps an alternative source of trans-European identity: one simultaneously international and domestic, yet whose ideological claims to power are significantly different from the roman capital with its associations of "Dignity" and "stateliness" and imperial expansion.

Elizabeth Tudor's humanist education in multiple hands, writing and sewing, should be seen as exceptional if not entirely unique. Yet, even in this royal text one finds a hierarchy of proper female pedagogy that self-consciously privileges sewing before writing as an acquired skill. The manuscript *Miroir*'s manipulation of competent and incompetent hands suggests the ideological work necessarily in play when sewing is conjoined with reading and writing. Its display of skillful sewn letterforms—whether in thread or in ink—in specific contrast to its "vnperfyte" roman and italic capitals, makes a claim for Elizabeth occupying an unthreatening position of age, rank, and gender at the same time that it demonstrates an awareness and deployment of a range of graphic literacies and transnational alphabets.[42]

The implications of sewn letters are thus equally significant, I would suggest, for concepts of literacy as the ability to write as well as to read. The limited survival of sewn letters and signatures is hardly going to correct statistical analyses of signatory records in the seventeenth century. However, they can serve as the kind of sources that recent scholars of women's reading practices have recommended examining as alternatives to the limitations of such material.[43] At the same time, feminist scholars may need to recognize the challenge that such sources represent to the historical claims of an absolute separation of reading and sewing from writing that have formed one of the most effective counters to studies of signatory records in the assessment of women's literacy. In other words, we need to become attuned to the ways that, in the early modern period, inscribing letters with a needle could be seen as analogous to, or indeed continuous with, inscribing letters with a pen.

While learning to read letters and to sew them is widely thought to have occurred simultaneously for girls in the Renaissance, learning to write is commonly seen by scholars of early modern literacy as a later and more rarefied skill. Eve Sanders and Margaret Spufford each cite several examples of schools before the mid-seventeenth century where girls were taught to read and sew simultaneously but not to write, both in England and on the Continent.[44] Whereas in late sixteenth-century France writing instruction seems to have been explicitly forbidden for girls by ecclesiastical authorities, in England and Italy access to writing-literacy appears to have been more a function of the limited time and opportunity girls had for advanced study in the "petty" or elementary schools, as well perhaps as to a paucity of female instructors.[45]

However, we also find repeated scenes in early modern drama that represent women teaching girls simultaneously to read, write, and sew. In the anonymous English play *The Wit of a Woman* (London, 1604), the schoolmistress Balia surveys and corrects the written as well as sewn work by her four female charges, none of which is particularly accomplished:

> Well *Merilla,* let me see your Cushin-work: oh Lord heere is a great fault, in trueth your colours are not wel mingled, besides it is not euen laid.
>
> . . . .
>
> Now *Gianetta,* what haue you written? looke you, a faire maide, and make such foule blottes, and not a streight line? all awry, all awry, I pray you let it be mended. (A3[v])

As a result of such simultaneous instruction, however, one of the girls' suitors can later boast of his lover, "Faith mine, her mistresse sayeth, hath an excellent hande at her needle, and for an apt hand to writing: I must confese, shee is worthy prayse" ($B3^{r}$).

Likewise the banished Queen Eulalia of Richard Brome's eponymous *The Queen and the Concubine* (London, 1635)—forced in exile to earn her living as a schoolmistress—inspects both the "Sampler" and the "writing book" of her students, praising one for her clean work and cautioning the other not to get ahead of herself: "No child you must not Joyn-hand yet: you must your letters and your minums better first. Take heed, you may Joyn-hand too soon, and so mar all; still youth desires to be too forward" ($G3^{v}$–4^{r}).[46]

The suggestion of untoward or dangerous erotic behavior associated with precocious writing—"Joyn-hand" being script but also unsanctioned marriage—recurs throughout the early modern period, so commonly in fact that it engenders a counterargument against lascivious needlework. In his 1616 *Asylum Veneris*, Daniel Tuvill makes the connection between surreptitious sewing and writing explicit. To those who believe that for women "The Pen must be forbidden them as the Tree of good and euill" and that the act of writing "is a Pandar to a Virgine Chastitie," he argues "But if this be their feare, let them likewise barre them the vse of their needle." "With this did *Philomela* fairely character those foule indignities, which had bin offered hir by *Tereus*," he reasons, adding, "and why then may not others expresse their loues, and their affections in the like forme? . . . Affection is ingenious, and can impe them, as it pleaseth hir" (88).

To return to the allusion to Philomel from *Titus Andronicus*, Marcus's unfortunate niece Lavinia is remembered not only for her ability with the needle but also for her habits of reading "Sweet Poetrie and Tullies Oratour" ($F4^{r}$) to her young cousin Lucius. Unlike my earlier examples, Shakespeare's account asserts the separation of writing from sewing and reading, however, revising this traditional Ovidian scene of women's textual communication and insisting on Philomel's status serving *not* as a paradigm, an "example of a woman to work by."

In Arthur Golding's version of the *Metamorphoses* (1567), Philomel conveys the story of her rape not just by handiwork but also by "weaving purple letters . . . which bewraide / The wicked deede." Marcus refers to this particularly female form of rubrication—"weaving purple letters"—when he exclaims upon seeing the handless Lavinia: "Fair Philomel, why she but lost her tongue." Instead, for Lavinia, his

> lovely niece, that mean is cut. . . .
> A craftier Tereus . . .
> . . . hath cut those pretty fingers off
> That could have better sewed than Philomel. ($E2^{v}$)

Lavinia's disfigurement precisely denies the heroine the possibility of using sewn letters to tell her story. Rather, *Titus Andronicus* substitutes an alternate technology for sewing, a fairly grotesque parody of elementary writing instruction, an etiology reminiscent of Geoffroy de Tory's claim that bovine Io founded the formative letters of the Greek alphabet after her rape by scraping and imprinting her hooves in the dust, creating an iota and an omega. Likewise, Lavinia is invited to imitate her uncle's inscription in "this sandie plot." Marcus provides his niece with a new "pen to print [her] sorrowes plaine"—the familial staff that when inserted in Lavinia's mouth and guided by her handless limbs allows her to write the Latin *Stuprum*—"Rape"—"Without the help of any hand at all" (F4v). This fantasy of an origin for writing that conflates voice, pen, and print, erasing both manual and auditory difference, resembles etiologies of creating standardized copying hands cited by Jonathan Goldberg, even as it erases another site of copying and *copia*, the sampler, as a means of expression.[47]

In Marcus's hands this new writing becomes a means to resolve the ostensible "mystery" of Lavinia's violation, just as for Philomela and Procne sewn letters provide the manner by which a crime is revealed. John Taylor's *The Needles Excellency*, in contrast, celebrates needlework as a source of secrecy, "Poesies rare, and Annagrams," emblems and mottos, variations on nominal letters that, as Taylor puts it, offer "Significque searching sentences from Names" (A1v). Carrying meaning both significant and to be sought out by the reader, sewn letters are one source for George Puttenham's "cognizance, emblemes, enseignes and impreses"—"two or three words of wittie sentence or secrete conceit . . . such as a man may put in letters of gold and send to his mistresses for a token, or cause to be embrodered in scutchions of armes, or in any bordure of a rich garment to giue by his noueltie maruell to the beholder." Puttenham sees no need to distinguish between the medium on which such words and figures appear—metal, paper, cloth—or indeed whether they "rest in colour or figure or both, or in word or in muet shew." Rather, "The vse and intent is one . . . and that is . . . to insinuate some secret wittie, morall and braue purpose presented to the beholder, either to recreate his eye, or please his phantasie, or examine his iudgement or occupie his braine or to manage his will either by hope or by dread."[48]

As noted earlier, scholars have begun to trace needlework as a potential form of artistic publication for women in the early modern period, charting the trajectory of visual images transposed from emblem books, title pages, and print illustrations onto pillows, bed hangings, and mirror frames—images stored, in the interim and for future use, in samplers such as Bostocke's. Helena's oft-cited recollection of her girlhood sewing with Hermia in *A Midsummer Night's Dream* offers a vision of just such female pictorial creativity:

> We Hermia, like two Artificiall gods,
> Haue with our needles, created both one flower,
> Both on one sampler, sitting on one cushion,
> Both warbling of one song, both in one key;
> As if our hands, our sides, voices, and mindes
> Had beene incorporate.

As Jones and Stallybrass have written, the speech uses the language of emergent Protestant marriage ceremonies for the "incorporation" of the two women through their collaborative sewing, a rite, I would add, placed decisively in the past, memorializing but only in nostalgic form their erotic affection as well as their semidivine art.[49] In similar terms, the opening sonnet of Ostaus's 1561 *La vera perfezione del disegno per puntie ricami*, or *The true perfection of design for embroidery stitches*, praises his patron the Venetian "Gentildonna" Lucretia Priuli for "l'ingegno donnesco" ("the feminine wit") that "far con l'ago, quanto / Da Poeta o Pittor mai fusse espresso" ("makes with the needle, that which by Poet or Painter was never before expressed"). Indeed, asserts Ostaus ingratiatingly, "Here one sees that Woman greatly resembles the Creator" ("Qui si uedra, che s'assomiglia tanto / La donna al Creator") (A3^{r}). Giovanni Antonio Tagliente's 1531 *Esemplario nvovo che insegna a le donne a cuscire, a raccamare et a disegnare* (*New edition instructing women how to sew, embroider, and design/draw*) carries on its frontispiece an image of two women working on the same embroidery frame, in this case on what looks like an ecclesiastical piece, which bears a striking similarity to Helena's description of twin hands and minds producing one work.

What is again occluded in Shakespeare's account of Hermia and Helena's needlework—and affirmed by contrast in Italian manuals such as those of Ostaus and Tagliente—is the presence of letters, indeed of writing, in conjunction with sewing. The embroidery handbooks produced in Venice that were translated and distributed throughout Europe repeatedly provide instructions on how to make ciphers, alphabets, phrases, and pithy sentences. Ostaus's text, for example, includes several alphabets mapped for reproduction in different stitches: plate 12 has been directly linked to a sample of mid-seventeenth-century "whitework" now in the Victoria and Albert Museum. Giovanni Antonio Tagliente explicitly offers instruction in the "punto scritto," or "the writing stitch," advertising that in addition to "flowers of various styles, . . . trees, . . . vases, fountains, landscapes with antique histories . . ." in his book "you will find letters—antique majuscules, and the french letters, and many other sorts of designs and letters for sewing and embroidering enciphered letters, or other verses however one might wish, and as you will amply see in the present work" (A1r). Tagliente is, of course, best known for his introductory reading and writing manuals widely circulated in the sixteenth century, the latter of which promise to provide "many diverse sorts of letters to satisfy the various appetites of men." His embroidery guides are equally invested in letter formation and alphabetical literacy, however. Both texts provide illustrations of gothic or "French" letters to copy and include patterns for almost identical rebuses of hearts and eyes accompanied by capitalized verses. Even more strikingly, the sewing manual of 1531 uses the same plates of exemplary roman majuscules that appear in the earlier writing manuals of 1524. Similarly, Tagliente recycles the illustration of sharpening tools for quills for the sewing guide, in keeping with his categorization of both writing and sewing as "disegno."

Unlike his writing manual, however, Tagliente's guide to sewing offers itself explicitly as a pedagogical tool to women. To the "magnanimous and beautiful women and most chaste young ladies" ("magnanime, & bellissime donne, & castissime damigelle") whom he identifies as his readers, he advises a specific autodidactic project, similar to the methods by which one acquires handwriting: "make it your work first to learn the small and easy designs, and most of all learn the first example, which is provided in the first illustration, which is a picture. And then go on to the second group and thus follow the other illustrations" ("fa di mestiero prima ad impararare . . . gli disegni piccoli, & facili . . . che sopra tutto impariati lo primo esempio, lo qual de la e disgnato neella primatauola, che e un quadro. Et poi lo presente secondo gruppo, & cosi seguitando le altre tauole . . .") (A1v). Looking at such "quadri," or "pictures," is a form of reading, in his terms: at another point in the text, he tells his female readers, "you will read this design in the histories of the wise ancients" ("Leggesi nelle historie delli saui antichi questo disegno") (A3r). Tagliente also strategically employs an alphabetical notion of what it means to be literate, however, imagining his female audience not only as readers but also as aware of the pedagogy of literacy. Acquiring the skill to "design a complete / whole figure" ("disegnare una figura intiera") resembles the process of learning the alphabet, he argues: "as it would be, say, if one wanted to learn how to read: first one would have to give primary attention to recognizing the letter A, and then the letter B and thus to follow from the beginning to the end." ("come sarebe a dire, uno vuol imparar leggere, imprima ha di mestieri dar principio a cognoscere la lettera A, et dopo la lettera B, & cosi dal principio per insin al fine bisogna seguire") (D2v). To an even greater extent than the English translations of Continental manuals, then, equivalent Italian guides to sewing and writing such as Tagliente's suggest the extent to which difference in medium could be seen as secondary to a consistent pedagogic program for literacies and an overarching notion of the copying copious hand in the production of what was regarded as a continuum of texts.

I do not want to idealize the limited possibilities that needlework offered women in this or later periods. The opposition of (acceptable) sewing to (immoral) writing was not simply an attempt by male-authored conduct manuals to keep women from their books but also a frequent sore point for early modern women writers who themselves self-consciously rejected the needle for the pen. The Italian reformist Olympia Morata wrote angrily in a 1540 letter from Ferrara, "since letters surpass all human affairs, what women's spindles and needles . . . will be able to call me away from the gentle Muses? I have closed my ears against these women's spells just as Ulysses did at the Sirens' rocks."[50]

Nonetheless, it is important to recognize that sewing and writing do not seem to have been regarded necessarily as the separate activities often so described by recent scholars of literacy and as represented in certain early modern—specifically Shakespearean—texts. These examples suggest that the conjunction or separation of sewing and writing forms part of the contestatory ground of literacy itself in the period, rather than simply the raw material with which histories of literacy can now be correctly or incorrectly written. Furthermore, if sewing could serve as a form of writing for women, a way to comment on, and differentiate between, a range of texts in this period, we need to begin to consider needlework as the site of potential intersection of visual and what have been thought of as more traditionally verbal literacies, sewn letters as a potential form of contextual and textual commentary. We must begin to *read* sewn pieces, asking what would be legible and to whom in these sites—that is, who was literate in sewn letters and what did they read there?

Helena's specific image of *sides* formerly incorporate, among "hands, sides, voices, mindes," should remind readers of *another* prelapsarian fantasy, one (arguably *the* one) on which the marriage ceremony is based. We find that fantasy forcefully rendered in a 1607 cover to a Book of Common Prayer and Bible (Untermyer Collection, Metropolitan Museum of Art, New York), to which the anonymous needleworker has added an inscription as a guide to the depiction of Genesis: on the front, in roman capitals, set off by a cartouche that lends it space and prominence, appear the words "A DREAME." What exactly is being "dreamt" here: a paradise of marital harmony at the moment of its demise or, as Eve is holding two apples, a reverie of female power and forbidden knowledge about to be realized? Or does the cover comment on the fantastical nature of the biblical account as a whole, its demonization of Eve that early modern female historians from Christine de Pisan to Amelia Lanyer attempt to counter and revise? However we choose to read this rubric, we *read* it, in the most traditional sense—as we would read an annotation written in the margins of a printed picture or a caption printed below an illustration. The sewn commentary—A DREAME—and its image carry at least equal authority as those other couplings of word and image, I would argue: the combination of capitalization—spacing—and position—in the center of the frame—renders this phrase visually the work's title, conditioning our reading of its cover image, and potentially of the contents within, asking us to consider it, in short, as writing and to decipher its relationship to the text it envelops.

By attending to such examples when they are recorded through sewing, this essay has tried to suggest some of the ways that the examination of seemingly unconventional sites of lettering might add to or refigure notions of literacy for early modern women. Most broadly, the consideration of sewn letters usefully complicates what has at times become a constricting dualism of reading and/or writing in discussions of early modern literacy. The lettering in samplers serves as memorials not only of pedagogic practice and subject formation, not only of exchanges of gift and service economies, but also of affective and social relations. These sewn relations are idiosyncratic perhaps; they are nonetheless valuable if what we seek to glimpse is not simply the extent but also the experiences of female literacy in the early modern period.

Notes

1. Thomas Heywood, *The Rape of Lucrece: A True Roman Tragedie* (London, 1608), E4v.

2. Heywood does make this act of literacy somewhat ambiguous by having Lucrece suggest that during Colatine's absence she is required as a dutiful wife to act the part of "husband."

3. Giovanni Ostaus (Venice, 1561), facsimile reproduction in Giovanni Ostaus, *La Vera Perfezione del Disegno per Punti e Ricami: Riproduzione della edizione di Venezia del 1561 dall'esemplare della Biblioteca Corsiniana in Roma* (Bergamo: Istituto Italiano D'Arti Grafiche, 1909), A2v.

4. Most notably, Erasmus, in *De recta Graeci et Latini sermonis pronunciatione* (1528) includes an account of the origins of letters as serpent's teeth sown by Cadmus, as an analogy of how to disseminate alphabetical learning to children.

5. William Shakespeare, *The Most Lamentable Romaine Tragedie of Titus Andronicus* (London, 1594), E2v.

6. Cited in Betty Ring, *Girlhood Embroidery: American Samplers & Pictorial Needlework, 1650–1850*, 2 vols. (New York: Knopf, 1993), 1:10.

7. Maria Fossi Todorow, *'Imparaticci'—'Samplers': Esercizi di ricamo delle bambine europee ed americane dal Seicento all' Ottocento*, Palazzo Davanzati, June 26–November 26, 1986 (Florence: Centro Di, 1986), 11.

8. John Taylor, *The Needles Excellency* (London, 1624), A2r.

9. Ann Rosalind Jones and Peter Stallybrass, *Renaissance Clothing and the Materials of Memory* (Cambridge: Cambridge University Press, 2000), 144, 170.

10. On the ideological implications of "literacy" vs. "literacies," and the contestatory nature of such knowledge and its definitions in the early modern period, see Margaret W. Ferguson, *Dido's Daughters: Literacy, Gender, and Empire in Early Modern England and France* (Chicago: University of Chicago Press, 2003), esp. 1–13 and ch. 1.

11. See in particular the influential work by Rozsika Parker, *The Subversive Stitch: Embroidery and the Making of the Feminine* (London: Women's Press, 1984; New York: Routledge, 1989), 5 and passim. See also the introductory essay by Jennifer Harris to the exhibition "Embroidery in Women's Lives, 1300–1900" (Whitworth Art Gallery, 1988), 10.

12. Rozsika Parker cites a 1619 listing for "coventry blue thred to make letters in needlework on the bed sheets" (Parker, *Subversive Stitch*, 1984, 85) as evidence of the "practical application[s]" of such alphabets. However, Parker also argues for an emerging interpellative function for samplers, manifested by what she identifies as the new phenomena of signing and dating such pieces (86).

13. On the hornbook, see Andrew Tuer, *History of the Horn Book* (1897; New York: Benjamin Blom, 1968). For an analysis of development of the hornbook and primer alphabet as a symbolic system in the early modern period, see Patricia Crain, *The Story of A: The Alphabetization of America from The New England Primer to The Scarlet Letter* (Stanford, Calif.: Stanford University Press, 2000), 20 and passim.

14. Crain, *Story of A*, 21. See also Anne Ferry, *The Art of Naming* (Chicago: University of Chicago Press, 1988), 129.

15. Margaret Spufford, "First Steps in Literacy: The Reading and Writing Experiences of the Humblest Seventeenth-Century Spiritual Autobiographers," *Social History* 4.3 (October 1979): 407–35, 417.

16. Ibid., 435.

17. While Jonathan Goldberg, *Writing Matter: From the Hands of the English Renaissance* (Stanford, Calif.: Stanford University Press, 1990), 135, claims that "[w]ith Coote's list, it appears that any place of business might have been a schoolroom in Elizabethan England," in fact, the dedication indicates that fabric workers and needleworkers of both genders were more greatly associated with literacy instruction than were other trade workers.

18. Francis Clement, *The Petie Schole* (London, 1587), 9.

19. From its earliest written appearances in English, "lore" indicated both that which was learned and learning itself—information and erudition simultaneously—as well as alluding to the act of teaching that learning to others. See *The Oxford English Dictionary Online* (Oxford: Oxford University Press, 2005).

20. William Hawkins, *Apollo Shroving* (London, 1627), B3r.

21. Armando Petrucci, *Public Lettering: Script, Power, and Culture*, trans. Linda Lappin (Chicago: University of Chicago Press, 1993), 18. For wall lettering in England in particular, see Tessa Watt, *Cheap Print and Popular Piety, 1550–1640* (Cambridge: Cambridge University Press, 1991).

22. Joseph Moxon, *Mechanick Exercises, or, The Doctrine of Handyworks Applied to the Art of Printing: A Literal Reprint in Two Volumes of the First Edition Published in the Year 1683* (New York: Typothetae of the City of New York, 1896), 225.

23. According to the *OED*, 2 ed.: "3.a. Of textile materials, esp. silk: Manufactured; spun. b. Decorated or ornamented, as with needlework; elaborated,

embellished, embroidered"; 1.b. and 1.c. "Shaped, fashioned, or finished from the rough or crude material; cut." See also 4.1617: "Who likes, approves, and usefull deems This work, for him 'tis wrought."

24. Cited in Harris, "Embroidery in Women's Lives," 12.

25. Cited in Parker, *Subversive Stitch*, 75–76.

26. The other exception being the interlaced *V*'s that form the *W*'s in the piece. Interestingly, these letters were commonly used as a signatory mark in certain parts of England, in place of a mark of trade or a name. See Wyn Ford, "The Problem of Literacy in Early Modern England," *History* 78 (February 1992): 22–37, 34.

27. For the frequency of the classical *I* in Continental early modern needlework, see also Giulia Piccolomini's signed whitework sampler in Todorow, *Imparaticci*, and a seventeenth-century Spanish or Portuguese pattern book, overstitched throughout, with a roman capital IESVS.

28. Reproduced in Jones and Stallybrass, *Renaissance Clothing*, 157. For more on James I and the roman capital, see Bianca F.-C. Calabresi, "'Alphabetical Positions': Engendering Letters in Early Modern Europe," *Critical Survey* 14.1 (spring 2002): 9–27. On the typically mixed classicism of England in this period, see *Albion's Classicism: The Visual Arts in Britain, 1550–1660*, ed. Lucy Gent (New Haven, Conn. and London: Yale University Press, 1995).

29. Jones and Stallybrass, *Renaissance Clothing*, 158.

30. See Goldberg, *Writing Matter*, 159–62, for a summary of such techniques.

31. Among others, Maureen Quilligan, "Elizabeth's Embroidery," *Shakespeare Studies* 28 (2000): 208–14; and Lisa M. Klein, "Your Humble Handmaid: Elizabethan Gifts of Needlework," *Renaissance Quarterly* 50. 2 (summer 1997): 459–93. For a different perspective on the book's function, see Frances Teague, "Princess Elizabeth's Hand in *The Glass of the Sinful Soul*," *English Manuscript Studies 1100–1700: Writings by Early Modern Women* 9 (2003): 33–48.

32. For a balanced analysis of the translation, and of the relationship between author, translator, and recipient, see Anne Lake Prescott, "The Pearl of the Valois and Elizabeth I: Marguerite de Navarre's *Miroir* and Tudor England," in *Silent but for the Word*, ed. Margaret Hannay (Kent, Ohio: Kent State University Press, 1985), 61–76.

33. Even as they note a disparity between the work's sewn cover and its rather awkward italic hand, critics—most notably Maureen Quilligan—determine that this piece ultimately acts to display Elizabeth's "verbal mastery," with later printed versions "merely replicat[ing] in monumentally public form the authority the . . . object implicitly had within it" (Quilligan, "Elizabeth's Embroidery," 209).

34. According to Klein, "Your Humble Handmaid," 481, the interlaced letters on the front cover "emulate Katherine's characteristic signature, 'Kateryn the Quene KP,' in which the loop of the 'P' reaches back to intersect the 'K.'"

35. Likewise, George Puttenham writes that such plays on letters constitute "a meete study for Ladies. . . . They that vse it for pleasure is to breed one word out of another . . . where upon many times is produced some grateful newes or matter to them for whose pleasure and seruice it was intended" (George Puttenham, *The Arte of English Poesie* [London, 1589], II.90).

36. See Clement, *Petie Schole*, 61; and Simon Daines, *Orthoepia anglicana: or the first part of the English grammar, etc.* (London, 1640), 76/M2v, for consistent emphasis on capitalization of proper names from the late sixteenth to the mid-seventeenth centuries.

37. Goldberg, *Writing Matter,* provides the most thorough discussion and assessment of this pedagogic process. See also "Breeding Capital," ch. 2 of Richard Halpern, *The Poetics of Primitive Accumulation: English Renaissance Culture and the Genealogy of Capital* (Ithaca, N.Y.: Cornell University Press, 1991), for an Althusserian-inflected reading of early modern hands from which my questions about the relationship of economic and cultural capital derive.

38. "Le Maiuscole Cancellaresche, escono tutte dalli tre Tratti onde escono letre piccole, Tuttauia per che in uero non hanno regola ferma, si fanno giuditio dell' occhio, auuertirete che i tratti siano gagliardi et sicuri, senza Tremoli. Come qui uedete" (Giovambattista Palatino, LIBRO NVOVO D'IMPARARE A SCRIVERE TUTE SORTE LETTERE ANTICHE ET MODERNE DI TVTTE NATIONI, facsimile of the 1540 edition in *Three Classics of Italian Calligraphy,* [New York: Dover Publications, 1953], 152).

39. Ludovico degli Arrighi, *La operina di Ludovico Vicentino, da imparare di scrivere littera cancellarescha,* facsimile of the 1522 edition in *Three Classics of Italian Calligraphy,* 22.

40. *The Mirror of The Sinful Soul: A Prose Translation from the French of a poem by Queen Margaret of Navarre, Made in 1544 by the Princess (Afterwards Queen) Elizabeth, then eleven years of age,* facsimile reproduction (London: Asher and Co., 1897). The manuscript is also reproduced and its potential nationalist implications discussed in Marc Shell, *Elizabeth's Glass with 'The Glass of the Sinful Soul' (1544) by Elizabeth I and 'Epistle Dedicatory' & 'Conclusion' (1548) by John Bale* (Lincoln and London: University of Nebraska Press, 1993).

41. On the faithfulness of Elizabeth's translation and the significance of slight variants between the texts as a result, see Prescott, "Pearl of the Valois," 68–69; and Shell, *Elizabeth's Glass,* 108–9.

42. That Elizabeth used majuscules strategically has recently been noted by Janel Mueller and Leah Marcus, who note her "practice of substituting majuscule for miniscule letterforms" that began to appear shortly after her ascendancy to the English throne. They observe that such word-medial and word-final capitals "typically occur in the closing phrase of a letter or an inscription, just before the queen's elaborate signature." (See *Elizabeth I: Autograph Compositions and Foreign Language Originals,* ed. Janel Mueller and Leah S. Marcus [Chicago: University of Chicago Press, 2003], xix–xx.) In the context of Elizabeth's earlier manuscript, then, one might read this as a strategic emphasis of the queen's own nominative power that culminates in her self-nomination as Regina.

43. See, for example, Heidi Brayman Hackel, "The 'Great Variety' of Readers and Early Modern Reading Practices," in *A Companion to Shakespeare,* ed. David Scott Kastan (Oxford: Blackwell, 1999), 139–57, and *Reading Material in Early Modern England: Print, Gender, and Literacy* (Cambridge: Cambridge University Press, 2005), ch. 5; Sasha Roberts, "Reading in Early Modern England: Contexts and Problems," in *Reading in Early Modern England,* ed. Sasha Roberts, *Critical Survey* 12.2 (2000): 1–16; Eve Rachele Sanders, *Gender and Literacy on Stage in Early Modern England* (Cambridge: Cambridge University Press, 1998), 142 and passim.

44. Sanders, *Gender and Literacy,* 227–28; Spufford, "First Steps in Literacy."

45. Ferguson, *Dido's Daughters,* 67–68, 78.

46. Lena Cowen Orlin's "Three Ways to Be Invisible in the Renaissance: Sex, Reputation, and Stitchery," in *Renaissance Culture and the Everyday,* ed. Patricia Fumerton and Simon Hunt (Philadelphia: University of Pennsylvania Press, 1999), 181–203, provides a useful catalog and a critical analysis of sewing in early modern English plays.

47. Goldberg, *Writing Matter*, 182.
48. Puttenham, *Arte of English Poesie*, II.85, 90.
49. Jones and Stallybrass, *Renaissance Clothing*, 153.
50. *Olympia Morata: The Complete Writings of an Italian Heretic*, ed. and trans. Holt N. Parker (Chicago: University of Chicago Press, 2003), 90.

Chapter 5

The Female World of Classical Reading in Eighteenth-Century America

CAROLINE WINTERER

Death by classics? For twenty-year-old Eliza Lucas (c. 1722–93), who presided over a prosperous indigo plantation in colonial South Carolina, the idea seemed ludicrous. An avid reader of Plutarch's *Lives*, she scoffed at the warnings of an older woman from the neighborhood, who advised her that rising at 5 A.M. to read Plutarch would send her to an early grave—or worse, wrinkle her skin and "spoil" her marriage. After narrowly preventing the older woman from hurling the toxic text into the fireplace, Lucas cheerfully polished it off and then begged a male friend to send her some Virgil. An extreme instance of devotion to classical reading, perhaps, but Eliza Lucas (later Pinckney) was not atypical among elite, white American women in the eighteenth century, who began in increasing numbers to read classical literature. This chapter will investigate how and why they embarked on this project, focusing most especially on women's own stated reasons for reading the classics as articulated in diaries, letters, magazines, and books.[1]

Few intellectual projects have been so wrapped in paranoid rhetoric for so long as classical study, a branch of learning that seemed to possess infinite capacities to illuminate, refine, and ennoble men and an equally dependable ability to corrupt women. Since the Renaissance, classical learning had been as much an academic subject for boys as a male puberty rite. Boys learned Latin and Greek in school not just so that they could master the judicious statecraft and heroic deeds of the ancients but also as a combative initiation rite into the mysteries and privileges of languages, exemplars, and sayings that gentlemen knew and ladies did not. In this world the gold standard of erudition was Greek, the silver Latin: to know and use these languages with grace and agility was to sit among the gods of Olympus, dispensing wisdom both philosophical and political. Both languages were so difficult to acquire that they remained the realm of privileged boys and men who had the time and tutoring to learn them. The occasional, highly privileged girl might be taught Greek and Latin and encouraged to emulate classical female worthies, but this was often done in the spirit of virtue-building busywork—a kind of lexical embroidery. Advanced study of the classical languages was discouraged for women lest they "appear threateningly insane and requiring restraint," as the fifteenth-century Italian humanist Leonardo Bruni put it. A woman, he observed, should leave "all public severity to men." The classically learned woman also became dangerously unfeminine, a *virilis femina* or an *homasse* (man-woman). The Renaissance humanist conversation about classical civic virtue was both the language of politics and the idiom of exclusion. Colonial Americans inherited this classical project, and few women in the seventeenth century (barring spectacular exceptions such as Anne Bradstreet) were taught Greek, Latin, or classical history and literature.[2]

By the mid-eighteenth century a change was afoot that brought growing numbers of elite women into the sphere of classical learning long cherished by men. The cause of this new opportunity for female classical learning was the establishment in colonial America of salons and tea tables, where groups of men and women could gather for conversation, reading, society games, and the like. Modeled on British precedents—which were modeled on French versions—this new colonial "polite" society created a whole new arena for sociability between the sexes. But what to say there? And how to say it? Being polite required a whole new social register. "Politeness," explains Lawrence Klein of the situation in England, "tended to bring all modes of apprehension—spiritual, cognitive, aesthetic—within the horizon of gentility and cast all such spiritual, intellectual, or creative endeavours as a species of gentlemanly accomplishment." In feats of steely self-control, polite people strove to appear languid and easy, restrained and learned.[3]

For this dazzling project of cultivating gentility, classical learning became imperative. Long associated with the pinnacles of masculine learning, judgment, and statecraft, classical learning now became a conversation, like the weather, to which all could contribute, each in his or her own measure. The shift in the function of classical erudition was not easy, trying both men and women in different ways. From men, it required restraint: a polite man had to resist the urge to trumpet his classical learning pedantically. Pedantry was a minor offense in the scholarly republic of letters but a mortal sin in the mixed company of the salon, where he would be written off both as an eye-rolling bore and as a scholar, two attributes believed to be incompatible with the ideal of the gentleman.

For women, the effort bordered on the impossible. Politeness demanded that elite women contribute elegant conversation appropriate for the ears and minds of both sexes. Women now had to acquire, without formal schooling, a grasp—however tenuous—of the ways and means of people who had lived two thousand years before. But they had to do so within narrow boundaries. Ancient history was acceptable for women, but the classical languages were not; admiring the heroism of Cicero or Scipio was acceptable, but tying that heroism to prescriptions for modern statecraft was not; reading about ancient orators was acceptable, declaiming aloud less so. A woman's conversation should be ornamental but not instructive in its own right; she should have enough learning to take an interest in her companion's conversation but not be so learned as to surpass his grasp of the subject.

This precarious balance between feminine frivolity and petticoat pedantry was difficult enough to achieve that magazines and books rushed in to fill the void with advice. Published mostly in Britain and then imported to or reprinted in the colonies, these texts conjured a vision of what many of them called a "female world" of conversation in which the proper deportment of women was essential. The idea of a female world had first formed in the French courts to describe the salon culture governed by women. Taking root in England, it spawned such publications as the anonymous *Wonders of the Female World* (1683), which discussed exemplary historical and mythological female figures from classical antiquity. The frontispiece envisioned this female world as a classical one, with Clio, Athena, and Lucretia clustered around the bubbling "font of Helicon" as the "Hill Parnassus" squatted in the distance.[4]

One early help for navigating this female world was the *American Magazine and Historical Chronicle*, published in Boston between 1743 and 1746 and filled with reprints of articles originally published in London. It contained many articles that discussed how women might acquire some classical learning—but not too much. One author in June 1745 encouraged women to emulate the learned women of Greece and Rome, such as Cornelia, mother of the Gracchi (who had "contributed much to the Eloquence of her Sons"); the daughter of Loelius (who "express'd in her Conversation the Eloquence of her Father"); and the daughter of Hortensius (who delivered an oration before the Triumvirs). Such a woman was "the Honour of her Sex," and this reading would inoculate her against the "too prevailing Custom of Cards, Visitings, and other Ways of killing the Time." But while a woman's classicized conversation with men could let her sparkle and shine, it could easily cross the line into unattractive pedantry. "Shun learned Clacks, and Females talking Greek," admonished a 1744 article that gave advice to a young woman just after her marriage.[5]

Advice books were another source of information for young women on how to navigate the treacherous terrain of classical conversation in mixed company. Hester Chapone addressed this question head-on in her popular *Letters on the Improvement of the Mind, Addressed to a Young Lady*, first published in 1773 in London and reprinted in the United States beginning in 1782. Chapone recommended ancient history as the most profitable kind of classical learning for young women and viewed ancient texts as didactic purveyors of morals. "It is thought a shameful degree of ignorance, even in our sex, to be unacquainted with the nature and revolutions of their governments, and with the characters and stories of their most illustrious heroes." Homer for Greece and Virgil for Rome, declared Chapone as she described "heroic actions and exalted characters." Like others, Chapone cautioned women against undertaking the ancient languages; they were not useful to women, and the essentials of knowledge they imparted were equally available in English, French, or Italian translation. She also expressed fear that the learned woman would threaten men: "The danger of pedantry and presumption in a woman—of her exciting envy in one sex and jealousy in the other—of her exchanging the graces of imagination for the severity and preciseness of a scholar, would be, I own, sufficient to frighten me from the ambition of seeing my girl remarkable for learning."[6]

In this female world of advice books and magazine chatter about classical literature, actual libraries housing classical books loomed like Parnassus, a fantastic place of wonders reached only with difficulty and perseverance. With the exception of the few circulating libraries, which did allow women, in general books and libraries were controlled by men. Sarah Logan experienced the effects of this firsthand. She was the daughter of the prosperous Quaker merchant James Logan (1674–1751), whose library numbered in the thousands of volumes. Logan was among the most accomplished humanists in America during the colonial period. Like many of his male contemporaries, he did not believe that girls should be taught to read Latin or Greek but thought highly enough of the sterling morals imparted by (some) classical authors that he believed girls might profitably read them in English. With his daughters in mind he produced an English translation of Cato's moral sayings, published as *Cato's Moral Distichs* (1735). The book may not have been as appealing to young women as Logan had hoped since it exactly translated advice intended primarily for boys: "Regard not Woman's Passions, nor her Smiles / With *Passion* she ensnares, with Tears beguiles," read one saying. Logan's lovingly prepared *Distichs* was not one of the three books in the library with the explicit ownership mark of his oldest daughter, Sarah.[7]

The Virginia planter William Byrd II (1674–1744) of Westover, James

Logan's contemporary, also used his library as a kind of reward system for the women in his life. On the one hand, as a man lunging relentlessly at genteel propriety through his own acquisition of Greek and Latin, he sought compatible erudition in a mate. He told his second wife, Maria Taylor, that he had fallen in love with her in part because she knew Greek. "When indeed I learned that you also spoke Greek, the tongue of the Muses, I went completely crazy about you," he wrote her in a letter. "In beauty you surpassed Helen, in culture of mind and ready wit Sappho." His first wife, Lucy Byrd, put her name in a classical book in the Westover library, the Englished version of the Greek-language meditations of the Roman emperor Marcus Aurelius, entitled *The Emperor Marcus Antoninus: His Conversation with Himself* (1701). Even so, such privileges could be revoked on a whim. On December 30, 1711, Byrd noted in his diary that he had quarreled with Lucy "because I was not willing to let her have a book out of the library."[8]

A lonely old age as a spinster: this is what awaited the female classical pedant, if moralists were to be believed. Women who learned Greek and Latin risked alienating spouses and other women, their learning a sign of their "rapid advances towards *manhood*," as one author in a *Lady's Magazine* of 1793 put it. The author regaled readers with the story of the tragic decline of a woman who put aside her sewing and painting to take up the "toga virilis" of Greek and Latin. After boring her husband and friends with her "female pedantry," she ended up living alone with her cats, the object of pity and ridicule. Women did not necessarily take this lying down. The Philadelphia-area poet Hannah Griffitts (1727–1817), who never married, mockingly addressed one of her poems to Sophronia, a Roman woman who was said to "hate men" and "love Greek" so much that she never married.[9]

Four works in particular stand out in the female world of eighteenth-century American women's classical reading: Charles Rollin's *Ancient History*, Alexander Pope's *Iliad* and *Odyssey*; and Fénelon's *The Adventures of Telemachus*. Popular with men, they also captured the attention of women, who declared their frequent reactions to these works in diaries, letters, and magazines. Several things deserve mention about the texts from the outset. First, although they were about the Greco-Roman past and so "classical" in the broadest sense of that term, they were all originally written in a modern vernacular. They were part of what we might call a "vernacular classical" tradition, a category that was rapidly encroaching on the cultural reverence for ancient texts in Greek and Latin. Two of the texts in this vernacular classical trinity (Rollin and Fénelon) were originally published in French in France and were immediately translated into English in Britain. A few American women notably read the works in both languages: there is a bit of evidence to suggest a linguistic hierarchy within this vernacular classical world, with some women taking pains to point out that they read Rollin or Fénelon in French, a sign of their doubly Olympian accomplishment. Second, women linked these books to the expanding eighteenth-century Atlantic trade in goods, not just reading the books but surrounding themselves with a veritable gallery of related artifacts that they bought either ready-made or crafted themselves. They made embroideries and watercolors based on the books' engravings; some women covered rooms in their homes in theme wallpapers. As Catherine Kelly shows in her essay in this volume, women moved easily between the bookish culture of letters and the material culture of accomplishment, seeing them not as opposed but as parallel paths to the formation of sensibility and taste. Classicism for eighteenth-century American women was at some level a system of signs and symbols that helped to articulate and promote a female cultural elite. Third, all three texts were eminently compatible with the project of cultivating female piety. Some ancient texts, such as Ovid's *Metamorphoses*, to take a prominent example, were deemed problematic for women because of their frank depiction of the adulterous, bestial, and homosexual romps prominent in Greco-Roman mythology.[10] By contrast, the three works most popular among women presented fewer problems and in some cases were explicitly promoted as conducive to forming Christian piety.

Charles Rollin's *Ancient History* (thirteen volumes, 1730–38), a staple of American men's reading in the eighteenth century, was also prized by women, for whom it was viewed first and foremost as a source of both information and pleasure. These two goals were seen as mutually reinforcing, helping to drape the didacticism of history in pleasant garb. Abigail Adams, who mentioned Rollin in her letters to John Adams, found "great pleasure and entertainment" in its pages. In 1797 twelve-year-old Julia Cowles, who was attending a female academy in Connecticut, wrote in her diary for weeks on end about the exciting goings-on of the Romans and Assyrians depicted in Rollin's *Ancient History*. She struggled along with him to mesh classical history with holy writ: "Rollin says he thinks it very strange that so many large cities [were] built so soon after the flood." Magazines for women by the early 1800s increasingly assumed that their female readers had read Rollin's *Ancient History*. They cited certain well-known passages and related them to current events, as the *Ladies' Weekly Museum* did in 1817 when it compared a sea serpent apparently sighted off Gloucester, Massachusetts, with the one described in Rollin's description of the first Punic War.[11]

Rollin's *Ancient History* was also one of the books that women were specifically urged to teach to their children, recommendations that began in the eighteenth century and were still going strong decades later.

While describing her own reading of Rollin, Abigail Adams "perswaided Johnny [John Quincy] to read me a page or two every day." Half a century later, in 1827, another mother weighed in on the utility of Rollin in the *American Journal of Education*: "At twelve, permission to peruse Rollin's Ancient History has been asked as a very great favor." The South Carolina plantation mistress Alice Delancey Izard (1746/47–1832) trumped them both, advising her son Ralph Izard, Jr., in 1803 to read Rollin in French: "I wish you to have a good general knowledge of ancient, as well as modern history. Mr. Rollin's Ancient & Roman history is the best I know, & it would give me great pleasure to send it to you. Borrow it, if you can, & read it with attention. The French edition is much superior to the translation, & I believe you sufficiently Master of that language to understand a book so well written." Believing that women should guide rather than govern men, Alice Izard had long turned to classical models to understand a mother's proper relationship with sons. While in Rome in 1775 she posed for John Singleton Copley for a lavish double portrait that shows her sitting with her husband, Ralph Izard, and a sketch (possibly hers) of the sculpture group "Papirius Praetextatus and His Mother," which is depicted in the background of the painting. The parable concerns a young man who refuses to divulge Senate secrets to his mother, an act for which he is rewarded by the Senate.[12] (See Figure 5.1.)

Rollin was recommended for men too, but why specifically was he so popular among women? Rollin not only spun out an exciting and readable narrative of republics rising and falling with the virtue of their peoples but, just as important, Rollin also seemed to possess a sterling character that was believed to be conveyed in his writings. "Good Mr. Rollin" was what fifteen-year-old Maria Trumbull Hudson (1785–1805) called him. Such views were widely propagated in American magazines even in the colonial period. The works of Rollin "inspire the love of virtue, and respect for religion," asserted an anonymous contributor to the *American Magazine* in 1745. An 1807 article in the *Port Folio*, notifying its readers of a new edition of Rollin's history appearing in Boston, praised him as an "elegant scholar and a primitive Christian" who linked "moral sentiment with historical tradition."[13]

Also in the group of prized female classical texts were Alexander Pope's rhyming English verse translations of Homer's *Iliad* (1715–20) and *Odyssey* (1725–26). The most popular translations of Homer in the colonies, Pope's *Iliad* and *Odyssey* sold nearly twenty thousand copies in 1774 and were steady sellers before and after. Women were a key component of Pope's American popularity, recording their thoughts about his epics in their diaries and letters. Some women read Pope in a solitary moment, as did twenty-four-year-old Elizabeth Drinker, who noted in

Figure 5.1. John Singleton Copley (American, 1738–1815), *Mr. and Mrs. Ralph Izard (Alice Delancey)*, 1775. Oil on canvas. Overall: 174.6 x 223.5 cm. (63³/₄ x 88 in.). Framed: 203.2 x 254 x 10.2 cm (80 x 100 x 4 in.). Museum of Fine Arts, Boston. Edward Ingersoll Brown Fund, 03.1033. Photograph © 2007 Museum of Fine Arts, Boston.

her diary in 1759 that she had "begun to read Pope's Homer; the Iliad" after a crowded morning in church. Other women had Pope's *Iliad* read to them by men; one was seventeen-year-old Sally Wister of Germantown, Pennsylvania. Her suitor, she noted in her diary in 1778, picked up "Homer's Iliad, and read to us." Wister did not mention that this *Iliad* was Pope's (perhaps it did not need mentioning?) but knew the text well enough that she could recall in her diary the precise lines read to her, from Book 17. Of all the classical texts eagerly read by the Massachusetts slave Phillis Wheatley (1753–84)—an impressive list that included Horace, Virgil, Ovid, and Terence in Latin—the hands-down favorites were the two epics of Pope, whose style she imitated to international fame in her *Poems on Various Subjects, Religious and Moral* (1773).[14]

Lavishly illustrated, Pope's epics inspired a parallel visual culture for women. In 1810 Maria Bissell, who attended a Connecticut academy, made a silk embroidery of the frontispiece of an 1808 Boston edition of

Pope's *Iliad,* which depicted the teary parting of Hector and Andromache. However, like Rollin, Pope also found favor among women because his epics—and indeed, other writings—could be read as confirmations of Protestant morality. Both Drinker and Wister were Quakers; Wister, like other American women in the eighteenth century, quoted from Pope when she needed an apposite phrase about mercy or sympathy.[15]

Third in the category of favorite classical reading for eighteenth-century women was the best-selling book *Les Aventures de Télémaque* (1699), by the French pastor François de Salignac de la Mothe-Fénelon (1651–1715). The book was a publishing sensation in Europe and America. One of the most important works of political theory of the eighteenth century, it had gone through 150 editions by 1830, not including some 80 translations.[16] Read by American women and men both in French and in English translation, the book also spawned a parallel "female world" of images and objects, from paintings and wallpaper to embroideries and even a shell grotto. Here was a book—and especially a story—that captured the imaginations of American men in one way but inspired American women in quite another.

Like Rollin, Fénelon had impeccable moral and literary credentials to recommend him to his American audience. He spent ten years as the Superior of the Nouvelles Catholiques, a society for the instruction of young female converts, before writing the *Traité de l'Education des Filles* (1687), first translated into English in 1699. In many ways Fénelon was entirely a traditionalist when it came to the education of girls. These, he reckoned, were corruptible creatures beset by natural character flaws such as timidity, false modesty, and a propensity for putting passion over reason. Such failings demanded an education rich in didactic moralism to inspire them to inhabit their homey orb in a way that was modest, simple, and amiable. This education would include perhaps a little Latin and definitely a lot of Greek and Roman history, which were storehouses of exempla such as the mother of the Gracchi, who "contributed very much to the forming of the Eloquence of her Sons, who became afterwards so great Men."[17]

This pleasure principle—robing the didactic lessons of history in fetching tales—resulted in the work for which he was best known, *Les Aventures de Télémaque,* written while he was tutor to the young dauphin, the grandson of Louis XIV. The tale was directly inspired by the peregrinations relayed in Homer's *Odyssey.* It follows young Telemachus, son of Ulysses, as he leaves Ithaca and his mother, Penelope, to search for his father, who has not yet returned from the Trojan War. Telemachus is accompanied by his guide, Minerva, who has assumed the shape of a man named Mentor. Along the way Telemachus learns valuable lessons about kingship and self-mastery. The work was popular initially because it was viewed as a satire of the excesses of King Louis XIV of France (a charge Fénelon denied), and Fénelon was banished to the obscurity of a pastorate in Cambrai.[18]

Fénelon's *Telemachus* resonated deeply among revolutionary Americans, who found two themes of the story to be particularly relevant to their own struggles against King George III. On the one hand they could see in Telemachus's search for his father a parallel to their own search for a new father figure to replace the displaced king. They also followed young Telemachus in his journey of self-discovery, learning the lessons in self-mastery essential for republican self-government.[19]

Fénelon's *Telemachus* also found a lasting audience among American women: among only three books inscribed by Sarah Logan of Philadelphia with her autograph was an edition of Fénelon's *Les Aventures de Télémaque* (Amsterdam, 1719). "Sarah Logan her Book 1723," reads the inscription in the small calf duodecimo.[20] Some women, from the evidence we can glean in writings and artifacts, seemed to have been finding something different in *Telemachus* than men were seeing, something that resonated more deeply in their own lives than the tale of prodigal sons and the cultivation of male autonomy and authority.

Elizabeth Graeme Fergusson (1737–1801) may have known *The Adventures of Telemachus* better than any other American in the eighteenth century, man or woman. Born into an elite Philadelphia family, she was raised both in the family's house in the city and in their summer home of Graeme Park, twenty miles north of Philadelphia. Fergusson's mother took great pains with her youngest daughter's education, and as Fergusson reached her maturity the house at Graeme Park became a kind of literary salon, attracting such Philadelphia luminaries as Benjamin Rush and Benjamin Franklin to soirees of learned conversation. Calling herself "Sophia" (among other names) and Philadelphia the "Athens of North America," Fergusson hoped to plant what she called the seeds of art and learning in America, aspirations she frequently turned into published odes.[21]

Fergusson seems to have been especially captivated by *Telemachus*, viewing aspects of her life through its lens. She called her much older friend Richard Peters her "Mentor" in one of her odes and worried that a long parting from her husband "exceeds that of the celebrated Ulysses and Penelope." In 1760, at the age of twenty-three, she began an English verse translation of *Télémaque*. She had few female classical translators as models from which to work. There were, of course, two European greats: in France, Anne Dacier (d. 1720), translator of Homer's *Iliad* from Greek into French; and in England, Elizabeth Carter (1717–1806), translator of Epictetus. However, Fergusson, moving a text from French into English, was charting the newer waters of British America's vernacular classical world. It is unclear what motivated Fergusson's translation besides intellectual and literary interest, but a romantic rupture may have given the project some steam. She had been engaged for five years to William Franklin, son of Benjamin Franklin, but in 1759 he jilted her while in England. Fergusson continued to work on the translation over the next several decades, especially after the deaths of her mother and sister, when the work seems to have distracted her from her grief. Throughout she worried that her translating work would make her what she called "a *Classical* pedant, or what is much Worse a *female* one."[22]

The manuscript was complete by the early 1790s, and she wrote in it that she hoped to "have it printed." Despite encouragement from her friend Elias Boudinot, Fergusson ultimately declined publication, citing the "delicacy of [her] Situation" (the fear of a woman having to collect subscriptions for publication). She may not have seen the decision to forgo publication as a failure. In choosing to keep the manuscript form of her translation, Fergusson stood in a particularly female tradition of eighteenth-century belles lettres in America. Leaders of the female-centered colonial salons circulated manuscripts unintended for print as a way to enrich the salons' literary networks and to distinguish their intellectual pretensions from the sometimes gossipy and banal conversations of the tea tables.[23]

One particular episode in *Telemachus* seized the imaginations of eighteenth-century American women: the moving story of Telemachus's stay on the island of Calypso. Calypso was a lovely nymph who lived on an island somewhere in the balmy Mediterranean. The island was truly paradisiacal, a place of gentle winds and fragrant forests, of sunny beaches broken by the shade of mossy grottos. In league with Venus, Calypso had already seduced Ulysses waylaying him for a time on his journey home to Ithaca before he finally escaped her charms. When Telemachus and Mentor arrive, she sends other nymphs from the island to detain Telemachus. Calypso falls in love with Telemachus; Telemachus falls deeply in love with the nymph Eucharis; jealous complications ensue, and it becomes clear to the ever-reasonable Mentor that the love-struck Telemachus will be ensnared on the island of Calypso forever. It is only when Mentor pushes Telemachus off a cliff into the churning sea below that the spell is broken. Telemachus, released from the slavery of passion, is at liberty to resume his journey.

Here was the classic eighteenth-century setup: Venus and Calypso, embodiments of passion, conspire unsuccessfully to stymie Minerva, the embodiment of masculine reason and sober deeds. But might not some female readers have been cheering for Calypso, representative of the scope and limits of women's possibilities for action? Calypso ruled her balmy island, a "female world" like the one women were creating through their classical reading, polite conversation, and silk embroideries. Calypso was a formidable figure in her own right, leading her band of nymphs and commanding men with her wiles and her beauty.

On the other hand, Calypso's plight was truly heartbreaking, doomed as she was to lose lover after lover, a victim of the competing agendas of Venus and Minerva. Her jealousy, rage, and especially her loneliness are repeatedly and movingly evoked in *Telemachus*: she is a nymph, but her despair is human. Her little world was defined by men, who suddenly landed on her beaches and just as suddenly sailed away. Calypso's role was that of the ideal woman conversationalist in the salon, who modulated her speech and silence to meet the needs of her male companion. Comparing Calypso's role to women's ideal role in conversation, one author in an 1806 issue of the *Companion and Weekly Miscellany* put it this way: "Yet would she, like Calypso, wish to hear Tellemachus o'er and o'er again." Calypso's beauty never faded, but she was ultimately powerless to detain the heroes of Greece on their quest for other goals than eternal love. Her island might be a paradise and a way station, but it was, like all islands, lonely and dependent. One Philadelphia woman in the 1760s seems to have been especially captivated by the grotto of Calypso as a kind of female world. She made a small grotto entirely of shells and dedicated it to Calypso, whose name means "the Concealer." Imaginatively sprawling but physically confined, the shell grotto of Calypso may have spoken more meaningfully about the closed lives of American women than did the expansive adventures of Telemachus and Mentor.[24]

The Philadelphia woman's shell rendering of the grotto of Calypso was just one of many objects made by or for American women in the late eighteenth and early nineteenth centuries that ruminated in some way on the Calypso of Fénelon. The subject was a favorite among neoclassical painters. Angelika Kauffman, the British painter of many female classical subjects, completed a canvas entitled *Telemachus and the Nymphs of Calypso* around 1782. In England in 1773 Benjamin West painted a version of Telemachus's stay on Calypso's island, a painting known in America and which continued to be discussed in magazines read by women in the early 1800s. In England fans depicted the theme, though it is unclear whether any of these made it to America. At least one girl in a female academy in America rendered the scene in silk embroidery. Frances Mecia Campbell, who attended Mrs. Saunders and Miss Beach's Academy in Dorchester, Massachusetts, created the work from what was probably a book engraving while she attended the academy in 1807. As American women began to decorate with wallpaper, they turned to such designers as the French paper designer Joseph Dufour, whose most popular motif in the American market, entitled *Télémaque*, depicted Minerva tossing Telemachus off the cliffs in the magnificent setting of the island of Calypso. It was expensive paper for only the most elite households, requiring eighty-five colors and a huge swath of wall for full effect. It was the paper chosen by Rachel Jackson, wife of President Andrew Jackson, to adorn the walls of the entry hall of their grandly classical Tennessee plantation, the Hermitage.[25]

The female world of classical reading in eighteenth-century America rapidly took on historically specific characteristics. Resting on the increasing social prestige of a vernacular classical tradition, the female world partook of the same books favored by elite, literate men while also cultivating themes that seemed to bear more clearly on women's particular social and intellectual situations. Whatever the stated fears that classical reading would turn women into petticoat pedants, wrinkly spinsters, and dissipated pagans, in fact most women recorded a seamless meshing of classical reading with ideals of female piety, submission, and decorum.

The imperial crisis of the 1760s and 1770s forever changed the female world of classicism by giving it a newly politicized, republican edge. To be sure, underneath these new republican meanings that women attached to classicism there persisted the older world of desultory reading, gentility, and piety that would endure well into the nineteenth century. But republican revolution also catapulted certain strands of women's classicism into the realm of political symbolism. Women's republicanized classicism gave them a voice with which to articulate some of American women's first political questions about their place in the new Republic. Elite women married to patriots latched onto the republican ideal of the Roman matron, who was chaste, sober, dignified, and dedicated to the selfless service of Rome. Abigail Adams began to sign her letters to John Adams as "Portia" (wife of the Roman senator Brutus) in 1775, and Mercy Otis Warren adopted the republican, Roman pen name of "Marcia." Other women of this time posed in portraits as Roman matrons; Warren eventually published the first Roman play in America, linking the fragile, easily corrupted new nation to Roman imperial destiny in *The Sack of Rome* (1790).

A major influence on American women's formulation of the republican Roman matron was the classically educated historian of Britain Catharine Macaulay (1731–91). In an age when history writing was lauded as the noblest form of writing for men (but seen as totally inappropriate for women), Macaulay published the multivolume *History of England from the Accession of James I to that of the Brunswick Line* (1763–83), a highly partisan history of royal absolutism in England. Radical Whigs on both sides of the Atlantic praised the text not just for its congenial political message but also because Macaulay seemed to have transcended the limits of female ability: women wrote poems, not histories.

Here was a new creature on the female classical landscape, a woman whose reading about antiquity taught her the love of liberty and pushed her into the masculine work of history writing. Macaulay's *History* in fact encouraged such a view. "From my early youth," she wrote, "I have read with delight those histories which exhibit Liberty in its most exalted state, the annals of the Roman and the Greek Republics." The lesson she took from this history reading was the need for liberty, and "Liberty became the object of a secondary worship" for Macaulay. Like other girls of her elite status, Macaulay had had a tutor, but she had quickly realized the limits of ornamental female accomplishments and wandered instead into her father's library. Exactly what she read there remains a mystery, but when Elizabeth Carter met Macaulay, she commented that Macaulay's conversation raced around "the Spartan laws, the Roman politics, the philosophy of Epicurus, and the wit of St. Evermond." The result, according to Carter, was "an extraordinary system."[26]

In revolutionary America, the patriot Mercy Otis Warren took Macaulay as an intellectual model, corresponding with her and eventually using some of Macaulay's ideas in her own *History of the Rise, Progress, and Termination of the American Revolution* (3 vols., 1805), the first history ever published by an American woman, and one highly laudatory of republicanism. Even John Adams, who told Warren that history was no work for a "lady," praised the remarkable accomplishment of Catharine Macaulay. Abigail Adams, too, wondered how Macaulay achieved "eminence in a tract so uncommon." Adams wrote to a friend in 1771 that she had "a curiosity to know her Education and what first prompted her to engage in a Study never before Exibited to the publick by one of her own Sex and Country." Warren and her elite, patriotic crowd actually met Mrs. Macaulay (as they called her), but others more removed from this inner circle could connect her history to "liberty" and republicanism through one especially important image of her that circulated in the colonies. This was the frontispiece to the third volume of her *History*, which cast her in profile as a Roman matron: austere, learned, and republican. In fact, it was through Macaulay's *History* that American men and women were introduced to some of the first instances of classical imagery crafted in deliberately simple style to mimic the Roman austerity that Americans associated with revolutionary ideals of liberty.[27] (See Figure 5.2.)

Catharine Macaulay was also a zealous promoter of improved classical education for girls. Her *Letters on Education* (1790), addressed to a fictional recipient named Hortensia (a name shared by the ancient Roman

Figure 5.2. Catharine Macaulay depicted as a Roman matron in the frontispiece to volume 3 of her *History of England* (1767). Special Collections Research Center, University of Chicago Library.

woman who had dared to address the Forum), included this prescription: Plutarch's *Lives*, Livy, Sallust, Tacitus, Epictetus, Seneca, Virgil, and Terence. She supplemented this with Rollin's *Ancient History* ("in French"), Fénelon's *Telemachus*, and those transatlantic Whig favorites Addison's *Cato* and the *Spectator*. Lest her listing be interpreted as applying only to boys, she made a careful note at the end: "But I must tell you, Hortensia, lest you should mistake my plan, that though I have been obliged (in order to avoid confusion) to speak commonly in the masculine character, that the same rules of education in all respects are to be observed to the female as well as to the male children."[28]

The American Revolution gave women's classicism in America a newly politicized edge that helped them to envision themselves as proper subjects of republicanism. As self-styled modern Roman matrons, they had duties to the republic as important as those of the American men styling themselves Cincinnatus or Cato. Like Roman matrons, they would educate themselves and their children to the service of the *novus ordo seclorum.* But underneath this spectacular new, republicanized classicism persisted the older, belletristic world of classicism, of charming Rollin and lovely Telemachus wallpaper. Women, in fact, linked both old and new classicisms in the new project of being educated women of the Republic. An 1805 article in the *Evening Fire-Side* magazine showed how both Macaulay and Rollin could be put to useful ends. Stating that Macaulay's reading in the "annals of the Greek and Roman republics" made "liberty the idol of her imagination," the author praised the two books that had republicanized Macaulay: Rollin's *Ancient History* and *Account of the Roman Republic*, which not only "first lighted up that spark in her mind" but also gave "the tone to her sentiments and character" through the subsequent period of her life.[29] The spark of republicanism mixed with the beauty of sentiment: here was the legacy of the eighteenth-century female world of classicism.

Notes

This chapter is adapted from Caroline Winterer, *The Mirror of Antiquity: American Women and the Classical Tradition, 1750–1900* (Ithaca, N.Y.: Cornell University Press, 2007). It is used by permission of the publisher.

1. Eliza Lucas to Mary Bartlett, c. March–April 1742, in *The Letterbook of Eliza Lucas Pinckney, 1739–1762*, ed. Elise Pinckney (Chapel Hill: University of North Carolina Press, 1972), 33. Pinckney later made sure her daughter studied Latin; see Mary Beth Norton, *Liberty's Daughters: The Revolutionary Experience of American Women, 1750–1800* (Ithaca, N.Y.: Cornell University Press, 1980), 262.

2. Walter Ong, "Latin Language Study as a Renaissance Puberty Rite," *Studies in Philology* 56 (1959): 103–24; Anthony Grafton and Lisa Jardine, *From Humanism to the Humanities: Education and the Liberal Arts in Fifteenth- and Sixteenth-Century Europe* (Cambridge, Mass.: Harvard University Press, 1986), 33; Margaret L. King and Albert Rabil, Jr., eds., *Her Immaculate Hand: Selected Works by and about the Women Humanists of Quattrocento Italy* (Binghamton, N.Y.: Center for Medieval and Early Renaissance Studies, 1983); *virilis femina*: Natalie Zemon Davis, "Gender and Genre: Women as Historical Writers, 1400–1820," in *Beyond Their Sex: Learned Women of the European Past*, ed. Patricia LaBalme (New York: New York University Press, 1980), 158; *homasse*: Bonnie Smith, *The Gender of History: Men,*

Women, and Historical Practice (Cambridge: Cambridge University Press, 1998), 16.

3. David Shields, "British-American Belles Letters," in *The Cambridge History of American Literature,* vol. 1, *1590–1820,* ed. Sacvan Bercovitch (Cambridge: Cambridge University Press, 1994), 339; Lawrence E. Klein, "Politeness and the Interpretation of the British Eighteenth Century," *Historical Journal* 45 (December 2002): 889.

4. The term "female world" is used in this sense in "How to Converse with Mankind," *Boston Weekly Magazine* March 9, 1743, 10; "On the Style of Dr. Samuel Johnson," *Universal Asylum* (April 1791): 237; "The History of Narcissa," *Massachusetts Magazine* (March 1792): 179; Carlos, "Useful Hints and Advice to the Ladies," *Weekly Museum,* May 5, 1792, n.p.; Terpander, "Thoughts on the Neglect of Morality in Choice of Husbands," *Massachusetts Magazine* (April 1795): 56; and Misogamos, "Arguments in Favor of Celibacy," *American Universal Magazine,* March 6, 1797, 302. On French salon culture, see Carolyn Lougee, *"Le Paradis des Femmes": Women, Salons, and Social Stratification in Seventeenth-Century France* (Princeton, N.J.: Princeton University Press, 1976); Dena Goodman, *The Republic of Letters: A Cultural History of the French Enlightenment* (Ithaca, N.Y.: Cornell University Press, 1994); and Anon., *The Wonders of the Female World* (London: Printed by J. H. for Thomas Malthus, 1683), frontispiece.

5. "Of Illustrious Women," *American Magazine and Historical Chronicle* (June 1745): 245, 248; Anon., "Advice to a Young Lady Just after Her Marriage," *American Magazine and Historical Chronicle* (December 1744): 699.

6. Hester Chapone, *Letters on the Improvement of the Mind, Addressed to a Young Lady* (1773; repr. Hagerstown, Md.: William D. Bell for Gabriel Nourse, 1818), 2:195.

7. Kevin Hayes, *A Colonial Woman's Bookshelf* (Knoxville: University of Tennessee Press, 1996), 10–16; Edwin Wolf, 2nd, *The Library of James Logan of Philadelphia, 1674–1751* (Philadelphia: Library Company of Philadelphia, 1974), ix; Frederick B. Tolles, "Quaker Humanist: James Logan as a Classical Scholar," *Pennsylvania Magazine of History and Biography* 79 (1955): 418–19; James Logan, *Cato's Moral Distichs. Englished in Couplets* (Philadelphia: Benjamin Franklin, 1735), 11.

8. Hayes, *Colonial Woman's Bookshelf,* 9; Louis B. Wright and Marion Tinling, eds., *The Secret Diary of William Byrd of Westover, 1709–1712* (Richmond, Va.: Dietz Press, 1941), 461.

9. "On Female Authorship," *Lady's Magazine* 2 (1793): 69–72, quotations from 69 and 72; Karin Wulf, *Not All Wives: Women of Colonial Philadelphia* (Ithaca, N.Y.: Cornell University Press, 2000), 46.

10. Marie Cleary, "'Vague Irregular Notions': American Women and Classical Mythology, 1780–1855," *New England Classical Journal* 29 (2002): 222–35.

11. Abigail Adams to John Adams, August 19, 1774, in *Adams Family Correspondence,* ed. Herbert Butterfield et al. (Cambridge, Mass.: Harvard University Press, 1963), 1:143; Julia Cowles, 19 July 1797, in *The Diaries of Julia Cowles: A Connecticut Record, 1797–1803,* ed. Laura Hadley Moseley (New Haven, Conn.: Yale University Press, 1931), 12; "Sea Serpent," *Ladies' Weekly Museum,* August 30, 1817, 279. For an overview of men's reading of Rollin, see William Gribbin, "Rollin's Histories and American Republicanism," *William and Mary Quarterly* 29 (October 1972): 611–22. Abigail Adams does not mention which edition of Rollin she is reading, but Butterfield (143n2) notes that the library of John Adams contained the fifth edition (London, 1768), which suggests that the colonists kept abreast of recent editions from the metropole.

12. Abigail Adams to John Adams, August 19, 1774, in *Adams Family Correspondence,* 1:142–43; A Mother, "Thoughts on Domestic Education," *American Journal of Education* (September 1827): 567; Alice Izard to Ralph Izard, Jr., January 5, 1803, Ralph Izard Family Papers, 1778–1826, Library of Congress. On Alice Izard's attitudes toward female submission, see Jeffrey Robert Young, *Domesticating Slavery: The Master Class in Georgia and South Carolina, 1670–1837* (Chapel Hill: University of North Carolina Press, 1999), 118. The identification of the sketch and statue of Papirius Praetextatus in Copley's painting is from William B. Dinsmoor, "Early American Studies of Mediterranean Archaeology," *Proceedings of the American Philosophical Society* 87.1 (July 1943): 75. For the view that the sketch was made by Alice Izard and a confirmation of the identification of the statue, see Maurie D. McInnis, "Cultural Politics, Colonial Crisis, and Ancient Metaphor in John Singleton Copley's *Mr. and Mrs. Ralph Izard,*" *Winterthur Portfolio* 34 (summer/autumn 1999): 95, 102–4.

13. Maria Trumbull Hudson to Jonathan Trumbull, December 14, 1800, in *A Season in New York 1801: Letters of Harriet and Maria Trumbull,* ed. Helen M. Morgan (Pittsburgh: University of Pittsburgh Press, 1969), 63; "M. Crevier's Answer to Mr. Voltaire," *American Magazine* (December 1745): 541; "Rollin's Ancient History," *Port Folio,* November 21, 1807, 331.

14. Frank Luther Mott, *Golden Multitudes: The Story of Best Sellers in the United States* (New York: Macmillan, 1947), 316; Elizabeth Sandwith Drinker, December 4, 1759, in *The Diary of Elizabeth Drinker,* ed. Elaine Forman Crane (Boston: Northeastern University Press, 1991), 1:40; Sally Wister, June 3, 1778, in *Sally Wister's Journal: A True Narrative,* ed. Albert C. Myers (Philadelphia: Ferris and Leach, 1902), 165; Julian Mason, *The Poems of Phillis Wheatley* (Chapel Hill: University of North Carolina Press, 1989), 3–4.

15. Betsy Ring, *Girlhood Embroidery: American Samplers and Pictorial Needlework, 1650–1850,* 2 vols. (New York: Knopf, 1993), 1:215. Wister quotes a few stanzas from Pope's *Universal Prayer* ("That mercy I to others show, That mercy shew to me") in her diary for June 3, 1778 (*Sally Wister's Journal,* 168).

16. The first English translation as *The Adventures of Telemachus, the Son of Ulysses* appeared in London in 1699; the first American edition was published, with engravings, in New York by T. and J. Swords in 1794. There were at least forty editions published in the United States between 1794 and 1900; eleven of those were by 1800. By 1773 a London edition with French and English on opposite pages was available. See *National Union Catalog,* 169: 352, 356–59.

17. James Herbert Davis, *Fénelon* (New York: Twayne, 1979), 42–45; François de Salignac de la Mothe-Fénelon, *Instructions for the Education of a Daughter, by the Author of Telemachus* (London: Jonah Bowyer, 1707), 231.

18. Davis, *Fénelon,* 90–111.

19. Jay Fliegelman, *Prodigals and Pilgrims: The American Revolution against Patriarchal Authority, 1750–1800* (Cambridge: Cambridge University Press, 1982), 46–49.

20. Wolf, *Library of James Logan,* 169; Hayes, *Colonial Woman's Bookshelf,* 10.

21. Martha Slotten, "Elizabeth Graeme Fergusson: A Poet in the Athens of North America," *Pennsylvania Magazine of History and Biography* 108 (1984): 260, 262.

22. Mentor and Ulysses quotes are from ibid., 271, 267. Pedant quote is from Anne Ousterhout, *The Most Learned Woman in America: A Life of Elizabeth Graeme Fergusson* (University Park: Pennsylvania State University Press, 2004), 295.

23. Quotations from Ousterhout, *Most Learned Woman,* 321. On unpublished

manuscripts, see David Shields, "The Manuscript in the British American World of Print," *Proceedings of the American Antiquarian Society* 102 (1992): 403–16.

24. Rario, "The Pedestrian: Number IX," *Companion and Weekly Miscellany*, January 11, 1806, 83. On the work of female conversation in the salon, see Goodman, *Republic of Letters*, 103–4. On the shell grotto, see Susan Stabile, *Memory's Daughters: The Material Culture of Remembrance in Eighteenth-Century America* (Ithaca, N.Y.: Cornell University Press, 2004), 20–22.

25. West's *Calypso* is discussed in "The Calypso," *Port Folio*, February 11, 1804, 46; *Philadelphia Repository*, January 5, 1805, 7; and "The Artist—No. II. Benjamin West, Esq. President of the Royal Academy," *Port Folio*, October 1811, 334–35. On British fans, see Charlotte Schreiber, *Catalogue of the Collection of Fans and Fan-Leaves of the British Museum* (London, 1893), 6, 41, 60. Campbell's embroidery is reproduced in Wendy Cooper, *Classical Taste in America, 1800–1840* (New York: Abbeville Press, 1993), 257. *Télémaque* wallpaper is reproduced in Catherine Lynn, *Wallpaper in America: From the Seventeenth Century to World War I* (New York: Norton, 1980), 205, 211, 219.

26. Catharine Macaulay, *The History of England from the Accession of James I to that of the Brunswick Line*, 3d ed. (London: Edward and Charles Dilly, 1769), 1:v–vi; Elizabeth Carter quoted in Bridget Hill, *The Republican Virago: The Life and Times of Catharine Macaulay, Historian* (Oxford: Clarendon Press, 1992), 11; and Catharine Macaulay, *Letters on Education* (London: C. Dilly, 1790; repr. Oxford: Woodstock Books, 1994), 129–30, 142. For more on Macaulay as a female history writer, see J. G. A. Pocock, "Catharine Macaulay," in *Women Writers and the Early Modern British Political Tradition*, ed. Hilda L. Smith (Cambridge: Cambridge University Press, 1998), 243–58; Philip Hicks, "The Roman Matron in Britain: Female Political Influence and Republican Response, ca. 1750–1800," *Journal of Modern History* 77 (March 2005): 35–69.

27. Rosemarie Zagarri, *A Woman's Dilemma: Mercy Otis Warren and the American Revolution* (Wheeling, Ill.: Harlan Davidson, 1995), 54–55, 152; Abigail Adams to Isaac Smith, Jr., April 20, 1771, in *Adams Family Correspondence*, 1:77; Catharine Macaulay, *The History of England from the Accession of James I to that of the Brunswick Line* (London: J. Nourse, R. and J. Dodsley, and W. Johnston, 1767), 3: frontispiece. On the arrival of "republican" icons in revolutionary America, see W. H. Bond, *Thomas Hollis of Lincoln's Inn: A Whig and His Books* (New York: Cambridge University Press, 1992); Frank Sommer, "Thomas Hollis and the Arts of Dissent," in *Prints in and of America to 1850*, ed. John D. Morse (Charlottesville, Va.: University Press of Virginia for the Henry Francis du Pont Winterthur Museum, 1970), 111–59, and Caroline Winterer, "From Royal to Republican: The Classical Image in Early America," *Journal of American History* 91 (March 2005): 1264–90.

28. Macaulay, *Letters on Education*, 129–30, 142.

29. "Memoirs of the Life of Catherine [*sic*] Macaulay Graham," *Evening Fire-Side*, January 5, 1805, 28. Judith Sargent Murray praises Macaulay because she "wielded successfully the historic pen" *(The Gleaner: A Miscellaneous Production in Three Volumes* [Boston: L. Thomas and E. T. Andrews, 1798]; repr. in Sheila Skemp, *Judith Sargent Murray: A Brief Biography with Documents* [New York: Bedford Books, 1998], 129).

Chapter 6

Reading and the Problem of Accomplishment

CATHERINE E. KELLY

In 1789 students at the Bethlehem Female Seminary, arguably America's most prestigious school for girls, concluded their first public examination with a "dialogue in verse" that summed up their educations. Standing before trustees and town dignitaries, ten speakers enumerated the different branches of their learning, citing the "uses and delights" of each. Not surprisingly, the students first praised reading, which deepened a young woman's connections to an intimate circle of family and friends, connected her to a larger world, and anchored her in the wisdom of the "Holy Scriptures." The girls also described their accomplishments: vocal and instrumental music, which generated songs of praise along with the more tactile pleasures of holding the "sweet guitar"; drawing, which served as the basis of both painting and ornamental needlework; and "tambour work," along with the homelier arts of sewing and knitting. The dialogue confirmed what the examination had already demonstrated, for the audience had listened to two days of recitation, participated in a prayer service accompanied by music and song, and inspected samples of student writing and drawing.[1] At the Bethlehem Female Seminary the most prominent "daughters of Columbia" claimed identities as sophisticated and discerning readers, and they did so within an intellectual and cultural context that laid a heavy emphasis on "ornamental accomplishments."

How are we to understand the relationship between reading and accomplishment that obtained at Bethlehem Female Seminary and at scores of other female academies during the founding decades of the American Republic? For the most part, Americanists have cast one as the antithesis of the other. The distance between reading and accomplishment is the distance between the intellectual and the vacuous, between the abstract and the merely mechanical, between power and dependence. If participation in the community of letters offered women a toehold in an emergent public sphere, accomplishments only mired them in domesticity. From this perspective, reading and education more generally signal the promise and the possibility of the American Revolution. Accomplishments register promises betrayed and possibilities foreclosed.[2]

But these juxtapositions would have made little sense to eighteenth- and early nineteenth-century Americans, who generally did not view reading as an alternative to accomplishment, much less as a cure for it. This essay reexamines the relationship between the two by locating women's reading in the context of their accomplishments and vice versa. By paying close attention to the connections between reading and accomplishment that obtained both in published discourse and at women's academies and seminaries, we gain a new understanding of the culture of letters and the culture of accomplishment. More important, we gain a clearer sense of the ways in which reading, especially women's reading, was embedded in a variety of other polite practices. A close focus on the relationship between reading and accomplishment illuminates the complex and sometimes contradictory intersection of texts, images and objects, and performance that characterized Anglo-America in the long eighteenth century. Just as important, we can see the ways in which cultures of reading and accomplishment *together* contributed to the contradictory, contested gender dynamics that marked the public sphere and political culture in the early American Republic.[3]

Reading and Accomplishment in Early National Literary Culture

In the enormous published discourse on female intellect and manners that appeared in the years following the Revolution, reading and accomplishment were problematized in remarkably similar ways. There was a broad consensus that the republican woman should possess both education and accomplishment. The problem lay in determining how much and what kind. Writers of all stripes warned of the dangers of excess, of too much reading or refinement. One anonymous writer insisted that although a woman might love reading, she must ensure that she was "no book-worm, no recluse, no pedant." Another decried the genteel education that produced a coquette who knew only how to "squeak if not sing. . . . kiss a lap dog with propriety, and . . . faint away judiciously." Indeed, the print culture of the federal period contains a rogue's gallery of bluestockings and coquettes—women whose misguided educations had ruined them for society, to say nothing of marriage. Too much learning produced a pedant; too much refinement produced a coquette; and too little of either produced a drudge. As the Reverend

John Bennett observed in his popular *Letters to a Young Lady*, it was a "narrow, middle path betwixt the extremes."[4]

Determining that path was all the more difficult given that writers and educators disagreed about *which* books and *which* accomplishments were most likely to foster virtuous womanhood. Most obviously, Americans debated the merits of novels. Bennett, for example, insisted that "they corrupt all principle," creating a "sickly sensibility." As late as 1809 a trustee of the Philadelphia Academy for the Instruction of Ladies warned students there that novels lead to "weak intellects and depraved dispositions," however "hackneyed" the censure might seem. But Hannah Webster Foster, the author of two novels, cautioned readers against condemning "all novels indiscriminately," for "some of them are fraught with sentiment; convey lessons for moral improvement; and exhibit striking pictures of virtue rewarded; and of vice, folly, and indiscretion punished." As Cathy Davidson has pointed out, this issue took on special urgency for female readers, who were deemed especially susceptible to fiction's influence, which simultaneously supplanted reason with fantasy as decorous behavior with unrestrained sexuality.[5]

Not surprisingly, these arguments over the propriety of novel reading and the power of print more generally were deeply implicated in broader debates over female intellect. Should a woman's reading cultivate her imagination, her reason, or both? How could parents and teachers cultivate the female mind without sacrificing the feminine virtues?[6] Bennett championed the "elegant studies," which demanded less "abstraction" than a sustained engagement with "politics, philosophy, mathematics, or metaphysics." But another writer took issue with those who would confine women's reading "to such books as are directed to the imagination or fancy." In a world that "teem[ed] with the solicitations of passions, or the temptations of artifice," a young woman surely needed books that inculcated "firmness" of mind.[7]

Just as writers debated the sort of reading that guaranteed a woman's virtue, so too did they debate the accomplishments that fitted her for the Republic. "Accomplishment" included a battery of skills ranging from the explicitly performative arts of singing, instrumental music, and dancing to a mastery of French and perhaps Italian, to a variety of visual arts, including fine penmanship, drawing, painting, quillwork, japanning, and especially ornamental needlework. Indeed, even reading, especially the art of reading aloud, could be counted as an "accomplishment." Not surprisingly, needlework—which joined the "useful and the beautiful" and which was exclusively women's province—generated the least criticism among the educators and pundits who sized up the welter of potential attainments. Certainly, commentators disagreed about just how much of a young lady's needlework should be devoted to, say, tambour as opposed plain sewing. However, as one observer put it, so long as a woman's "passionate fondness" for "tambour work, embroidery, and the like" did not eclipse her attention to everyday sewing, knitting, and spinning, the most ornamental needlework remained an "innocent passion."[8]

Dancing and music, which placed young women on display, were altogether more problematic. Hannah Webster Foster surely spoke for many when she described them as "perhaps the most fascinating, and of course, the most dangerous of any accomplishment." Though "polite and elegant," music and dancing could "allure their fond votaries from that purity and rectitude which are the chief embellishments of female character." Such was the case with the musically gifted Levitia, Foster's cautionary counterheroine, whose well-intentioned parents had "spared no pain nor expense" to provide her with a top-flight musical education. Once addicted to the flattery that followed performance, however, Levitia becomes a creature of "unbounded wants," a "garden, in which the useful plants are overrun and choaked by noxious weeds." Predictably, Levitia falls victim to a foreign-born impresario who seduces her with the promises of a stage career and the public "palm of applause." Indulged heedlessly, the pleasures of music and movement might combine with the pleasure of self-display to excite women's sexual passion. After all, as the Reverend Bennett pointed out, "a woman, who can spark and engage the admiration of every beholder at a ball, is not always content with the graver office of managing a family."[9]

If these reservations were common, they were hardly universal. In an address before the prestigious Philadelphia Young Ladies' Academy in 1787, John Swanwick especially encouraged young women in the study of instrumental music, which served to "attach all persons to their homes," not least because no lady could drag a pianoforte through the city streets. The author of *The Female Guide,* published in 1793, credited dancing and music with contributing to a broader social good: singing contributed to "sublime public worship." Dancing dispelled prejudice, no small achievement in the rancorous political climate of the 1790s.[10]

We would do well to read these debates over excess and variety—over how much and what kind—in the context of the eighteenth-century consumer revolution. If the broad discourse on reading, accomplishment, and femininity derived partly from transatlantic concerns about gender, on the one hand, and the American preoccupations with republican virtue, on the other hand, it also commented on the transformation of material life. Over the course of the eighteenth century growing numbers of middling and wealthy Americans were able to purchase access to an expansive print culture; these same Americans purchased the training and props that constituted accomplishment. Anxieties about moderation, virtue, and femininity have a long history in Anglo-American culture. However, the linked discourses on reading and accomplishment took shape, circulated, and intensified in a world that included growing numbers of books and magazines, tambour hoops, dancing masters, and pianofortes. The urgency that suffused discussions of texts and tambour derived from writers' recognition of the circulation of objects, ideas, and appetites in a protean consumer market and, more fundamentally, from their calculation of the near impossibility of regulating that circulation.[11]

Negotiating a path through the stacks of novels, magazines, paint boxes, and embroidery skeins that confronted a young woman was obviously a complicated, even hazardous, business. While the twinned cultures of print and accomplishment posed difficult choices, those same cultures simultaneously offered young ladies an entreé into the worlds of sensibility and taste. "Sensibility" was less a single quality than a composite of them; it demanded particular feelings—delicacy, transparency, and compassion—tempered by intelligence and reason. Taste married sensibility's feeling to reason's discernment, and as Americanists have come to recognize, these linked constructs cast a long shadow over the early Republic. The culture of feeling shaped manners and material culture, belles lettres and private correspondence, family life and political culture. If true sensibility was understood to be natural, it could also be cultivated. Consider "Louisa," the model of womanhood advanced by the Reverend John Bennett in his *Letters to a Young Lady*. Louisa's "exquisite sensibility" manifested itself in her "artless, undesigning, unstudied manner." Here was a young woman who "never affects to be anything, but what she is." At the same time, this "exquisite sensibility" was surely enhanced by her reading, which typically included "Addison's papers on the pleasures of imagination; several pieces of Miss Seward; Mason's English garden; Ariosto, with Hoole's translation; Webb's enquiries into the beauties of Painting, together with a collection of poems." Louisa culled these texts for epigrams, which she systematically transcribed into a commonplace book. As Bennett put it, the collected verse and prose formed "a very elegant bouquet" that cast a "delicious fragrance on her character and virtues." Just as reading and writing honed Louisa's sensibility, Bennett hoped that reading *about* Louisa "would communicate some traits of resemblance" to the fictive reader of his *Letters* and to real readers.[12] Not every girl could hope to attain Louisa's "exquisite sensibility," but the right reading definitely improved her chances.

Academic Accomplishments

Toward this end, women's academies and seminaries offered a curriculum that was deeply concerned with the cultivation of sensibility and taste. By the close of the eighteenth century, many of these schools had embraced a significant portion of the Anglo-American canon on taste, and a wide-ranging preoccupation with aesthetics ran through the entire academy experience. To understand the connections between beauty, sensibility, and pleasure, to understand the standards of taste that governed the production of polite letters and fine arts, students were directed year after year to the same familiar treatises: Henry Home, Lord Kames's *Elements of Criticism*, Alexander Jamieson on rhetoric and belles lettres, Archibald Alison's *Essays on the Nature and Principles of Taste*, Joseph Addison's collected essays, and the entire run of the *Spectator*, which commentators agreed offered young ladies an especially good model of taste and style. Above all else, students read Hugh Blair's *Lectures on Rhetoric and Belles Lettres*, often memorizing and reciting long passages in order to develop their capacity for discernment and to improve their own literary style. Sarah Pierce, founder of a prestigious female seminary in Litchfield, Connecticut, put it this way: the goal of reading rhetoric and applying its principles to composition was to "foster imagination" and "to create or direct taste."[13]

If students' reading engaged literary aesthetics, it also addressed the visual arts. After all, taste obtained not only in letters but also in painting, sculpture, and architecture. As no less an authority than Joseph Addison had explained, the pleasures of the imagination "arise from visible Objects, either when we have them actually in our View, or when we call up their Ideas into our Minds by paintings, Statues, Descriptions, or any the like Occasion." Accordingly, the extensive study of Addison or Blair was supplemented with other books and prints aimed at sharpening what we might call "visual literacy." The library of the Bethlehem Female Seminary, for example, included "Da Vinci on Painting," *Paston's Sketch book*, and *Smith on Drawing*, while the library of the Dorchester, Massachusetts, school operated by Mrs. Saunders and Miss Beach boasted "fine Drawings" along with "English and French Books."[14]

All of these books and prints helped initiate young women into the "Republic of Taste," which not only set the agenda for aesthetic criticism but also connected that criticism both to the discourse of civic humanism and, less obviously, to the demarcation of social distinctions. Like an education in letters, an education in art was intended to cultivate the values and behavior that marked the virtuous citizen. Within the Republic of Taste, art was valorized insofar as it inculcated the virtues necessary for republican society—discernment, sensibility, and most important, disinterestedness. As Elizabeth A. Bohls has pointed out, for eighteenth-century thinkers, precisely because art honed the "capacity to abstract from the particular to the general" it could help citizens "overcome differences between private interests . . . at the fundamental level of perception." However, the disinterestedness that resulted owed much to interest itself. In Jay Fliegelman's formulation, eighteenth-century notions of a "universal standard of taste" underscored the distance between those who possessed the ability to recognize the standard and those who did not. As he notes, that distance was measured in morality, culture, and class.[15]

Of course, questions about the connections between taste and civil society were not special to the United States. On the contrary: like the texts that sought to define its boundaries, the Republic of Taste was a transatlantic phenomenon. It derived from a constellation of shifts in politics, aesthetics, literary culture, class structure, and consumer markets that extended well beyond the boundaries of any particular nation. The precise meanings attached to those shifts varied among nations and over time. Through the early national period Americans collapsed the Republic of Taste into the American Republic, slighting transatlantic contexts in order to invest discussions of aesthetics and manners with singularly national resonances. No matter that these books were written by foreigners and consumed on both sides of the Atlantic; Blair's *Lectures on Rhetoric and Belles Lettres* and "Davinci on Painting" prepared young women to enter and serve a distinctly *American* Republic of Taste.[16]

Efforts to cultivate students' sensibility and taste and to harness those qualities to the needs of the Republic extended well beyond immersing them in an aesthetic canon. The overwhelming majority of female academies and seminaries offered some kind of instruction in accomplishments including drawing and painting and most especially ornamental needlework. Although parents paid extra for this training, it proved remarkably popular. In fact, it was the income generated by these skills that kept many schools afloat.[17] Accomplishments were desirable not because they countered book learning, as so many historians have assumed, but because they enhanced it. At least through the 1820s Americans viewed women's instruction in reading, writing, geography, history, and the myriad ornamental branches of learning as part of a single, integrated project.

Both reading and accomplishments were deemed to be particularly suited for inculcating what one writer called the "noble principle of emulation," which stood at the center of eighteenth-century learning.[18] Like the fictional Louisa, whose reading fills her commonplace book and by extension her heart, young women copied appropriate models in the hope that they might transcend mere mimicry and internalize the style and substance of their betters. A schoolgirl's commonplace book might have included her own observations, poetry, and even drawings, but it was largely devoted to "improving" extracts drawn from published sermons, conduct manuals, essays, and poetry.[19] The same schoolgirl looked to popular prints, usually selected by her teacher, for the subjects of her needlework; she then stitched her subject in a design and a style that were also specified by the teacher.[20] This concern with emulation was made explicit by one man who was dismayed by his ward's lack of progress at the Bethlehem Female Seminary. "Her unwillingness to undertake any of the ornamental branches, shews her totally devoid of that emmulation, without which nothing can be acquired almost induces me to believe that she is not compos mentis," he fumed. Never mind that the girl displayed "no taste for the arts," for the arts fostered the habits that undergirded other kinds of study. "I want her mind exercised by every possible means," he continued, demanding that the girl be kept at "worsted work" and that she begin drawing lessons immediately.[21]

Reading and accomplishment were joined in more obvious ways. For example, the same themes and turns of phrase that young women recorded in commonplace books and schoolgirl essays to demonstrate their mastery of belles lettres were embroidered on samplers. Both media were dominated by inscriptions testifying to women's religious faith and practice. But samplers, like commonplace books, also testified to young women's participation in a transatlantic community of letters. If quotations from Isaac Watts were especially popular, girls also selected verse from Alexander Pope, Oliver Goldsmith, Thomas Cowper, John Bunyan, and John Milton.[22] With both needle and pen girls praised nature, whose "beauteous works" when "fitly drawn" will "please the eye and the aspireing mind / To nobler scenes of pleasure more refined." They aspired to immortal friendships that might "outlive . . . the stars survive . . . the tomb."[23] Anticipating death, young women also anticipated the passing of time, youth, and beauty. In prose and embroidered inscriptions they reminded themselves that only virtue and intellect withstood the test of time. As one young woman wrote, "Rear'd by blest Education's nurturing hand / Behold the maid arise her mind expand / Deep in her heart the seeds of virtue lay / Maturing age shall give them to the day." As another put it, "Beauty will soon fade away, / But learning never will decay."[24]

All of these lines, culled from late eighteenth- and early nineteenth-century samplers, could as easily have been drawn from copybooks of the same period. Indeed, the 1802 "diary & composition & extract book" kept by fifteen-year-old Mary Bacon while she was an academy student included carefully transcribed poems and essays elaborating each of these themes. Bacon wrote several essays and letters on the connections between education and female virtue, praising the woman "who has improved her time—cultivated her mind—and stored it with useful knowledge." The "useful knowledge" that Bacon prized included a familiarity with polite verse, for along with her essays and letters she transcribed poems on "Green fields," "Winter," "Friendship," "The beauties of friendship," "Plato's advice," "The Sailor's Consolation," and "The Woman of Merit Described."[25]

Explicitly literary themes also dominated young women's pictorial embroidery and painting. Students' most extravagant creations typically displayed their familiarity with belles lettres and with print culture more generally. The characters and plots of much-loved books, mediated by imported, engraved prints, provided scores of young women with fodder for needlework and paint. Many students, for example, looked to illustrations from James Thomson's perennially popular book of verse, *The Seasons*, for inspiration. "Schoolgirl" artists, like British and Continental painters and engravers, were especially keen to depict "Autumn," when the gentleman Palemon admits his love for rustic Lavinia. (See Figures 6.1 and 6.2.) Still others chose themes that testified to their patriotism as well as to their mastery of polite culture. In 1804 the student Mary Beach created a large needlework copy of a Bartolozzi engraving taken from Angelica Kauffman's painting of Cornelia, mother of the Gracchi. Cornelia was a figure revered in the early Republic for her eloquence as well as her maternal strength. In choosing Cornelia, Beach (or her teacher) signaled republican commitments and familiarity with the cosmopolitan world of engraved prints. So too with Nancy H. Lincoln, whose large representation of the Washington family was taken from a London engraving copied from the Jeremiah Paul group portrait. The connections between engraved and printed matter on the one hand and women's ornamental work, on the other, are most arresting in so-called "print work" that appeared in the United States around the turn of the century and used a monochromatic color scheme to mimic the effect of engraved prints.[26]

In academies and seminaries American girls and young women moved easily between the literary and visual arts, between the culture of letters and the culture of accomplishment. In the process they both revealed and elaborated the connections between the two. Even embroidery, the accomplishment most maligned by contemporary scholars, drew women into a world of letters, sensibility, and taste. Far from excluding women from the eighteenth-century culture of sensible letters, women's mastery of accomplishments, especially their skills in the visual arts, helped signify their participation in that culture. Obviously, this interpretation goes a long way toward rehabilitating women's accomplishments, but it should also complicate our understanding of both women's participation in the community of letters and their connections to political culture. More important, it can illuminate the relationship between the two.

He saw her charming, but he saw not half

The charms her downcast modesty conceal'd.

Autumn.

Figure 6.1. "Autumn." Illustration from James Thomson, *The Seasons: With the Castle of Indolence* (1804). Library Company of Philadelphia.

Figure 6.2. Needlework picture depicting Palemon and Lavinia. Created by Sarah Ann Hanson while she attended the Moravian Seminary for Young Ladies in Lititz, Pa. Pictorial embroidery of silk, chenille, spangles, paint, and ink. Private collection. Photograph courtesy of Old Salem Museum and Gardens.

Let us return, for a moment, to women's artistic productions, to their paintings and embroideries. The historian Steven Bullock has pointed to the ways in which Federal-era Masons elaborated a rich visual language calculated literally to impress their version of republican society upon the minds of Americans.[27] As Bullock has argued, Masonic imagery could be drawn without academic training and read without a classical or cosmopolitan education. Indeed, it combined "moral elegance with semiotic simplicity" in order to reach the broadest possible audience. The rich visual culture that was elaborated at academies and seminaries worked in precisely the opposite way: it was calculated to display students' classical and cosmopolitan learning. It trumpeted their access to exclusive visual resources and expensive materials. Pictures of Palemon and Lavinia or of Cornelia, mother of the Gracchi, clearly demonstrated young women's skill, learning, and taste at the same time that they anchored virtuous female accomplishment in an exclusive world of expensive books and printed images. These pictures, with their tiny stitches and delicate washes of color, inscribed the American Republic not as a Republic of Letters but as a "Republic of Taste," where virtue resided in the propertied discernment of the connoisseur rather than the earnest, workaday morality of the artisan. This was hardly a neutral substitution. The literary critic Michael Warner has argued that in the years following the Revolution growing numbers of Americans laid claim to print culture as a means of articulating their citizenship and defining their place in an emergent public sphere.[28] However, if these men and women aggressively pursued books and periodicals, they did not gain access to costly illustrated books; they enjoyed far less exposure to fine, imported engravings. Female students' grandest productions underscored the fact that print cultures, like the citizens who participated in them, were not created equal. Culled from expensive sources, fashioned in silk and watercolor, and executed by graceful young ladies, "schoolgirl" art ensured that the highly restrictive Republic of Taste would work as a counter to the more protean Republic of Letters.

Accomplishment, Performance, and the Public Sphere

Women's prominent and public role in the construction of an American Republic of Taste allowed them to stake out territory within the public sphere, for display and performance were central to young women's literary and artistic endeavors. A mastery of reading, for example, meant a mastery of reading aloud. Female readers were instructed not only to heed "pronunciation, accent, and cadence" but also to adjust their delivery to "the number and extent" of their audience.[29] Girls' commonplace books were hardly private documents, or secret testimonials to the construction of an authentic inner life. Instead, they were usually written under the watchful eye of a teacher, often as a requirement for graduation, and later circulated among family and friends. This scrutiny was deemed so fundamental that in 1814 two students at Sarah Pierce's Litchfield Academy forfeited the opportunity to receive academic prizes because they refused to submit their journals for public inspection. The "ornamental branches" obviously yielded finished products that could be displayed. Paintings and embroideries were generally framed, often at great expense. Indeed, the imperative to display girls' accomplishments was so strong that frame making began to employ significant numbers of artisans when and where schoolgirls began to make art.[30]

More to the point, academy examinations and exhibitions allowed young women to display the fruits of their learning before a public audience in a formal and highly ritualized setting. In the years following the Revolution, with the growing insistence on the connections between the quality of education and the health of the Republic, public examinations became more common for male and female students alike. Exhibitions were intended both to demonstrate that students were fit to join a republican culture and to provide an idealized picture of that republican culture. In other words, the academy exhibition was the public sphere writ small.

Like the examination held at the Bethlehem Female Seminary in 1789, these events were literally public performances that displayed young women's learning, sensibility, and suitability for civic life. The ceremonies typically took place in school halls, drawing townsmen and townswomen into the schools proper and underscoring the public ends of private education. They were regularly covered by the local press, making the proceedings available even to those who were unable or unwilling to attend. Although it is difficult to know for certain exactly who turned out for academy exhibitions, scattered evidence suggests that they were popular entertainments among educated women and men. Salem's indefatigable minister William Bentley made a point of attending academy examinations along with Harvard's commencement. *Port Folio* editor Joseph Dennie attended the annual exhibitions at the Philadelphia Young Ladies' Academy. Harriet Beecher Stowe recalled that the "literati of Litchfield," Connecticut, regularly turned out for exhibitions at Sarah Pierce's academy.[31]

Whoever they included, audiences were treated to oratory, declamations, and recitations that took place in physical spaces adorned with visible symbols of girls' education and sensibility. Samples of penmanship, composition, drawing, painting, and embroidery—even commonplace books and diaries—were set out for audiences to assess and appreciate. The students as well came in for a fair measure of inspection. Observers reported that at Susanna Rowson's academy, the "ladies [were] attired with the greatest simplicity; no ornament whatever appearing among them." At Bethlehem's 1789 examination, the girls sat "in the form of a half-moon, and were mostly dressed in white." In 1814 the instructor John P. Brace noted that the Litchfield "girls were all arranged in their best apparel" around the schoolroom. Only after the visiting "ladies and gentlemen had looked as long as they pleased" at the girls and the room could he announce the students' "credit marks."[32] Indeed, looking at Jacob Marling's 1816 depiction of a celebration at the Raleigh Academy, it is not hard to imagine that the young ladies who assembled to exhibit their learning and talent bore a marked

Figure 6.3. Jacob Marling (American, 1774–1833), *The May Queen (The Crowning of Flora)*, 1816. Oil on canvas, 30 1/8 x 39 1/8 in. Chrysler Museum of Art, Norfolk, Va. Gift of Edgar William and Bernice Chrysler Gabisch. 80.181.20.

resemblance to the painted and embroidered figures that were exhibited on paper and canvas. Taste, grace, and learning were fused in virtuous feminine publicity. (See Figure 6.3.)

Displays of skill and sentiment drew young women into the public sphere alongside their commonplace books, sketches, and samplers. But if women assumed a prominent public role, it was an inherently ambiguous one. Whatever else they suggested, women's paintings and embroideries summoned to mind the threatening specter of luxury, commodities, and consumption—the same specter that haunted the public discourse on reading and accomplishment. This specter was made manifest at examinations, not only in the skills and supplies that schoolgirl artists purchased but also in the ways in which the finished products emulated luxury goods. Even more ominously, women's accomplishments suggested the ways in which selfhood, or more to the point, self-fashioning, was bound up with consumption. In other words, women's public presence was articulated through images, objects, texts, and performances that simultaneously connected them to republican refinement and to luxurious consumption—connections made all the more potent by the resemblances between students and their subjects. Women's literary and artistic work thus simultaneously maintained the boundaries of the Republic of Taste and raised questions about the legitimacy of women's claims to membership within that republic.[33]

In the cultural and political landscape of the early American Republic, the values and practices of both reading and accomplishment resonated with the deep tensions and contradictions that shaped American republicanism and that came to occupy center stage in American civic culture by the 1780s. By trying to think in new ways about the relationship between reading and accomplishment, we can learn a great deal about the gender dynamics of a period that is attracting new attention from Americanists interested in the public sphere, in consumer culture, in political life, and—of course—in reading. Certainly, the culture of letters and the culture of accomplishment can help illuminate a period of American history marked by both a sense of expansive opportunity and sharp foreclosure. More broadly, thinking about reading and the problem of accomplishment reminds us to think not only about the ways that reading—and education generally—set women at odds with society but also about the ways that women's reading operated in society. Finally, an exploration of reading and the problem of accomplishment reminds us that in our efforts to conjure the historic female reader, we would do well to try and see her in the context of the objects, images, and books that surrounded her.

Notes

1. William Cornelius Reichel, *A History of the Rise, Progress, and Present Condition of the Bethlehem Female Seminary with a Catalogue of Its Pupils, 1785–1858* (Philadelphia: Lippincott, 1858), 53–56.

2. See esp. the arguments made by Linda K. Kerber, *Women of the Republic: Intellect and Ideology in Revolutionary America* (Chapel Hill: University of North Carolina Press, 1980), 139–261; Mary Beth Norton, *Liberty's Daughters: The Revolutionary Experience of American Women, 1750–1800* (New York: Little Brown, 1980), 256–94; and Barbara Miller Solomon, *In the Company of Educated Women: A History of Women and Higher Education in America* (New Haven, Conn.: Yale University Press, 1985), 14–26. Kerber goes furthest, extending her anger over women's exclusion from institutions and disciplines into contempt for women's training in the ornamentals. See, for example, her caption for Mary M. Franklin's embroidered map of the world: "Teachers at girls' academies frequently translated formal learning into familiar media. In Pleasant Valley, New York, a schoolgirl embroidered a map of the world. Did the effort improve her knowledge of geography?" (Kerber, *Women of the Republic*, 216–17). More recently Margaret Nash, *Women's Education in the United States, 1780–1840* (New York: Palgrave Macmillan, 2005), 41–45, has argued that accomplishments were not the distinguishing features of female education but were, in one form or another, part of

the curricula for male and female students. However, she does not explore the relation between book learning and accomplishment. Sally Schwager, "'All United Like Sisters': The Legacy of the Early Female Academies," in *To Ornament Their Minds: Sarah Pierce's Litchfield Academy, 1792–1833*, ed. Catherine Keene Fields and Lisa C. Knightlinger (Litchfield, Conn.: Litchfield Historical Society, 1993), 12–19, has suggested that contemporary historians who deride ornamental education have been influenced by nineteenth-century feminists such as Elizabeth Cady Stanton, who derided their own educations. Historians, however, seem equally influenced by others, like eighteenth-century iconoclast Benjamin Rush and nineteenth-century reformers Catharine Beecher and Emma Willard, who worried that the frivolous dimensions of the ornamental arts would corrupt practical and evangelical aims of women's education.

3. The literature refining and elaborating Jurgen Habermas's analysis of the public sphere, *The Transformation of the Public Sphere: An Inquiry into a Category of Bourgeois Society* (Cambridge, Mass.: MIT Press, 1989), is large and growing too fast to be fully cited here. For critical discussions of Habermas's concept of the public sphere, see, for example, the essays collected in Craig Calhoun, ed., *Habermas and the Public Sphere* (Cambridge, Mass.: MIT Press, 1992). For Americanists' attention to and interventions in these debates, see David Waldstreicher, review of Craig Calhoun, ed., *Habermas and the Public Sphere, William and Mary Quarterly*, 3rd ser., 52 (1995): 175–77; David S. Shields, *Civil Tongues and Polite Letters in British America* (Chapel Hill: University of North Carolina Press for the Omohundro Institute of Early American History and Culture, 1993). On women in the public sphere, see esp. Dena Goodman, *The Republic of Letters: A Cultural History of the French Enlightenment* (Ithaca, N.Y.: Cornell University Press, 1994); Dena Goodman, "Public Sphere and Private Life: Toward a Synthesis of Current Historiographical Approaches to the Old Regime," *History and Theory* 31 (1992): 1–20; Shields, *Civil Tongues and Polite Letters*; Jan Lewis, "Politics and the Ambivalence of the Private Sphere: Women in Early Washington, D.C.," in *A Republic for the Ages: The United States Capitol and the Political Culture of the Early Republic*, ed. Donald R. Kennon (Charlottesville: United States Capitol Historical Society and University Press of Virginia, 1999), 122–51; and Fredrika J. Teute, "Roman Matron on the Banks of Tiber Creek: Margaret Bayard Smith and the Politicization of Spheres in the Nation's Capital," in ibid., 89–121.

4. "A Female Portrait," *Juvenile Port-Folio and Literary Miscellany*, August 3, 1816; "Modern Female Education," *Weekly Visitor, or Ladies' Miscellany*, February 1, 1806; Rev. John Bennett, "Elected Prose; Letter III," *American Museum or Universal Magazine*, August 1791. Bennett was the author of the hugely popular *Letters to a Young Lady on a Variety of Useful and Interesting Subjects*, which went through more than ten editions between 1790 and 1820 and was still in print in 1856, was published serially in the *American Museum or Universal Magazine*, and was transcribed into the commonplace books of students in at least one female seminary. See extracts from Mary Bacon's journal reprinted in Emily Noyes Vanderpoel, *Chronicles of a Pioneer School: The Litchfield Female Academy, Litchfield, Connecticut, 1792–1833* (Cambridge, Mass.: Harvard University Press, 1902), 72–76.

5. Rev. John Bennett, "Letters to a Young Lady; Letter XXIII," *American Museum or Universal Magazine*, June 1792; James Milnor, "Speech before the Philadelphia Academy for the Instruction of Young Ladies," *Port Folio*, May 1809. Hannah Webster Foster, *The Boarding School; or, Lessons of a Preceptress to her Pupils* (Boston: I. Thomas and E. T. Andrews, 1798), 23—significantly, Foster advances

this argument in a didactic novel in which these words are spoken by the headmistress of a boarding school to her pupils; Cathy N. Davidson, *Revolution and the Word: The Rise of the Novel in America* (New York: Oxford University Press, 1986), esp. 83–150.

6. Mary Kelley, "'Vindicating the Equality of Female Intellect': Women and Authority in the Early Republic," *Prospects: An Annual of American Cultural Studies* 17 (1992): 1–28, has adroitly traced the ways in which shifting assessments of women's intellect measured equality against gender difference.

7. Bennett, "Elected Prose; Letter III"; Anon., "Desultory Observations on the Education and Manners of the Fair Sex," *Boston Magazine,* February 1796.

8. Professor Meiners, of Gottingen, "On the Education and Accomplishments of Females," *Lady's Weekly Miscellany,* March 31, 1810.

9. Foster, *Boarding School,* 42; Bennett, "Letters to a Young Lady; Letter IX," *American Museum or Universal Magazine,* March 1792. On the expansion of music in the colonies and the early Republic, see Cynthia Adams Hoover, "Music and Theater in the Lives of Eighteenth-Century Americans," in *Of Consuming Interests: The Style of Life in the Eighteenth Century,* ed. Cary Carson, Ronald Hoffman, and Peter J. Albert (Charlottesville: University Press of Virginia, 1994), 307–53. Richard Leppert, "Social Order and the Domestic Consumption of Music: The Politics of Sound in the Policing of Gender Construction in Eighteenth-Century England," in *The Consumption of Culture, 1600–1800: Image, Object, Text,* ed. Ann Bermingham and John Brewer (London: Routledge, 1997), 514–34, emphasizes the patriarchal dimensions of women's musical accomplishments.

10. John Swanwick, *Thoughts on Education, Addressed to the Visitors of the Young Ladies' Academy in Philadelphia, October 31, 1787* (Philadelphia, 1787), 15; James Cosens Ogden, *The Female Guide: or, Thoughts on the Education of that Sex, Accommodated to the State of Society, Manners, and Government, in the United States* (Concord, N.H.: Hough, 1793), 29.

11. The literature on the transatlantic consumer revolution is too large to be cited comprehensively. For surveys and overviews, see esp. John Brewer and Roy Porter, eds., *Consumption and the World of Goods* (New York: Routledge, 1993); Bermingham and Brewer, *Consumption of Culture;* and Cary Carson, "The Consumer Revolution in Colonial British America: Why Demand?" in *Of Consuming Interests,* 483–541. For American case studies, see T. H. Breen, *The Marketplace of Revolution: How Consumer Politics Shaped American Independence* (New York: Oxford University Press, 2004), and Richard Bushman, *The Refinement of America: Persons, Houses, Cities* (New York: Random House, 1992). For an insightful discussion of the intersection of literary culture, gentility, and the market, see Christopher Lukasik, "Breeding and Reading: Chesterfieldian Civility in the Early Republic," in *A Companion to American Fiction, 1780–1865,* ed. Shirley Samuels (Malden, Mass.: Blackwell Publishing, 2004), 158–67.

12. Bennett, "Letters to a Young Lady; Letter XX and Letter XIX," *American Museum or Universal Magazine,* May 1792; "Letters to a Young Lady; Letter XXII," ibid., June 1792; "Letters to a Young Lady; Letter XIX," ibid., May 1792.

13. Sarah Pierce, "Address at the Close of School, 29 Oct. 1818," in Vanderpoel, *Chronicles of a Pioneer School,* 177–78. Mary Kelley also recognized the inculcation of sensibility and taste in early national academies; see her *Learning to Stand and Speak: Women, Education, and Public Life in America's Republic* (Chapel Hill: University of North Carolina Press for the Omohundro Institute of Early American History and Culture, 2006), 17–19, 69–71.

14. Joseph Addison, *Spectator* (June 21, 1712); Kathleen Eagan Johnson, "'To

Expand the Mind and Embellish Society': The Educational Philosophy and Ornamental Arts of the Bethlehem Young Ladies Seminary, 1785–1840" (M.A. thesis, University of Delaware, 1978), 73. On Mrs. Saunders and Miss Beach's school, see Jane C. Nylander, "Some Print Sources of New England School Girl Art," *Antiques*, August 1976, 292–301.

15. Elizabeth A. Bohls, "Disinterestedness and Denial of the Particular: Locke, Adam Smith, and the Subject of Aesthetics," in *Eighteenth-Century Aesthetics and the Reconstruction of Art*, ed. Paul Mattick, Jr. (New York: Cambridge University Press, 1993); Jay Fliegelman, *Declaring Independence: Jefferson, Natural Language, and the Culture of Performance* (Stanford, Calif.: Stanford University Press, 1993), 73–75, 115–16. See also Eric Slauter, "The State as a Work of Art: Politics and the Cultural Origins of the Constitution" (Ph.D. diss., Stanford University, 2000); and Rochelle Gurstein, "Taste and 'the Conversible World' in the Eighteenth Century," *Journal of the History of Ideas* 61 (2000): 203–21. My understanding of the Republic of Taste owes much to John Barrell's remarkably influential study *The Political Theory of Painting from Reynolds to Hazlitt: "The Body of the Public"* (New Haven, Conn.: Yale University Press, 1986). The range of Barrell's influence and the influence of the civic tradition of aesthetics are both traced in Stephen Copley, "The Fine Arts in Eighteenth-Century Polite Culture," in *Painting and the Politics of Culture: New Essays on British Art, 1700–1850*, ed. John Barrell (New York: Oxford University Press, 1992), 13–37.

16. On the special importance of politeness and feeling for the American Republic, see, among many, David Waldstreicher, *In the Midst of Perpetual Fetes: The Making of American Nationalism, 1776–1820* (Chapel Hill: University of North Carolina Press, 1997), 53–107; and Gordon S. Wood, *The Radicalism of the American Revolution* (New York: Knopf, 1992), 189–212. On women's education as a register of political culture, see Kerber, *Women of the Republic*, 185–231; and Norton, *Liberty's Daughters*, 256–95.

17. For a fuller discussion of the numbers of schools offering such instruction, see Thomas Woody, *A History of Women's Education in the United States*, vol. 1 (New York: The Science Press, 1929). For general descriptions of the art made by female students, see Lynne Templeton Brickley, "Sarah Pierce's Litchfield Female Academy, 1792–1833" (Ed.D. diss., Harvard University, 1985); Fields and Knightlinger, *To Ornament Their Minds*; Suzanne L. Flynt, *Ornamental and Useful Accomplishments: Schoolgirl Education and Deerfield Academy, 1800–1830* (Deerfield, Mass.: Pocumtuck Valley Memorial Association, 1988); Betty Ring, *Let Virtue Be a Guide to Thee: Needlework in the Education of Rhode Island Women* (Providence: Rhode Island Historical Society, 1983); and Betty Ring, *Girlhood Embroidery: American Samplers and Pictorial Needlework, 1690–1850*, vols. 1 and 2 (New York: Knopf, 1993). On the financial significance of the ornamentals, see Brickley, "Sarah Pierce's Litchfield Academy"; and Woody, *History of Women's Education*.

18. Emulation, long overlooked in studies of early national letters and culture, is finally receiving its due. See J. M. Opal, "Exciting Emulation: Academies and the Transformation of the Rural North, 1780s–1820s," *Journal of American History* 91.2 (2004): 445–70; J. M. Opal, *Beyond the Farm: Ambition and the Transformation of Rural New England, 1770s–1820s* (Philadelphia: University of Pennsylvania Press, 2008); and William Huntting Howell, "'A more perfect copy than heretofore': Imitation, Emulation, and American Literary Culture" (Ph.D. diss., Northwestern University, 2005).

19. Schoolgirls' commonplace books rarely conformed to the formal catego-

ries that marked classical commonplace books; instead, they were compiled by accretion, mixing poetry, prose, records of daily experiences, and even artwork. Nevertheless, the point of keeping a commonplace book was the same as it had been for earlier generations of male students and men of letters: to cultivate taste and sensibility by emulating and internalizing the wisdom and judgment of other worthy minds. On the function of commonplace books in self-fashioning, see esp. Mary Thomas Crane, *Framing Authority: Sayings, Self, and Society in Sixteenth-Century England* (Princeton, N.J.: Princeton University Press, 1993). On the history and function of commonplace books, see Ann Moss, *Printed Commonplace-books and the Structuring of Renaissance Thought* (New York: Oxford University Press, 1996); and Sr. Joan Marie Lechner, *Renaissance Concepts of the Commonplaces: An Historical Investigation of the General and Universal Ideas Used in All Argumentation and Persuasion with Special Emphasis on the Educational and Literary Tradition of the Sixteenth and Seventeenth Centuries* (Westport, Conn.: Greenwood Press, 1962). Linda Kerber (*Women of the Republic*, 214) speculates that in the early Republic, journals or commonplace books initiated young women into a culture of print.

20. See esp. Ring, *Girlhood Embroidery*, 16–17, 22, and passim. Teachers were so influential in shaping students' needlework that art historians can tell where girls and women attended school from examining their embroidery. See, for example, Ring's discussions of the style of the Misses Patten who taught needlework in Hartford, Conn. (ibid., 202–10), or Abby Wright, who taught in South Hadley, Mass. (ibid., 159–65). On emulation and needlework, see Howell, "A more perfect copy than heretofore," 163–95.

21. Quoted in Johnson, "To Expand the Mind and Embellish Society," 37.

22. These arguments are based on data presented in Ethel Stanwood Bolton and Eva Johnston Coe, *American Samplers* (Boston: Massachusetts Society of Colonial Dames, 1921), which contains an appendix listing all the epigrams from eighteenth- and nineteenth-century samplers that the Society of Colonial Dames had been able to locate by 1921. While art historians agree that Bolton and Coe's list of samplers is not exhaustive, they also agree that it is representative.

23. Bolton and Coe, *American Samplers*, 265, 250.

24. Ibid., 268, 269.

25. Vanderpoel, *Chronicles of a Pioneer School*, 77.

26. Betty Ring has done more than any other scholar to trace the literary and print sources for schoolgirl art. On Mary Beach's version of Cornelia, mother of the Gracchi, see Ring, *Girlhood Embroidery*, 96; on Nancy Lincoln's "Washington Family," see ibid., 87; on print work, see ibid., 324–27.

27. Steven C. Bullock, "'Sensible Signs': The Emblematic Education of Post-Revolutionary Freemasonry," in *Republic for the Ages*, 177–213.

28. On the Republic of Letters, see Michael Warner, *The Letters of the Republic: Publication and the Public Sphere in Eighteenth Century America* (Cambridge, Mass.: Harvard University Press, 1990).

29. Foster, *Boarding School*, 17; A Lady, *The New Pleasing Instructor: or, Young Ladies Guide to Virtue and Happiness* (Boston: I. Thomas and E. T. Andrews, 1799), 10. On the refusal to circulate commonplace books, see Emily Noyes Vanderpoel, *More Chronicles of a Pioneer School, from 1792 to 1833* (New York: Cadmus Book Shop, 1927), 94.

30. On increasing numbers of frame makers, see Ring, *Girlhood Embroidery*, 1:22, 24. Families were willing to pay large sums to frame their daughters' work. For example, Caroline Stebbins's family paid five dollars to frame the embroi-

dered picture of Mount Vernon that she completed as a student at Deerfield Academy in 1806–7. For the cost of the frame, they could have purchased an additional half-year's tuition for instruction in reading, writing, and grammar. See Flynt, *Ornamental and Useful Accomplishments*, 21.

31. William Bentley, *The Diary of William Bentley: Pastor of the East Church, Salem, Massachusetts*, vols. 2–4 (Salem, Mass.: Essex Institute, 1905–14). For Dennie on the Philadelphia Young Ladies' Academy, see *Port Folio*, May 1809. For Stowe's comments on Litchfield's literati, see *Chronicles of a Pioneer School*, 182. It is likely that audiences grew to include more than local literati; by the 1800s, many schools were publishing broadsides that advertised the dates, times, and order of exercises for their exhibitions. On exhibitions as vehicles for emulation and competition, see Opal, "Exciting Emulation," 460–61.

32. Jane C. Giffen, "Susanna Rowson and Her Academy," *Antiques* (September 1990): 436–40; Reichel, *Bethlehem Female Seminary*, 76; "Extracts from the Private Journals of Mr. John P. Brace," in Vanderpoel, *More Chronicles of a Pioneer School*, 22.

33. Cf. feminist art historians Ann Bermingham and Anne Higonnet (Bermingham, "Elegant Females and Gentlemen Connoisseurs," and Higonnet, "Secluded Visions: Images of Feminine Experience in Nineteenth-Century Europe," *Radical History Review* 38 [1987], 16–36), who have suggested that what most distinguished the amateur artistic productions of eighteenth- and nineteenth-century (European) women was the extent to which their work was shrouded in privacy, the extent to which it was conceived, executed, and displayed within the domestic sphere.

Part III
Translation and Authorship

As the essays earlier in the collection suggest, reading is embedded in a range of social, textual, and material practices, and readers survive in the historical record only when some form of textual or visual production accompanied or followed their reading. Reading on its own, in other words, is invisible. In this final section of the volume the essays focus on textual production of various sorts: storytelling, testifying, translation, transcription, composition. Even as they attend to production in these various forms, this final cluster of essays affirms the connections between reading, speaking, listening, interpreting, and writing.

As the essays in Part I reveal, conduct manuals and other prescriptive literature in early modern England circumscribed girls' and women's reading. One seventeenth-century writer situated these prescriptions specifically in relation to both accomplishment and authorship, proposing appropriate reading for a gentleman's daughters: "In stead of Song and Musicke, let them learne Cookery and Laundrie. And in stead of reading Sir *Philip Sidneys Arcadia*, let them read the grounds of good huswifery. I like not a female Poetresse at any hand."[1] Girls should learn practical domestic work, that is, rather than aristocratic accomplishments, and they should eschew romance reading precisely because it might provoke them to write. Two generations earlier Margaret Tyler (fl. 1578) used the relationship between reading and writing to challenge such prohibitions in an early defense of female authorship. Significantly, her defense is based on women's right to translate texts. If men dedicate books to women, she reasons, women may read them, and if allowed to read, women should be permitted to respond by translating; for translation is a modest activity, an extension of reading, demanding more "heede then deepe invention or exquisite learning."[2] Indeed, early modern Englishwomen, like the American women studied here, published primarily in genres that relied explicitly on their readings of other texts: translations, compilations, refutations, and editions.[3]

Because the relationship between women's reading and writing was often complicated and sometimes obscured, this section of the volume imagines authorship and translation in broad terms: authorship imagined or documented, translation of texts, genres, and traditions. Just as the story of women's reading is not an unbroken, ever-upward trajectory toward expanding literacies, the story of female authorship and female storytelling is not a straightforward, teleological push toward ever greater liberties for women writers. As Ian Moulton demonstrates in his essay, the stereotypical, self-effacing female novelist of the nineteenth century owed far more to the prescriptive virtues codified in the Renaissance—silence, chastity, and obedience—than to the livelier models of female storytellers that prevailed in the medieval period. Bridging the oral culture of storytelling and the print culture of the novel is the Continental *novelle*, one of the first genres that European women began to dominate as authors. In its subject matter, characters, and language—vernacular, straightforward, familial—the *novelle* evokes female experience more than male scholarly authority. The translation of the Continental *novelle* into an English tradition, however, displaced female readers and storytellers from the center of the form.

While Puritan ideals would seem to invite women into the circle of literacy and exegesis, the story of colonial New England women's spiritual and intellectual lives is a "very mixed history," as Janice Knight observes, full of stereotypes and setbacks, dependent on partial and indirect evidence framed by a patriarchal culture. While Puritan ideals encouraged, indeed mandated, women's engagement with the Bible, their authority as readers and exegetes was challenged at critical moments of crisis and controversy. In her attention to Anne Hutchinson's trials, Mary Rowlandson's captivity narrative, and Mercy Short's demonic possession, Knight demonstrates the narrowing after the 1630s of the Puritan ideals of democratized religious authority and the expansion of literacy across gender and class boundaries. Further, she identifies the poignancy of the glimpses of these three women's inner lives, which are mediated through men's words. Rowlandson's best-seller is contained by her husband's sermon on her captivity and by Increase Mather's preface. To consider Hutchinson and, even more radically, Short in the context of authorship is to explore the complicated and profound way in which orality and textuality were intertwined in Puritan America, as in early modern England. Men recorded Hutchinson's words at her two trials, and our only record of Short's gestural reading of the Bible survives in Cotton Mather's account of his treatment of her. Reading in Puritan America, Knight argues, was a practice integrated with hearing and speaking, exegesis and action.

The status of textual authority and the relationship between women readers and male-authored texts figure prominently in Margaret Ferguson's discussion of Aphra Behn's theories of translation and specifically her 1688 translation of Fontenelle. God, Fontenelle, and Behn emerge in this treatise as translators and readers engaged in interpretive acts. Like the Puritan women in Knight's essay, Behn reads the Bible differently from her male opponents, and she moves away from orthodoxy in her interpretation and application of Scripture. Behn emphasizes the materiality of her Bible, rather than viewing Scripture as God's voice. Ferguson's essay explores translation in culturally specific terms, situating it within early modern notions of translation as a form of writing "reputed femelle" and opening up ways of understanding the relation between translation and original other than imitation or subversion. As she explores the gendered possibilities of fidelity in translation, Ferguson describes the triangulation Behn sets up between herself, her source texts, and her own readers.

Though she died 150 years after Behn, Deborah Logan, an elite and long-lived Philadelphia Quaker, engaged in two antiquarian and anachronistic practices with roots in early modern European habits of collecting that all the other women traced in this section would recognize: the curiosity cabinet and the commonplace book. Focusing on the poetry in her commonplace books, Susan Stabile examines the variety of modes in which Logan read: discovery, collection, transcription, supplementation, and annotation. Stabile argues that commonplace books, though kept by men and women in the early Republic, were gendered, their fragmentation and incompleteness mimicking women's domestic lives. She further suggests that this fragmentation demands a methodological response from its historians, a willingness—demonstrated by all the contributors in this section—to consider women's textual production on its own terms.

Notes

1. Thomas Powell, *Tom of all Trades: Or the Plaine Path-Way to Preferment; Being A Discovery of a passage to Promotion in all Professions, Trades, Arts, and Mysteries* (London, 1631), 47.

2. Diego Ortunez de Calahora, *The First Part of the Mirrour of Princely Deedes and Knightood,* trans. M[argaret] T[yler], 2d ed. (London, 1580); "Dedication and Epistle to the Reader" repr. in Moira Ferguson, ed., *First Feminists: British Women Writers, 1578–1799* (Bloomington: Indiana University Press, 1985), 56.

3. Barbara Lewalski, noting this tendency, is able to fit the "original" works by Elizabethan women into a footnote in *Writing Women in Jacobean England* (Cambridge, Mass.: Harvard University Press, 1993), 326n13.

Chapter 7

"Who Painted the Lion?" Women and *Novelle*

Ian Frederick Moulton

Popular Western stereotypes of female storytellers change remarkably when studied over the three centuries from 1500 to 1800. One of the most prevalent images of the female narrator before 1500, in the late medieval period, is memorably typified by Chaucer's Wife of Bath. The Wife is loud, forceful and bawdy; she reeks of sexual pleasure. By 1800, at the end of the period covered by this volume, the female narrator tends to be imagined as someone closer to Jane Austen—outwardly demure and proper, hiding her manuscript when visitors come to call lest her unladylike scribbling give offense.[1] Both stereotypes are familiar enough to modern readers; their limitations are fairly obvious, and each reflects the period that produced it. The Wife's passionate discourse conforms to medieval notions about the irrationality and sensuous nature of women, not to mention their reputed volubility. Jane Austen—or rather, a certain bloodless image of her—embodies all the feminine virtues appropriate to her social setting: modesty, decorum, chastity, and thrift.

What does not change from the fourteenth to the eighteenth centuries is the subject matter felt to be appropriate for women's stories: love, courtship, and as the Wife memorably puts it, "wo that is in mariage."[2] Perhaps this is not surprising; early modern gender ideology tended to divide the world into a masculine sphere of combat and aggression and a feminine sphere of sexuality and pleasure;[3] a masculine public sphere of politics and business, a feminine private sphere of family and household. However, even within the supposedly feminine sphere of sex, love, and marriage there was opportunity nonetheless for a wide variety of narrative approach and emphasis. A story about rape can be a leering and disturbing fantasy of male aggression or a sober cautionary tale; a story of adultery can be a celebration of sexual freedom or a moralistic defense of marriage; a courtship narrative can be a romantic fantasy or a serious lesson on the importance of careful choices.

This essay is about women's involvement with one particular narrative tradition, the *novella*, or prose tale, from the fourteenth to seventeenth centuries. It deals with women's relations to *novelle* as storytellers and authors as well as readers and auditors. More than any other early modern narrative genre, *novelle* were addressed to an imagined female readership, and a male-authored text written with a female audience in mind is a text shaped by women—if only indirectly. Although there is little direct evidence of how actual early modern women readers responded to *novelle*, there is much to be learned about cultural expectations for female readers from the way collections of *novelle* present themselves both to their female audience and to a larger public. In the period after 1500, women take increasing control of their own narratives; they intervene in male narrative traditions and reshape them to reflect their own concerns. In the case of *novelle*, women go from being imagined readers to actual readers, from imagined tale-tellers to actual authors.

* * *

> Experience though noon auctoritee
> Were in this world is right ynogh for me
> To speke of wo that is in marriage. (*The Wife of Bath's Prologue*, lines 1–3)

From the beginning, the Wife of Bath's prologue sets up an opposition between feminine "experience" and masculine "authority." In her view, women live life and experience its pleasures and sorrows. Men lock themselves away with books until they are too old to have fun, and then they sit in their drafty rooms writing tracts condemning women for being lascivious. The result is a written record that is nothing but a catalog of imagined female transgressions:

> For trusteth wel, it is an inpossible
> That any clerk wol speke good of wyves,
> But an if it be of hooly seintes lyves,
> N'of noon oother womman nevere the mo.
> Who peynted the leon, tel me who? (688–92)

The Wife often comically misinterprets the texts she alludes to, but here she uses Aesop to great effect. In Aesop, when a lion is shown a painting of a man killing a lion, the beast's first response is to ask who the painter was: If the painter had been a lion, the picture would be different.[4]

Like Aesop's lion, the Wife knows that the truth of a tale is often determined by its teller. She continues:

> By God, if wommen hadde writen stories,
> As clerkes han withinne hire oratories,
> They wolde han writen of men moore wikkednesse
> Than al the mark of Adam may redresse. (693–96)

The Wife is well aware that the ability to write stories gives literate men great power over illiterate women. Although the Wife tells stories, she does not write them. For her, the world of feminine experience is an oral world, characterized by chatting, laughing, shrieking, and whispering. She has the tongue of "a verray jangleresse" (638) and equates death with no longer speaking (810). She is opposed in every way to the masculine world of authority characterized by books and the sterility of solitary reading.

The climax of the Wife's autobiographical narrative is her confrontation with her fifth husband, Jankyn, a clerk who sits reading aloud from his book, lecturing her on the sinfulness of women. He tells her of Eve enticing Adam, Delilah betraying Samson, Xanthippe dumping a piss pot on Socrates' head, and Clytemnestra killing Agamemnon. The Wife's reaction to this tiresome and hateful catalog is to grab the book from Jankyn's hand, rip three pages out of it, and punch him in the face. Though he resists, she ultimately teaches her husband to govern his tongue, and she makes him burn his book (813–16). Feminine orality triumphs over masculine literacy.

The Wife's defeat of Jankyn the clerk is also, like the *Canterbury Tales*, a triumph of the vernacular over Latin, for though Jankyn lectures his wife in English, the books that clerks wrote and read in the fourteenth century were overwhelmingly in Latin. Medieval Latin was by definition a male language; girls were almost never taught to speak or write it, and it was the medium of all learned discourse. Though the Wife's speech is replete with citation of authorities, there is no way she could have read many of the books she cites. Her misquotations and misinterpretations of various authorities are thus not just a personal quirk or a sign of diminished intelligence; they are typical of most women's relation to learned texts in the late Middle Ages: jumbled, secondhand, and partial.

Despite the Wife's hostility to reading and her alienation from literate Latin culture, she is nonetheless an expert storyteller. Like the other pilgrims, she tells her tale, but alone in the *Canterbury Tales* she also tells the story of her life, the narrative of her "experience" with her five husbands. In doing so, she points not only to women's capacity as storytellers but also to their role as guardians of sexual knowledge: "She koude of that art the olde daunce" (*General Prologue* 476). Although she is more vulgar (and experienced) than the high-born ladies of Boccaccio's *Decameron,* by telling practical stories dealing with love, sex, and marriage the Wife exemplifies the role taken by women in the entire *novelle* tradition. Beginning with the *Decameron* (1353)[5] and continuing into the sixteenth century with volumes such as the *Heptaméron* of Marguerite de Navarre and the *Novelle* of Bandello, these collections of tales provide a crucial link between the traditional oral culture of storytelling and the modern literate culture of the novel. They also constitute a narrative genre that brings together femininity, storytelling, and sexuality in ways that have influenced women's fiction into the modern era.

Novelle were primarily a vernacular genre, written in various mother tongues, not in Latin. Unlike much poetry and almost all texts of theology, law, philosophy or medicine, *novelle* were written in a language women might read, and would understand if it were read to them. Women are crucial to the *novelle* tradition as interlocutors, storytellers, and as auditors. Seven of Boccaccio's group of ten storytellers are women, and he always refers to his readers as "ladies." Many of Bandello's *Novelle* are dedicated to female readers, and the collection as a whole is addressed to the memory of Ippolita Sforza. In the works attributed to Marguerite de Navarre and Jeanne Flore, women are not only represented as active participants in fictional dialogues; they also appear as authors of the text.

The centrality of women to *novelle*—both as imagined participants and as actual authors and patrons—has profound implications for our understanding of female reading and knowledge in the early modern period. Not only are readers of *novelle* often explicitly gendered female, but the world of women and women's possible role in the larger world are arguably the primary subjects of *novelle.* Of course, men read *novelle* too; indeed, men probably read them more than women did. Nonetheless, *novelle* are a genre that from the beginning addresses itself primarily not to men but to women (at least rhetorically),[6] and it is one of the first genres that women authors take as their own. If we are to understand the construction of female readership in early modern Europe, we must understand what it is to be a reader of *novelle.*

Written in simple, vigorous, vernacular prose, *novelle* are realistic and domestic: they are about ordinary people, not supernaturally gifted heroes; they occur in real places such as Florence, Lyon, and Sicily, not in Arcadia, Troy, or Faerie Land. They concern themselves not with the place of mankind in the universe but with relationships between individuals—often sexual or familial relationships. They rarely deal with war and seldom describe combat in any detail. While some tales are amoral and others pointedly moralistic, *novelle* tend to be worldly and cynical in tone. They value wit and practical skill. Rather than tracing their genealogy to classical myths and legends, *novelle* are drawn from oral folk culture.[7] Though many have long and distinguished literary pedigrees, they tend to present themselves as "true" stories—not works of fiction.[8] Although in the Victorian period it was fashionable to translate Boccaccio into a pseudo-medieval dialect, full of "haths," "thees," and "forsooths," more recent translators have stressed the "contemporary and completely fresh tone" of Boccaccio's prose.[9] In fact, this "fresh" language has more in common with medieval women's language than men's: it is vernacular and straightforward, the antithesis of Latin rhetoric. It is the language of lived experience, not written authority.

Novelle are women's literature in more than their language. Women are central to the action in many tales, and many have female protagonists.[10] This is not to say that the representation of women in *novelle* is particularly broad in its scope: Women in *novelle* are primarily sexual beings—even in collections attributed to female authors.[11] Not that all women in *novelle* are lustful or unchaste, but in *novelle* the central issues for women are always sexual ones: chastity, marriage, adultery, and rape. Sometimes women's sexuality is seen as a threat; other times it is celebrated. Some female characters are virgins; others are sluts. Some are faithful lovers; some are adulterous wives. Some are innocent; others are knowingly seductive. However, they are never asexual. Indeed, they are always heterosexual: there is little mention of homoeroticism or autoeroticism in *novelle*.

The notion that stories dealing with love and sex are appropriate feminine reading goes beyond *novelle*. Ariosto's flirtatious epic *Orlando Furioso*, for example, frequently addresses itself to female readers. However, *novelle* focus on issues surrounding female sexuality more than any classical literary genre did. Though some of the most famous tales—such as the story of Ser Cepparello, which opens the *Decameron*—have little to do with either women or sex, as the genre develops, female sexuality comes to be its central concern. In the *Decameron*, 67 percent of the stories deal with sexual relations in one form or another.[12] In Marguerite's *Heptaméron*, the figure is closer to 90 percent.[13] Sexual issues are also paramount in other major collections, such as *Les Cents Nouvelles Nouvelles* and Bandello's *Novelle*.

That Marguerite de Navarre's *Heptaméron* is, if anything, more relentless than Boccaccio in its sexual focus raises serious questions about the function of *novelle* as a genre and their role in the lives of the women who read them. One should not necessarily assume that in the early modern period open discussion of sexuality and female desire is positive for women. Modern feminism has often seen the frank expression of women's sexuality as self-evidently liberating since it provides a healthy corrective to Victorian ideas about ideally sexless women. However, in the early modern period no such formulation existed. In *novelle* women are active lustful subjects as well as passive objects of desire. The nineteenth-century denial of female sexuality can, in fact, be seen in part as a feminist response to earlier notions that women were controlled by their animal desires and thus incapable of functioning equally as rational members of society. Some Victorian "feminists" argued that women's innate purity rendered them morally superior to men, and thus entitled to respect and various forms of social power and responsibility.[14] As the debates between characters in the *Heptaméron* reveal, in the early modern period women were empowered not by arguing that they were sexual beings but by asserting that they were capable of overcoming their natural desires.

Like much else in the genre, the way women are represented in *novelle* was largely defined by Boccaccio's *Decameron*, the first vernacular text in any genre to achieve pan-European circulation and popularity.[15] Like its author, the *Decameron* is deeply contradictory in its attitudes toward women. Although toward the end of his life Boccaccio stipulated in a letter that the *Decameron* should be kept away from women,[16] he nonetheless consistently represents the audience of the *Decameron* as female: he always refers to his readers as "donne," never as men. Indeed, at the beginning of the fourth day, Boccaccio offers a spirited defense against his (presumably male) detractors, who have accused him of wasting his time writing *novelle* to please women instead of writing Latin poetry for a male audience (249).

How are we to read Boccaccio's ostensible devotion to women's pleasure? Certainly the collection is not always flattering in its portrayal of women, and in many tales women are harshly treated. The fact that none of the hundred tales in the *Decameron* deals with female friendship or companionship suggests that Boccaccio was primarily interested in women as they relate to men. Given the culture in which Boccaccio was writing, this is hardly surprising, but it has profound effects on the way women are portrayed not only in the *Decameron* but also in the tradition of *novelle* as a whole. When Virginia Woolf lamented the lack of female friendship in fiction prior to the twentieth century—and this despite the fact that many novels were written by women—she was indicting a tradition of narrative fiction that has its beginnings in Boccaccio's *novelle*.[17] The *Decameron*'s male-centered perspective relegates women to the traditionally feminine sphere of sexuality, courtship, marriage, and procreation.

In the preface to the *Decameron*, Boccaccio suggests that the collection was written primarily to help women recover from lovesickness. He reflects that men are more easily cured of lovesickness than women, for they have so many more nonerotic pastimes available to them: Men "can take a walk and listen to or look at many different things; they can go hawking, hunting, or fishing; they can ride, gamble, or attend to business" (3). Women, on the other hand, are denied these forms of mental and physical relief: "They, in fear and shame, conceal the hidden flames of love within their delicate breasts" (2). Women lack the social power to act on their desires: "restricted by the wishes, whims, and commands of their fathers, mothers, brothers, and husbands, they remain most of the time limited to the narrow confines of their bedrooms." If women are afflicted with love-melancholy, it will fester within them, unless they can purge it with "nuovi ragionamenti" (new discussions). Boccaccio's collection of amorous tales will give them the purgative they require. Reading *novelle* will provide women with distraction, moral precepts, and imaginative release.

But to what end? The alternative title of the *Decameron* is *Prencipe Galeotto* (Prince Galahad), an allusion to the book of romance that seduces—and damns—Paolo and Francesca in Dante's *Inferno* (5.137). In Arthurian legend Galahad was the knight who first brought the adulterous Lancelot and Guinevere together. If Boccaccio's book is a "Galeotto," then, far from being a remedy for love-sickness, it is a pander that will lead young women to illicit affairs. Thus the *Decameron* is both a *Remedia Amoris* and an *Ars Amatoria*—a cure for love-melancholy and a guide to adultery.

Despite this ambivalence, the collection has, I would argue, a serious educational function. At the outset Boccaccio invokes the Horatian principle of *utile dulce*: "in reading [the *Decameron*] the ladies . . . will, perhaps, derive from the delightful things that happen in these tales both pleasure and useful counsel, inasmuch as they will recognize what should be avoided and what should be sought after" (3). Because *novelle* tend to avoid theological and philosophical issues, many critics read this statement as tongue-in-cheek and contend that the tales were written and read primarily as light entertainment.[18] However, although *novelle* are often hilarious, they also have the potential to be profoundly educational, not least for their female readers. After all, they provide women with knowledge about sexual situations without potentially hazardous sexual experience; in *novelle* women can read about the consequences of sexual relationships and sexual desire, without engaging in actual sexual activity.

While Boccaccio's presumably virginal female storytellers maintain a certain modesty, they are not lacking in sexual knowledge, including knowledge about the gendered power dynamics and social consequences of sexual relationships. Although they object to the subject chosen for the seventh day—tricks wives have played on their husbands—they have no trouble coming up with stories about clever ways to commit adultery and to be revenged on jealous husbands. It is true that most of the bawdiest tales are told by the three men in the group, but while some tales have proved shocking to readers over the years, at no time is it suggested in the *Decameron* that any are unfit for feminine ears. Though the women might be somewhat reticent to tell bawdy tales, they blush and giggle in response to those of the men, and such stories are clearly presented as appropriate for a group of unsupervised, unmarried, respectable young men and women.

Granted, the occasion of the tale-telling in Boccaccio is anything but normative; the young people come together only to escape the plague, and they retreat to their villa at "a time when going about with your trousers over your head was not considered improper if it helped to save your life" (686). Safely removed from the horrors of the Black Death, the ten young people create an alternative society that is largely organized by women and in which women share power more or less equally with men. The very idea of passing the time by telling stories comes from Pampinea, the most articulate of the women, and she is unanimously elected to rule the group for their first day. This alternative society of storytellers is admittedly temporary, and its elaborate structure resembles the rules of a game rather than a utopian republic, but it nonetheless marks the space of tale-telling as a largely feminine one. This feminine space is represented symbolically by the enclosed garden in which the group meets initially, as well as by the hidden "Valley of Ladies" where the young women retire to bathe (412–13) and where the group meets to tell the bawdy tales of the seventh day.

In the *Decameron* the space of the *novelle* is defined as a space of feminine play. The play is not irresponsible but rather is mature and structured. It is not didactic or moralizing but does give intelligent, sensitive, practical readers much to think about. The *novelle* are not feminine play as women might imagine it, but as imagined by a male author whose attitudes toward women, while ambivalently positive, are nonetheless pervaded by the misogyny of his society. Seen within the context of his entire career, Boccaccio's attitudes toward women are wildly inconsistent. The praise of women in the *Decameron* must be balanced against the deep misogyny of his final vernacular work, *Corbaccio* (1365). In addition, although he wrote a compendium of famous women's lives, it was written in Latin, and few women could read it.

Boccaccio's contradictory attitudes toward women are not idiosyncratic but reflect larger social contradictions. On the one hand, women are the idealized objects of masculine devotion; on the other, they are seen as physically, intellectually, and morally inferior. They are believed to be naturally sexual, but they must always be modest and chaste. The same contradictions are visible almost two hundred years later in the advice given "court ladies" in Castiglione's *Courtier* (3.5).[19] Entertaining conversation is the most important attribute of a cultured woman, but how can she be entertaining without being wanton and seductive? If noblewomen speak flirtatiously, this implies a wanton character. If they seem squeamish, they risk appearing hypocritical since everyone knows women love sexual conversation (3.5). In the end, *The Courtier* endorses one of the two habitual responses of the women in the *Decameron*: "when she finds herself present at such talk, she ought to listen with a light blush of shame." Giggling, however, is not encouraged.

Like the women in *The Courtier*, the female patrons of Bandello's *Novelle* are a silent audience; we do not know what they think of the tales the male author offers them. In other sixteenth-century collections of *novelle*, however, women do more than just listen while men tell tales about them. This is especially true of the two sixteenth-century French collections attributed to female authors: Marguerite de Navarre's *Heptaméron* (published in 1558) and the *Contes amoureux* (Amorous Tales) of Jeanne Flore (c. 1537). The authorship of both of these collections has been disputed—while Marguerite de Navarre is now given credit for full authorship of the *Heptaméron*, it was not published until nine years after her death and bears little stylistic resemblance to her other works, which are devotional poetry, not secular prose.[20] Nothing whatever is known of Jeanne Flore, but the name is almost certainly a pseudonym, possibly a feminine version of the name of the male Spanish author Juan de Flores.[21] Little is known of the circumstances of the collection's publication, and its textual history is fairly complicated. The surviving text is probably an abridged version of a lost work also attributed to Flore and entitled *Amour fatal*.[22] Only seven stories are told, though others (presumably lost) are referred to.

On one level, it does not matter who wrote the *Contes*; more important for our purposes is the fact that they were attributed to a female author and were presented to the public as such. The stories told in the *Contes amoureux* are all taken from other sources; but despite the fact that all the stories in the volume were originally told by male authors, the collection of *Contes amoureux* presents its readers with an imagined world that is almost entirely feminine. Whatever the gender of their author, the *Contes* continue to see *novelle* as resolutely feminine discourse. All the speakers are women. Toward the end of the day, six young men arrive to accompany the storytellers, but they do not speak.

This feminine world focuses exclusively on sexual concerns, and its highest value is sexual love and fulfillment. With one exception, all the speakers are united in their devotion to a religion of love, and their tales are dedicated to the proposition that it is always wrong to deny love's power. Women in "unequal marriages" are encouraged to take lovers, for if they remain faithful to their aged and impotent husbands, they will arouse the divine wrath of Venus and Cupid and be harshly punished. In fact, the text is characterized by the women's almost parodic devotion to sexual satisfaction.

Each of the tales focuses on the dire consequences of refusing sexual attraction. In the first, Rosamonde, a young and beautiful bride, is rescued from her hideous old husband Pyralius by her handsome lover Andro. In the second, Méridienne, a disdainful flirt, is crushed by a statue of Venus for refusing her suitor's love. In the third, a young woman who refuses all suitors is suddenly wracked by sexual desire just as she is married to an impotent old man: she commits suicide. The fourth tale is that of Narcissus, utterly self-absorbed and oblivious to his lover Echo. In the fifth, a young man named Nastagio has a vision of a ghostly woman who is continually torn to pieces by dogs as punishment for having refused her lover. The sixth tale is another story of a young wife rescued from her evil old husband by a handsome prince. The seventh is the tragic story of a cruel duke who kills his wife's lover and serves her his heart for dinner; the wife dies of grief, is buried with her lover, and their tomb becomes a lovers' shrine.

The overall effect of the *Contes* is hard to ascertain. On one level, by encouraging women to pursue true love and sexual fulfillment the text seems to provide a powerful endorsement of female sexual autonomy. Certainly it constitutes an impassioned protest against unequal marriages in which beautiful young women are sold off to impotent and ugly old men. However, the volume is more a polemic for sexual freedom than a debate on the issues surrounding women's sexuality, and as some critics have pointed out, its encouragement of adultery and sexual fulfillment stands to benefit young men as much as anyone else.[23] The *Contes* never take serious account of the severe social stigma attached to promiscuous women. They are blithely unconcerned with the consequences of sexual activity—either in terms of dishonor or the more basic questions of pregnancy or sexually transmitted disease—a major concern in the sixteenth century given the rapid spread of syphilis.

While it may be that "Jeanne Flore" was a woman who compiled and reworked a selection of tales in order to protest the miseries of enforced marriage and to assert the value of women's love and desire, it is equally possible that the entire collection is a male fantasy of female speech. Indeed, in their insistence that women's discourse is discourse about sexuality, the *Contes* bear a surprising resemblance to Pietro Aretino's *Ragionamenti*, also published in the mid-1530s. Granted, the tone of the *Contes* and that of the *Ragionamenti* could not be more different: Jeanne Flore writes in a formal, somewhat pedantic style, whereas Aretino revels in slang and street dialect. Jeanne Flore's women are heavenly aristocrats; Aretino's are whores and courtesans. However, these vastly different works concur in presenting women as primarily sexual beings. If anything, in its straightforward endorsement of sexual satisfaction Flore's text is much more simple-minded than Aretino's about the sexual dilemmas facing women.

Women's relation to sexuality is at the heart of perhaps the greatest sixteenth-century collection of *novelle*, the *Heptaméron* of Marguerite de Navarre. Unlike "Jeanne Flore," Marguerite uses her collection to reevaluate the relation of *novelle* to female knowledge and experience. In the *Heptaméron*, more than in any other collection of *novelle*, women have a multivalent role as tale-tellers, auditors, and participants in debate. The group of storytellers in the *Heptaméron* is divided equally between men and women—five each. They are in every way a more diverse group than that of the *Decameron*. Not all are young—Oisille is an elderly widow and Geburon an older man. Also there are a married couple, Parlemente and her misogynist husband, Hircan; Longarine, a young widow who has recently lost her husband; Dagoucin, a melancholy Platonist; Neifile and Ennasuite, two young, unmarried women; and Saffredent and Simontaut, two young, unmarried men.

Not only are the speakers more diverse than in other collections, but they are also much more deeply characterized. Each tale in Marguerite's collection is followed by a debate among the group about its significance. There is often strong disagreement, especially between male and female members of the group. The most dominant voices are those of the married couple, Parlemente and Hircan, who never agree on anything. Like Gasparo in *The Courtier*, Hircan is a fierce defender of masculine privilege. He consistently assumes that women are weak-willed, foolish, deceptive, and sexually obsessed. At times he argues that rape is an honorable and appropriately masculine activity.[24] Parlemente, in contrast to her choleric husband, is eloquent, sophisticated, and levelheaded. She frequently speaks in defense of women but insists (as some of the younger members of the group do not) on the need for self-control and personal responsibility.

Many commentators have seen Parlemente as a self-portrait of Marguerite, especially since Hircan bears a certain resemblance to Marguerite's second husband, Henri de Navarre. There is also something of Marguerite in Oisille, the elderly widow who is the group's conscience and spiritual leader. Reading Scripture is central to Oisille's life, but she also participates in the secular tale-telling. In her mix of worldly knowledge and spiritual devotion—a mix characteristic of Marguerite—Oisille can be seen as an idealized figure of the female reader and storyteller. She has sexual knowledge without being sexually obsessed. Her experience of "wo that is in mariage" has led her to spiritual wisdom. In a culture that often mocked old women, she appears as a natural leader and has the respect of all the members of the group, including Hircan.

In the *Heptaméron* storytelling represents a compromise between the sacred and secular worlds. As in the *Decameron,* the storytellers are brought together by misfortune. Traveling separately in the Pyrenees, the various characters are beset by a series of disasters: torrential rain, floods, and attacks by both brigands and bears. Harassed and bedraggled, one by one they take refuge at the Abbey of Our Lady of Sarrance. The floods have washed out the roads, and they are obliged to stay at the abbey for a few days until a new bridge can be built. To avoid boredom, Parlemente asks Oisille if she can suggest some pleasant way to pass the time. Oisille suggests the reading of holy Scripture. Hircan agrees that such spiritual exercise is worthwhile but insists that the body needs some exercise too. He asks Oisille to read Scripture to the group every morning and says they need to find some pastime "agreeable to the body" (67) to fill the afternoon hours. Hircan jokes that they should spend their afternoons having sex, but Parlemente replies that they should be more sociable: "let's leave on one side all pastimes that require only two participants, and concentrate on those which everybody can join in" (68). She suggests that they should imitate the young people in the *Decameron* and entertain each other by telling stories. The group eagerly agrees. Here again Marguerite differentiates between sexual knowledge and sexual obsession. Contrary to early modern stereotypes about insatiable women, it is Hircan who has trouble controlling his physical desires and Parlemente who can subordinate hers to the exigencies of civilized society.

The stories of the *Heptaméron* are thus a compromise between the spiritual pleasures of Bible reading and the bodily pleasures of sex. In contrast with meditation, which is solitary, and sex, which is for couples, the tale-telling is social and involves the whole group. As in Boccaccio, the impetus for the tale-telling, as well as its organization, comes from the women of the group. Also as in Boccaccio, the primary audience of the tales is at least rhetorically female. After each story as the speaker sums up, he or she inevitably addresses himself or herself to the ladies in the group, often using the phrase "Voilà Mesdames" (You see, Ladies) as a way of beginning discussion.[25] Like Boccaccio, Marguerite anticipates a female readership.

It is significant that, before spending the afternoon telling secular and often sexual tales, the group spends the morning listening to Oisille's Bible reading. That the group has a female spiritual leader is all the more remarkable in that they are, after all, in an abbey and there is no shortage of male clerics in residence. In fact, Oisille's personal devotion and study of Scripture are in stark contrast to the laziness and lack of spiritual discipline of the abbey's monks. Overall, the *Heptaméron* is extremely critical of the Catholic religious orders. Franciscans in the *Heptaméron* appear primarily as a sexual threat—an all-male community that repudiates marriage and preys on women.

Of course, Marguerite was critical of Catholic clergy and sympathetic to Protestant reformers. She wrote religious poetry and plays, and her court in Navarre sheltered John Calvin, Clément Marot, and Lefèvre d'Etaples, among others. When the *Heptaméron* was censored in its early publication, it was anticlerical tales, not bawdy or scatological ones, that were cut.[26] Women's moral and religious knowledge is paradoxical in works of the early modern period since women are encouraged to be devout, and even to read devotional texts, but not to meddle in theology or religious controversy. Likewise with political or social issues: ladies at court must remain attentive to social dynamics and codes of proper conduct, but they are not encouraged to shape those codes. Women are active participants in the *Decameron* and the *Heptaméron* but silent auditors in Castiglione's *Courtier.*

Marguerite's own involvement in theological controversy represents a special case; as queen of Navarre and older sister of the king of France, she occupied a social position that was anything but normative. However, even a woman as prominent as Marguerite did not engage in theological debates in Latin. Granted, she brings her religious beliefs and convictions to the *Heptaméron,* as well as to her devotional poetry. However, in *novelle* philosophical and theological concerns are explored through narrative, not through argument; through experience, not through authority.

As the Wife of Bath suggests, experience is not always pleasant. Although almost every story in the *Heptaméron* deals with sexuality on some level, in the words of the most recent English translator, sex in the *Heptaméron* "is rarely fun" (14). Many of the stories deal with actual or attempted rape; others deal with incest and illicit clerical marriages. The few happy couples one finds in the tales tend to be destroyed by larger social forces. Sexual relations are a source of misery in the *Heptaméron* because men's and women's needs and desires are seen as antithetical. Parlemente sums up the situation when she says of men, "All your pleasure is derived from dishonouring women, and your honour depends on killing other men in war. These are two things that are expressly contrary to the law of God" (305). If masculine honor is affirmed by rape, and feminine honor by chastity, how can men and women live together honorably? Parlemente accepts the need for women to submit to their husbands, but in return men have an obligation to act decently: "It is reasonable that the man should govern us as our head, . . . but not that he should abandon us or treat us badly'" (361). To this Oisille adds, "As the man claims to be wiser than the woman, so he will be the more severely punished [by God] if the fault is on his side."

In the *Heptaméron*, female virtue consists not in ignorance but in awareness of sexuality and its dangers. Good women know vice and avoid it. Sexuality, love, rape, courtship, and adultery are women's matters—they are what women should know about. Women's sexual behavior may be tightly controlled, but their knowledge of these matters is wide and deep. The fourth tale tells how a lustful courtier attempts to rape a young noblewoman by attacking her in her bedroom. She successfully beats him off, scarring his face with her teeth and nails. After this horrific experience the terrified young woman asks her wise, old lady-in-waiting what she should do next. The older woman advises her to remain silent and do nothing, for if people hear that the courtier attempts to rape her, she will be blamed for having incited him. In the debate that follows the tale Hircan criticizes the courtier for not having murdered the lady-in-waiting (97). Although a modern reader might decry the notion that the young woman should keep silent about the attempted rape, the tale demonstrates a keen insight into the dangerous sexual dynamics of courtly society. It offers women a model of both fierce resistance to male power and practical awareness of the need for social prudence. The lesson of the tale is only reinforced by a persistent legend, dating from Brantôme, that the young heroine "of birth so high . . . that there was no one higher in the land" is meant to be Marguerite (90). If so, her telling of the tale in the *Heptaméron* is an elegant and decorous way of getting the truth out.[27]

The debates between storytellers in the *Heptaméron* are impassioned but ultimately inconclusive. The collection is unfinished and ends abruptly following the seventy-second story. It is unclear what the final form of the text would have been, and there is some doubt as to whether the extant text represents Marguerite's own organizational scheme. Even so, a final reconciliation of male and female perspectives seems unlikely. Whenever tempers flare or controversy runs too deep, the remedy is to end the debate and tell another story. Though the depth of characterization of the tellers looks forward to the novel, they remain typically medieval in their resistance to change. They are iconic figures, and the stories they hear never convince them to alter their opinions.

The development of the novel form is a complex subject,[28] and there is no space here to explore it at any length. It is clear, however, that to a certain extent novels evolved from *novelle*. Like *novelle*, they focus on a realistic world; they are set in London and Paris, not Thebes or Camelot. Their protagonists are not epic heroes but "ordinary" people, of whatever social station. Their concerns are often the "feminine" concerns of *novelle*: marriage, adultery, chastity, and seduction. In France the connection between *novelle* and novels is reinforced by the fact that Madame de Lafayette's classic novel *La Princesse de Clèves* (1678) is in many ways a reworking of the story of Floride and Amador, the longest and most ambitious tale in the *Heptaméron*.[29]

Marguerite, "with whose stories," the narrator assumes, "you are familiar" (68),[30] makes a cameo appearance in *La Princesse de Clèves*. More importantly, the novel's exemplary heroine learns about virtue from her mother, who, like Marguerite's storytellers, tells her all about vice:

> Most mothers believe that it is sufficient to avoid talk of love matters to prevent young people from becoming involved. Madame de Chartres was of the opposite opinion: she often described love to her daughter; she showed her its attractions, the more easily to convince her of its dangers; she told her of men's lack of sincerity, their deceit and their faithlessness, and of the domestic misfortunes caused by such activities. She showed her, on the other hand, how much tranquility would be attached to the life of a respectable woman, and how much brilliance and grandeur might come to one who already possessed both beauty and birth, through the addition of virtue; but she also showed her how difficult it was to preserve that virtue, other than through extreme mistrust of one's own basic instincts and scrupulous dedication to that which, alone, can make for the happiness of a woman, namely to love her husband and to be loved by him. (21)

One could not find a better articulation of the politics of women's reading implicit in the *Heptaméron*. Thanks to this novel form of education, the Princess is able to keep firm control over her adulterous attraction for M. de Nemours. Knowing the ways of love from stories, she is able to resist temptation and maintain her integrity.

Virginia Woolf believed that the first significant women authors wrote novels because the genre was a new one, and thus less thoroughly masculinized than the epic or lyric poetry.[31] If the novel suited female authors, it was partly because it was descended from the *novelle*, a genre which addressed itself to women and provided them with a model for articulating their desires and concerns. Woolf points out that in the masculine literary tradition "a scene in a battlefield is more important than a scene in a shop."[32] This may be true in the *Iliad* or in *Henry V*, but it is not true in the *Decameron* or the *Heptaméron*.

The link between *novelle* and the novel is not as straightforward in the Anglo-American tradition,[33] not least because when the Continental genre of *novelle* was domesticated in England the notion that they were texts for and about women was greatly downplayed. For example, one of the most popular English collections, William Painter's *Palace of Pleasure* (1566), mixes "excellent *Novelles*" from Boccaccio, Bandello, and Marguerite de Navarre with "Pleasaunt Histories" from Livy. By conflating *novelle* with histories, Painter makes the genre a primarily masculine one, dealing with combat, royal politics, and male heroics: "In these histories (which by another terme I call *Novelles*) be described the lives, gestes, conquestes, and highe enterprises of great Princes, wherein also be not forgotten the cruell actes and tiranny of some. In these be set forth the great valiance of noble Gentlemen, the terrible combates of couragious personages."[34] Only after he lists these masculine subjects do we hear that the stories also deal with "the vertuous mindes of noble Dames, the chaste hartes of constant Ladyes, the wonderfull pacience of puissaunt Princes, the mild sufferance of well disposed Gentlewomen, and in divers, the quiet bearing of adverse fortune" (sig.*3^{v}).

Unlike most major texts of the *novelle* tradition, Painter's collection is addressed primarily to male readers: the volume is dedicated to the Earl of Warwick, who seems to Painter a logical guardian of female virtue: "To whom (I say) may constancie of Ladyes, and the vertuous dedes of Dames, more aptly be applied, than to him that hath in possession a Lady and Countesse of noble birth . . . whose curteous and countesse like behavior glistereth in court amongs the troupe of most honourable Dames" (sigs. *4^{r}–*4^{v}). Obviously such tales might more aptly be addressed to the ladies themselves.

When Painter does imagine female readers, his conception of them is far more moralistic than anything in Marguerite or Boccaccio: "Hath the Lady, Gentlewoman, or other of the feminine kinde a desire to behold a mirroure of Chastitie, let them read over the *Novelles* of the Lady Panthea, of the Duchesse of Savoie, of the Countesse of Salisburie, of Amadour and Florinda?" ("To the Reader," sig. ¶¶4^{r}). He also warns women to beware of scholars and learned men, who will always get the best of them: "If scornefull speache or flouting sport do flowe in the ripe wittes and lavishe tongues of womankinde, let them beware they doe not deale with the learned sorte, least Master Alberto with physicke drougues, or Philenio with Sophist art do staine their face, or otherwise offend them with the innocencie of their great Graundmother Eve when she was somoned from Paradise joy" (sig. ¶¶4^{r}). This is a long way from the *Heptaméron*. In fact, we are back to Jankyn and the Wife of Bath, but this time Jankyn is the hero and the Wife is told to keep her mouth shut.

Who painted the lion?

Notes

I would like to thank Heidi Brayman Hackel for inviting me to contribute to this volume. My essay profited greatly from reports by anonymous readers for the University of Pennsylvania Press. I am also grateful to Melissa Walter for offering many insightful suggestions. In addition, I would like to take this chance to acknowledge my great admiration for Margaret Ferguson, who first introduced me to the *Heptaméron*.

1. J. E. Austen-Leigh, *A Memoir of Jane Austen by Her Nephew*, ed. R. W. Chapman (Oxford: Clarendon Press, 1926), 102.

2. *The Wife of Bath's Prologue*, line 3. All references to the *Canterbury Tales* are to *The Complete Poetry and Prose of Geoffrey Chaucer*, ed. John H. Fisher (New York: Holt, Rinehart and Winston, 1977).

3. Ian Frederick Moulton, *Before Pornography: Erotic Writing in Early Modern England* (New York: Oxford University Press, 2000), 70–79.

4. In some versions the work is a statue, rather than a painting. See fable 59, "The Man and the Lion Travelling Together," in Aesop, *The Complete Fables*, trans. Olivia Temple and Robert Temple (New York: Penguin, 1998), 47.

5. While some collections, such as the thirteenth-century *Cento novelle antiche*, precede Boccaccio, the dissemination of the *Decameron* was so broad that it established the norms for the genre.

6. See Janet Levarie Smarr, "Boccaccio and Renaissance Women," *Studi sul Boccaccio* 20 (1991–92): 279–97. She concludes, "in sum, Boccaccio's writings in general were conceived of by both men and women as something of obvious interest to women, and were made available to them (at least to some of them) as soon as to men" (282–83).

7. On the sources for Boccaccio's tales, see A. C. Lee, *The Decameron: Its Sources and Analogues* (New York: Haskell, 1966). On the classical influence on *novelle*, see Robert J. Clements and Joseph Gibaldi, *Anatomy of the Novella: The European Tale Collection from Boccaccio and Chaucer to Cervantes* (New York: New York University Press, 1977), 1–25.

8. See *Heptaméron*, 69. All references to the *Heptaméron* are to the English translation by P. A. Chillon (New York: Penguin, 1984). Even the *Decameron*, which does not stress the veracity of its tales as much as other collections do, makes frequent mention of actual rulers and notable people.

9. *Decameron*, vii. All references to the *Decameron* are to the English translation by Mark Musa and Peter Bondanella (New York: Norton, 1983).

10. Thomas C. Bergin, *Boccaccio* (New York: Viking, 1981), 289, estimates that thirty-two stories in the *Decameron* have female protagonists and that women are essential to the action in forty-two others.

11. On the sexualization of women and the implications for female readers, see Mary Ellen Lamb, *Gender and Authorship in the Sidney Circle* (Madison: University of Wisconsin Press, 1990), esp. 72–89.

12. Bergin, *Boccaccio*, 279.

13. The exceptions are stories 28, 34, 44, 52, 55, 65, and 67—and all of these are very brief.

14. See, for example, Sarah Stickney Ellis, *The Women of England, Their Social Duties, and Domestic Habits* (London, 1838).

15. David Wallace, *Giovanni Boccaccio: Decameron* (New York: Cambridge University Press, 1991), 110–13.

16. Epistolo XXII (1373), *Tutte le opere di Giovanni Boccaccio*, ed. Vittore Branca, vol. 5.1 (Milan: Mondadori, 1992), 705.

17. Virginia Woolf, *A Room of One's Own* (New York: Harcourt Brace, 1957), 85–88. All references to Woolf are to this text.

18. Bergin, *Boccaccio*, 289; Ernest Hatch Wilkins, *A History of Italian Literature*, rev. ed. (Cambridge, Mass.: Harvard University Press, 1974), 109.

19. All references to *The Courtier* are to the English translation by Charles S. Singleton (New York: Anchor Books, 1959).

20. On the textual history of the *Heptaméron*, see the English edition edited

by Chillon, 7–10, and—in much greater detail—the French edition edited by Renja Salminen (Geneva: Librairie Droz, 1999), XI–LXXXII.

21. Laura Doyle Gates, *Soubz Umbrage de Passetemps: Women's Storytelling in the Evangiles des Quenouilles, the Comptes amoureux de Jeanne Flore and the Heptaméron, Inedita & Rara* 13 (Montreal: Editions Ceres, 1997), 64n4.

22. Jeanne Flore, *Contes amoureux*, ed. Gabriel A. Pérouse (Lyon: Editions de CNRS, 1980), 9–19.

23. Flore, *Contes*, 40; Gates, *Soubz Umbrage*, 76–77.

24. See also *Heptaméron*, 153, 219.

25. Cathleen M. Bauschatz, "'Voilà mes dames . . .': Inscribed Women Listeners and Readers in the *Heptaméron*," in *Critical Tales: New Studies of the Heptaméron and Early Modern Culture*, ed. John D. Lyons and Mary B. McKinley (Philadelphia: University of Pennsylvania Press, 1993), 104–22.

26. Pierre Gruget's 1559 edition, long taken as definitive, replaces stories 11, 44, and 46 with tales less critical of the Franciscans.

27. I am indebted to Melissa Walter for this point.

28. See Michael McKeon, *The Origins of the English Novel, 1600–1740* (Baltimore: Johns Hopkins University Press, 1987).

29. Timothy Hampton, *Literature and Nation in the Sixteenth Century: Inventing Renaissance France* (Ithaca, N.Y.: Cornell University Press, 2001), 109–49.

30. All references to *La Princesse de Clèves* are to the English translation by Michael G. Paulson and Tamara Alvarez-Detrell (New York: University Press of America, 1995).

31. Woolf, *Room of One's Own*, 80.

32. Ibid., 77.

33. The insularity of traditional accounts of the development of the novel in English can be seen in Ian Watt's *Rise of the Novel* (Berkeley: University of California Press, 1959), which refuses to see *La Princesse de Clèves* and other texts from seventeenth-century France as novels at all (30).

34. All references to William Painter's *Palace of Pleasure* are to the first edition (London, 1566).

Chapter 8

The Word Made Flesh: Reading Women and the Bible

JANICE KNIGHT

Throughout the trauma of captivity, Mary Rowlandson built her comfort on her Bible: it was at once sacred text and solacing icon, her "Guid by day," her "Pillow by night." In this reliance on Scripture, Rowlandson practiced the fundamental devotional act of her community. Protestantism has often been called a religion of the book; nowhere was this truer than in Puritan America, where reading the Bible was not only the legislated obligation but also the deepest desire of every believer. The union of *Sola Fides* and *Sola Scriptura*—the spiritual autonomy enabled by a new emphasis on experimental faith and a new availability of vernacular Bibles—not only democratized religious authority but also promoted the expansion of literacy across gender and status boundaries. Since a priesthood of all believers mandated immediate and personal knowledge of Scripture, reformers such as Thomas Cartwright preached that Bible study was the "necessary duty" of "all ages, all sexes, all degrees and callings, all high and low, rich and poor, wise and foolish." As early as 1642 New England law required that all "children & apprentices" be given "so much learning as may inable them perfectly to read the english tongue."[1]

But Protestant culture was deeply rooted in forms of transmission and expression that exceeded any narrow understanding of "the book" as a specifically printed artifact. At church and at home verses of Scripture were heard and repeated, becoming internalized first as oral memory. Children knew their Bibles long before they were able to decipher the printed book, a circumstance that sorted well with the Puritans' understanding of the text as divine dictation and their commitment to the value of the preached word. As David Hall has noted, the Bible was inscribed in a variety of devotional settings and practices: it was rehearsed aloud in prayers and sermons, meditated on privately as a written text, and in what might be called a convergence of the oral and the written, experienced as a "revelation" first delivered to the heart by the voice of the Holy Spirit and then confirmed in the reading of scriptural promises.[2] Moreover, the act of reading also included the arts of interpretation, of producing "readings" of Scripture and apprehending patterns of daily experience in light of sacred truths. In this broad sense, then, reading in Puritan America might be understood as a practice involving not just print artifacts but also various modes of hearing and speaking, of interpreting and acting in the world.

Expanding our understanding of "reading" practices to include orality, acoustics, and articulation, as well as interpretive arts that challenged conventions of typology and exemplarity, is particularly crucial for understanding "women readers" in early America. By focusing on the intersection between scriptural interpretation, lay authority, and gender politics in early America, this essay will reflect on the ways women read not only their Bibles but also their lived experiences in and through God's Word. In particular, it will focus on the uses of typology as a way of tracking the emergence of cultural norms enabling, shaping, and restricting women's reading practices. In the hands of conservative exegetes such as Samuel Mather, typology was understood as a "science" of reading that not only united the two Testaments but also governed interpretation of the symbolic dimensions of the literal text. More than mere resemblances or analogies, Old Testament persons, institutions, ceremonies, and events were divinely instituted prefigurations of things fulfilled in the New. Thus, Adam "typed" the Messiah; the exodus of the Jews foreshadowed Christ's journey in the wilderness. When applied more liberally, however, such types could serve as allegories for eternal spiritual states and for more immediate and personal struggles: Mary Rowlandson, for example, found her experience writ large in the trials of Job and in the promises delivered to David. The extension of typology encompassed but was by no means limited to such recapitulative identifications. Over time, the developmental logic uniting the two Testaments also authorized prospective readings of Puritan history in light of biblical schemata: Old Testament types not only were fulfilled in the life of Christ but also pertained to the present-day Church in the world, establishing "a literary-spiritual continuity between the two Testaments and the colonial venture in America."[3] New England was not only an antitype of Israel but also an anticipation of the New Jerusalem.

American Puritans were devoted to this extension of typology, voicing faith in God's express authorship not only of every aspect of daily life but also of their collective errand into the wilderness—the quotidian was read as providential; social and political events were figured in terms of a sacred mission. Authors as diverse as Edward Johnson and Edward Taylor routinely extended their reading of God's will from the Bible to the world, from text to experience, granting something like scriptural authority to lived events: experience itself came to have a signifying function that, in turn, required interpretation. Even while they elaborated this extension of typology, however, exegetes disagreed about its proper application and feared its potential dangers. In principle, all Puritans believed that there was a single "right reading" of Scripture on which communal consensus could be built. In practice, however, lay readers could and did produce divergent interpretations not only of sacred texts but also of their prophetic implications in the current world. And, when controversy emerged in this patriarchal religion, women often found themselves at its center, their competence and authority as readers questioned.

Scholarly work on typology has often obscured the implicit masculinization of that interpretive method, neglecting as well instances in which the logic of prefiguration became corporealized to the detriment of female hermeneuts. This essay considers two instances in which women readers figured centrally in transformations of Puritan typological self-understanding. First, the Antinomian Controversy offers a well-known case in which larger cultural debates about the authority of lay readers became narrowly feminized. In significant ways Anne Hutchinson's "crime" was a literary and a gendered one—as a woman, she was criminalized for interpreting her life in light of prophetic typology. One outcome of the Controversy was the transformation of Hutchinson from exegete *into* a secular type to be read, an American Jezebel. There were larger consequences as well: clerical authority was enhanced, and lay piety was brought under scrutiny in a routinization of religious self-expression.

Second, this essay explores how the figure of the captive woman—whether seized by Indians or possessed by Satan—was circulated as a new corporeal "type" of communal suffering and deliverance. Read in England as a tale of sensation, for New Englanders like Increase Mather, Mary Rowlandson's history disclosed "excellent textures of divine providence" pertaining to the larger community.[4] Similarly, the demonic possession of a young household servant, Mercy Short, was seen by Cotton Mather as emblematic of "such Works of Darkness . . . whereunto the people are now Enchanted"; her cure predicted a collective victory over Satan.[5] Just as the opinions and expressions of Hutchinson proved formative in the subsequent shaping of the genre of conversion testimony, so the pain of these women helped to produce and transform generic features of captivity and possession narratives.

"One Would Hardly Have Guessed Her to Have Been an Antitype of Daniel"

Anne Hutchinson and Her Bible

It might be fairly said that in 1637 theological disputes about the workings of grace turned on the opinions and reading practices of one woman. Though the origins and stakes of the Antinomian Controversy were multiple and diverse, with prominent ministers subjected to church discipline and men of standing banished for their opinions, retrospective accounts penned by the victors consistently foregrounded Anne Hutchinson as the principal agent in this cultural drama. The heat of their tirades strategically obscured the breadth and depth of theological disagreement among Bay ministers and congregants, redirecting attention to what seemed the unnaturally virile expressions of a naturally infirm female mind.[6] Governor John Winthrop's diatribe against the so-called Antinomians dilates on Hutchinson as "the head of all this faction," as "the breeder and nourisher of all these distempers," and as a woman "of a haughty and fierce carriage, of a nimble wit and active spirit, and a very voluble tongue, more bold then a man, though in understanding and judgment, inferiour to many women." Her "ayme" was the "utter subversion both of Churches and civill state"; her means was to spread "venome of these opinions into the very veines and vitalls of the People in the Country."[7]

To her critics, Hutchinson's doctrinal challenges were ineluctably bound up with dislocations in the domestic sphere: families were neglected, and "division betwixt husband and wife" proliferated.[8] What began as a theological dispute about the workings of grace transformed into a political debate about due deference. The anger felt by Winthrop and others, though localized as anxiety about eroding gender hierarchies, signaled a more global fear about preserving the order of proper "places" at home and at church, in the marketplace and in the courtroom. Hugh Peter put the matter succinctly: Hutchinson had "stept out of [her] place," had "*rather bine a Husband than a Wife and a preacher than a Hearer; and a Magistrate than a Subject.*" The results were deemed apocalyptic: "All things are turned upside down among us."[9]

Although multiple charges were brought against Hutchinson, most scholars agree that her conviction turned on her disclosure of the grounds of her assurance in God's "immediate revelations." Foregrounding questions of interpretive authority raised in her two trials rather than focusing on the content of Hutchinson's doctrines, I will argue that in a fundamental sense the Controversy turned on debates about the readerly prerogatives foundational to the priesthood of believers. The threat that the magistrates and ministers refused to ignore was constituted in the very way that Hutchinson read her Bible. And, while officials were unable to prove her guilty of the original charges they leveled, in the end they based her banishment on what they judged were her heterodox revelations.[10]

As many readers will know, Hutchinson was not the only "antinomian" brought before the civil court in November 1637. Her brother-in-law John Wheelwright had already been convicted for delivering a seditious sermon; other supporters, all adherents of John Cotton's more mystical brand of piety, had also been disenfranchised or banished. Hutchinson was called to answer an array of charges: that she joined the faction supporting Wheelwright; that she traduced ministers by saying that they preached a covenant of works; and that she convened an unlawful conventicle, teaching men together with women. Her defense to each charge was rooted in Christian liberties foundational to Protestantism: personal freedom in matters of conscience; individual discernment in spiritual questions; and importantly, reliance on the Bible alone as a spiritual guide.

Throughout two days of intense interrogation Hutchinson held the magistrates at bay; they were unable to prove that she had signed the petition supporting Wheelwright, sufficient not; nor could they discredit her teaching practices. The Bible became the arbiter in her dispute with Winthrop about her pastoral activities: Hutchinson not only provided explicit scriptural warrant for her practice but also demanded that Winthrop produce "a rule" from God's Word to support his objections.[11] Debate on this issue turned into a stalemate, with scriptural verses from one side met and countered by the other. In addition, though laywomen and laymen later lost their freedom to preach informally or to pose questions in church as a consequence of the Controversy, in this extraordinary exchange the Bible provided a level ground for a doubly disadvantaged laywoman to debate—and many would say to best—the sitting governor of the colony.

The second charge, that she had spoken "divers things" deemed "very prejudicial to the honour of the churches and ministers thereof," went to the theological heart of the larger controversy and brought Hutchinson into direct conflict with eminent preachers—not just about her doctrines but also about the precise wording and intent of statements she had made about their ministries.[12] It is not possible to chart out here the subtlety of the theological distinctions that Hutchinson made about indwelling and inherent graces, the *ordo salutis,* the freeness of grace, the status of works, and the seal of the spirit. Nor can I address the issues of confidentiality or the distinctions between public and private speech that surfaced in the trial.[13] What I do want to point out is that on every issue the rule of the Bible was the sole authority Hutchinson recognized, and it was her sole vindication. Her citation of specific verses often gave way to a more general defense: "If ever I spake that I proved it by God's word."[14] As she had done when debating Winthrop, for a time Hutchinson outflanked these university-trained ministers by recourse to scriptural rule, requiring that they swear an oath concerning the content of her speeches as a means to end the strife.[15] Since their allegations were grounded on partial and sometimes conflicting recollections of conversations they had had with Hutchinson several months before, the ministers were reluctant to risk violating the Third Commandment by submitting to such an oath. Their hesitancy gave Hutchinson the opportunity to call rebuttal witnesses, including John Cotton. His testimony upheld Hutchinson's version of these conversations, affirming that she maintained the fine but crucial distinction between condemning the ministers for preaching a covenant of works and merely observing that they simply did not preach the covenant of grace as clearly as did other ministers.

The two extant accounts of the trial differ significantly from this point about the order of events leading to Hutchinson's famous revelation.[16] In both accounts, however, the fierce dynamic of interrogation and rebuttal characterizing the trial to this point suddenly and inexplicably gave way to an uninterrupted space of near-soliloquy, in which Hutchinson volunteered the testimony that became the basis for her conviction. I believe that we cannot know what Hutchinson's motives may have been—whether confident of exoneration, she was seizing an opportunity to instruct her opponents; whether convinced of her eminent conviction, she desperately offered one last defense of her opinions; or whether she was deflecting attention away from her teacher John Cotton, who was becoming a new target of interrogation. In any case, her opponents seized upon her speech, claiming that a "marvellous providence of God" had "made her to lay open her self and the ground of all these disturbances to be by revelations."[17] Not surprisingly, Hutchinson offered a different view of the workings of providence, one that testified to the divine authorship not just of her "revelations" but also of her life's history, including her personal errand into the wilderness.[18]

Hutchinson declared that she would now provide the court with "the ground of what I know to be true." Retracing her spiritual history in England, she confessed that "being much troubled" by corruptions of the church and the flight of godly ministers to America, she "had like to have turned separatist." Rather than neglecting holy duties (countering her supposed antinomianism), she had kept a day of "solemn humiliation," retreating to meditation and prayer. It was then that God had intervened, guiding her to scriptural verses that soothed her spirit and resolved her doubts. Hutchinson's confession could stand as a model of regenerate reading. Disparaging any strength that might be claimed as the product of her fallible, weak, and corrupt human mind, Hutchinson instead waited patiently for God's guidance in directing her reading and assisting her understanding: "The Lord knows that I could not open scripture; he must by his prophetical office open it unto me." She was brought first one verse from 1 John and then another from Hebrews: "He that denies the testament denies the testator." A passive and inspired Hutchinson reiterated that it was God who opened the passage, "discovering" to her "which was the clear ministry and which the wrong" and endowing her with the power "to distinguish between the voice of my beloved and the voice of Moses"—that is, to discern those who preached the covenant of grace and those who preached the law.[19]

The magistrates certainly understood Hutchinson's testimony to constitute an admission of slander against the Bay ministers, but I would argue that in distinguishing between more and less efficacious preaching styles Hutchinson stood within the bounds of Protestant tradition, legitimately claiming the same high ground that her opponents had recently asserted against the prelates of Old England. Moreover, the methods whereby she arrived at spiritual conviction—holy exercises, humble submission to God's will, passivity before Scripture—placed her within the sanctions of orthodox reading practices. However, as I have shown elsewhere, normative practices were constantly under negotiation; definitions of orthodoxy were constantly redefined in a highly charged and mobile process of dialogic exchange. The climate of crisis in 1637–38 meant that what Hutchinson viewed as her freedom as a Christian was understood by magistrates and ministers, fearful of the precedent of Münster, as dangerously heterodox. Toleration was a value held neither by Hutchinson nor by her opponents, and the Antinomian Controversy renegotiated the fine balance between the centrifugal energies released by Protestantism and the desire for consensus among the community of saints.[20]

The magistrates recognized that, more than her critique of the ministry, the radiant dynamic of readerly authority described by Hutchinson constituted a fundamental challenge to worldly structures of deference. Her seemingly modest admission of creaturely incapacity without God's immediate aid was foundational to a new authority that transcended the limitations of the merely human, including Hutchinson's particular disadvantages as a laywoman. Hutchinson's understanding of grace as the immediate indwelling of the Holy Spirit activated a radical version of Paul's "new man." This reliance on "the Christ within" became the standard for female mystics, who recognized that renunciation of personal identity and the materiality of their own bodies could underwrite claims not only to spiritual equality but also to prophetic authority.[21]

Accordingly, the ground of debate shifted to more foundational issues of exegetical authority, the meaning of revelation, and the proper application of prophetic typology. Questions about the source of Hutchinson's knowledge, whether by "immediate voice" or "immediate revelation," went directly to the authority of the Book itself—whether revelation was closed or open, the product of inspired reading or the reception of extrascriptural voice. Defending Hutchinson's practice, Cotton explained that while the latter was repugnant, "tending to danger more ways than one," the former, if dispensed in and "according to a word of God," "are not only lawful but such as christians may receive." While acknowledging that the ministry was the usual means by which the Word was made effectual, Cotton also insisted on the legitimacy of unmediated revelation "in the reading of the word in some chapter or verse," when "it comes flying upon the wings of the spirit," when it is "breathed by the spirit of God."[22]

As her testimony unfolded, Hutchinson retraced a history of just this sort of divinely directed reading. Inspired by God, "by the voice of his own spirit to [her] soul," she was led to verses from Jeremiah, Daniel, and Isaiah that not only relieved her spiritual doubts but also explicated her current world, providing divine warrant for her actions and promising her God's prevenient care. In short, God discovered to her the ways in which her own life was embedded in or "typed" by sacred narrative patterns. While in England, "that place in the 30th of Isaiah was brought to [her] mind. . . . did much follow [her]," providing a scriptural gloss of her suffering under the corruptions of the church and the removal of godly teachers, and prescribing remedy in the form of her own removal: "The Lord giving me this promise and they being gone there was none then left that I was able to hear, and I could not be at rest but I must come hither." Again, passive before Scripture but actively interpreting her life in terms of it, Hutchinson's typological reading pressed the interpretive boundaries traditionally afforded the laity, shifting from allegorical identification to prophetic prescription.[23]

However, Hutchinson's reading did not rest with what—in other circumstances—might have been accepted as a personal version of the larger Puritan migration. Instead she shifted attention from Old England to New, applying the biblical script to condemn the practices of the court. With the whole of Isaiah 30 serving as her shadow text, Hutchinson implicitly cast herself as God's chosen one, leaving no alternative but to view the magistrates and ministers as false believers who "trust in oppression and perverseness." The prospective logic of her exegesis inevitably threatened destruction for the city on the hill: "this iniquity shall be to you as a breach ready to fall, swelling out in a high wall, whose breaking cometh suddenly at an instant" (Isa. 30:12–13). Finally making explicit the prophetic typology energizing her exegesis, Hutchinson testified to God's revelation that, like Daniel before her, she would suffer affliction for her steadfast piety and would enjoy deliverance from her persecutors. Either the transcriber or Hutchinson was so inspired by the power of this vision that her separation from God was verbally erased in a confusion of pronouns: "this place in Daniel was brought unto me and did shew me that though I should meet with affliction yet I am the same God that delivered Daniel out of the lion's den, I will also deliver thee." Summoning her full exegetical grandeur, Hutchinson famously cautioned the court: "Therefore I desire you to look to it, for you see this scripture fulfilled this day . . . consider and look what you do . . . if you go on in this course you begin you will bring a curse upon you and your posterity, and the mouth of the Lord hath spoken it."[24]

Winthrop took the full measure of Hutchinson's typological reaching, calling it "the most desperate enthusiasm in the world." Retailing her "fierce speech and countenance" and the "impudent boldnesse" of this "proud dame," he shrewdly reversed the roles of her prophetic script: "one would hardly have guessed her to have been an Antitype of Daniel, but rather of the Lions after they were let loose." Simply stated, Hutchinson's typological reading could only be had at the expense of the version upheld by the standing order; nothing less than the understanding of New England as a type of the New Jerusalem was at stake in her speech.[25]

Interpreting the prophetic dimensions of Scripture had always been deemed a dangerous enterprise, susceptible to the excesses of enthusiasm. Moreover, it was a practice traditionally limited to clerics and reserved for representation of corporate mission. And, while I would argue that gender was not the defining category in this battle over exegetical authority—as Roger Williams's experience made clear, any reader challenging the typological sacralization of the Puritan errand would have been discredited—it became a convenient wedge separating and stigmatizing Hutchinson's views. In a battle in which the principle of unmediated access to Scripture was embodied in the reading practices of one woman and the collective interpretation of the clergy was identical to that of the civil magistrates, the outcome was not hard to predict: Hutchinson was banished from the colony by the civil court; several months later she was excommunicated from the Boston congregation in her subsequent church trial.

While space does not permit discussion of this second trial, I would like to make a few observations relevant to the concerns of this essay.

First, despite legal sanctions, months of confinement, and ill health, Hutchinson remained sure of the sole authority of the Bible and of her rights and responsibilities as a reader. Even when interrogated by her beloved Cotton about her views on resurrection, Hutchinson rejected any but divine authority: "I desire to hear God speak this and not man. Shew me whear thear is any Scripture to prove it." Second, contrary to characterizations of her as haughty or intransigent, Hutchinson revealed herself as a true seeker, open to reflection, debate, and revision of her beliefs. When John Davenport and Winthrop (of all people!) brought convincing scriptural arguments, she modified her position on the mortality of the soul. It is testament to her integrity and purity of spirit that, regardless of the costs and without respect to persons, Hutchinson staked her life on enlightened reading of God's Word.[26]

"A LITTER OF BRATS HUNG UP AGAINST THE SUNNE"

At the conclusion of her court testimony, Hutchinson conceded to the magistrates, "you have power over my body, but the Lord Jesus hath power over my body and soul."[27] On this matter she indeed spoke prophetically, and not simply in terms of her banishment. Accounts of the Controversy written by the victors consistently reversed the logic of indwelling that liberated Hutchinson from the drag of corporeality, insisting instead that her beliefs were nothing more than the by-products of her corrupt female flesh. Scholars have long differed over how to judge the stakes and participants in the Controversy; some extol the moderation exercised by Winthrop, and others regard him as a repressive patriarch. I remain divided in my judgment to this extent: I believe that the theological debates were fought fairly and honorably by both sides and for the most elevated of stakes. However, the calumny systematically aimed at Hutchinson in the aftermath of the trials debased the very terms of the argument and reflects poorly indeed on the writers using such tactics.

A spate of histories, pamphlets, and tracts degraded Hutchinson's high beliefs with metaphors of illicit sexuality and bestialized maternity: she was an Eve who seduced her followers and a Jezebel who betrayed them. Her opinions were "a litter of brats," that when "hatched" went "crawling like vipers about the countrey."[28] Cotton Mather, marveling at her eminence, explained that "a *poyson* does never insinuate so quickly, nor operate so strongly as when *women's milk* is the *vehicle* wherein 'tis given."[29] As many readers will know, her detractors pressed this misogyny further, drawing the infamous analogy between Hutchinson's "monstrous births" and her theological "errors." Winthrop expended his greatest narrative skills and energy detailing the "monsters" delivered by Dyer and Hutchinson; others followed his lead. The callousness of this tactic and the relish with which they pursued it remains shocking today; at least one contemporary condemned their efforts as the products of a "sweatish and Feaverish zeal."[30]

The relationship her detractors projected between Hutchinson's body and her mind reached beyond the mere co-incidence of analogy, however, to become a corporealized countertypology. According to Thomas Weld, God communicated through Hutchinson not spiritually, as she claimed, but materially: "*God himself was pleased to step in with his casting voice . . . as clearly as if he had pointed with his finger.*" The relationship is providential: God's will becomes legible in and through Hutchinson's body, which itself becomes an exegetical object. However, the relationship is also prophetic. Her ideas *anticipate* their own bodily corruption; her deformed spirit is "fulfilled" in a grossly material antitype: "*as she had vented misshapen opinions, so she must bring forth deformed monsters; and as about 30. Opinions in number, so many monsters.*"[31] As her words are thus made flesh, she is made to stand as an obscene antitype of the incarnation itself. The fact that Hutchinson was convicted for her heterodox use of typology makes the hypocrisy and opportunism of Weld's analysis all the more stunning. Describing this analogy as "a monstrous conception of his brain, a spurious issue of his intellect," a critic of Weld turned the tables, aptly pointing out that "if any of the men he cals Familists, &c., had done so, would it not have been accounted irreligious? relishing of profanenes?"[32]

However, Weld's reading of the prophetic meaning of Hutchinson's suffering extended beyond her miscarriage; God's condemnation was confirmed in the manner of her death. Weld's "Preface," designed to bring narrative order to Winthrop's fragmented *"Short Story,"* recasts the Controversy in the familiar plot line of the jeremiad. Beginning with a celebration of Puritan errand, Weld's text writes the Controversy as the divine testing of God's chosen people, with final affirmation of their election coming in the form of Hutchinson's murder. Detailing the Indian attack that took the lives of Hutchinson and her family, Weld observes, "*Gods hand is the more apparently seene herein, to pick out this wofull woman, to make her and those belonging to her, an unheard of heavie example of their cruelty above al others.*" His next sentence, while perhaps referring to the resolution of the Controversy as a whole, gains spiteful resonance in the context of the massacre: "*Thus the Lord heard our groanes to heaven, and freed us from this great and sore affliction.*" His providential reading presses further still in "A Postscript" to his account: the renewal of God's allegiance is doubly confirmed by reports that two "*Sagamores (or Indian Princes)*" and their people have converted to Christianity and "*voluntarily submitted themselves to the will and law of our God and . . . put themselves under our government and protection.*" The mutability of typological practice is here made evident, as is the potential profanity of its application. The murder of English families was conventionally understood as God's chastening of New England; here it is rewritten as affirmation of the Puritan errand, sealed by these Indian conversions.[33]

Fifty years later ministers such as Cotton Mather were still casting Hutchinson as New England's Virago, still dismissing her doctrines as the diseased embodiments of "woman's wit." With Quakers and witches and rebellious servant girls abounding in the 1690s, all women seemed potentially to have defective minds—the disease of the "roving womb" plagued New England—and the best medicine was perhaps suggested by the title Mather chose for his history of antinomianism: *Hydra Decapitata.* His text followed the now-familiar strategy of obscuring the breadth of dissent by adopting Winthrop's pithy formula: *Dux Faemina Facta* (a woman the leader of the deed). And, while Winthrop was celebrated as our *Nehemiah Americanus,* taking pride of place in Mather's history of the New Jerusalem, *Magnalia Christi Americana,* Hutchinson was dismissed as our American Jezebel and consigned to the book's appendix along with other heretics.

While he was crafting his hagiography of the "founding fathers," Mather was also at work on a conduct manual for New England's daughters. A guide to "The Character and Happiness of a Virtuous Woman," Mather's *Ornaments for the Daughters of Zion* anxiously acknowledged a new range of options and activities available to his female readers in 1692. The lure of material luxuries and of cosmopolitan entertainments seemed to spell the decline of the piety embodied in the founding generation. Mather's admonitions to Zion's daughters ranged from warnings about the dangers of new fashions and the use of cosmetics to advice about how to win a virtuous husband. Not least, Mather prescribed proper reading material for his female congregants, urging them to give up the romances that had come into vogue and instead to return to Bible study. Virtue could still be cultivated by identifying with biblical models of womanhood, though the spectrum of acceptable types had narrowed. Now images of decorous femininity were to be found in the examples "a Lydia" or "a Tabitha," but readers were not encouraged to personal identification with these types. Rather, Mather's most comprehensive and corrosive pedagogy for his readers was provided by the narrative structure of *Ornaments*: organized along a taxonomy of the reproductive timeline, the text required that readers identify with generic female types—as maids, wives, mothers, or widows. This was a prescription Hugh Peter would have celebrated.

"NO NEW CREATURE BUT ONLY A MENDED MAN"

As a short appendix to these reflections on the Antinomian Controversy as a pedagogy for readers, I would like to suggest some of the more general changes it fostered in Puritan religious expression. Transcriptions of the conversion testimonies of Thomas Shepard's congregants provide the foundation for what we know of lay piety in these years. Many scholars have expressed surprise at the degree of depression and anxiety recorded in them. The testimonies display little of Hutchinson's spiritual self-confidence or exegetical independence; rather self-doubt and expressions of dependence on the ministry are the norm.

As I have shown elsewhere, after 1638 Shepard's sermons routinely constructed an audience that was earnest but unredeemed, on the path to salvation but never arriving.[34] His sermons emphasized human helplessness before sin and the efficacy of the ministry in preparing the heart of Christ. From their pews Shepard's flock listened and internalized this discourse; in one confession after another, candidates marked their spiritual growth primarily in terms of the lessons learned from recently preached sermons. Isabell Jackson's confession is representative: "In ministry out of Isaiah, Hear O Chick, I have brought up rebellious child, and I thought I was a rebellious wretch against God."[35] Shepard's ministry provided the necessary words of comfort: "but, said the minister, though thou can but sigh and breathe or chatter after the Lord. That did refresh that there should be any hope for such a poor creature as I am." These conversion narratives repeat a generic plot: congregants begin with laments of spiritual depression and self-doubt, cite recently preached Scriptures providing illumination and comfort, and most often conclude with modest expressions of hope. However, even the most sanguine narratives express continuing dependence on the ministry. Edward Hall, Mary Sparrowhawk, and many others testify to the importance of Shepard's sermons in helping them to "mourn" their unbelief, lifting their hearts "nearer to the Lord."[36]

I do not wish to be misunderstood: I am not challenging the poignancy or felt meaning of conversion for Shepard's congregants, sufficient nor am I suggesting that their statements conformed in any crude way to strictures of the new orthodoxy. The very means by which the laity first encountered Scripture as children involved this same process of internalizing the preached word. Rather, I would suggest that in the fraught context of controversy and the subsequently enhanced role accorded the ministry—not only in adjudicating scriptural interpretation but also in judging congregants' spiritual qualifications—laymen and laywomen came to experience and express themselves as subjects within a chastened religious discourse. The Bible, after all, is a living Word in many senses: it is a volatile, multivocal, lively text. And, while the multitude of scriptural types was fulfilled in the one Christ, each type embodied a unique set of affects and experiences available for identification, exemplification, and instruction. By the end of the 1630s the range of acceptable spiritual identifications had narrowed, reshaping the ways people came to understand their own lives and hearts.

From "Judea Capta" to "Pelican in Wildernes"

Mary Rowlandson's Captivity

On the face of it, the achievements of writers such as Anne Bradstreet and Mary Rowlandson argue the continued vitality of the expressive modes available to women in the post-Hutchinson decades. I believe that the radical spiritual and intellectual freedoms licensed by the highest Protestant ideals were still very much in play but were more narrowly channeled. Women still found sustenance and solace as readers, but certain interpretive practices were prohibited unless they were achieved through the guidance or with the approval of male clerics. Moreover, the figurative logic that had made Hutchinson's own body an object of typological interpretation was rehearsed throughout the century. First as captives among the Indians and then as demoniacs, the lives and bodies of women were circulated by male writers as material types for the spiritual progress of New England.

In the seventeenth century Mary Rowlandson's narrative was a best-seller on both sides of the Atlantic. Her history is still sufficiently well-known not to require recounting here; nor am I able in this foreshortened discussion to address the rich complexities and emotional registers of her powerful text or to engage with the substantial body of scholarship devoted to her narrative. However, since Rowlandson is the only female exegete after Hutchinson to enjoy a public forum, I cannot resist briefly commenting on a few of the ways Rowlandson remembered and interpreted her captivity through the Bible, and to reflect on how her experience was read by male clerics, including her own husband, as a type both for God's chastening and God's promised redemption of New England.[37]

As many scholars have noted, Rowlandson's text is contained—one might even say disciplined—by the two documents that frame it: the preface, most often attributed to Increase Mather; and the sermon delivered by her husband, Joseph Rowlandson, in November 1678. The doctrine of Joseph's sermon, "That the Lord may even forsake a People that have been near to him," implicitly casts Mary Rowlandson's captivity as the just punishment of an unfaithful nation; her deliverance promised the renewal of God's love.[38] The preface to her text makes this figural importance explicit, drawing a host of typological analogies that would have been heretical for Rowlandson herself to suggest: "this dispensation doth bear some resemblance to those of *Joseph, David,* and *Daniel.* . . . Stories whereof do represent us with the excellent textures of divine providence . . . worthy to be exhibited to, and viewed and pondered by all." The author casts Rowlandson as the "Handmaid," the "Servant" through whom the "awfull, wise, holy, powerfull, and gracious providence" of God is displayed. In a reversal of the litany of aspersions cast on Hutchinson, Rowlandson takes her place among God's "dear ones, that are as the Apple of his Eye, as the Signet upon His Hand, the Delight of His eyes."[39]

Yet, the author of the preface would have it both ways: as a figure of Judea Capta, Rowlandson is elevated; however, in herself, as a "modest gentlewoman," she personifies due deference. This is a wife, he carefully notes, who has not stepped out of her place; the preface stipulates that it is her status as "the precious yokefellow," "the dear Consort" of that "faithful Servant of God" the Reverend Mr. Rowlandson, that gives her story general importance. Moreover, the reader is repeatedly assured that "this Gentlewomans modesty would not thrust" her story into print. Rather those friends—presumably Increase Mather himself—who see in her experience "a dispensation of publick note, and of universall concernment" bring forth the publication.[40]

The degree to which Rowlandson consented to or participated in this grand typological reading of her personal suffering is an issue that I cannot address in this brief discussion. Her text reveals that she did identify her sufferings with the anguish of Job, David, and Daniel and that their histories gave voice and meaning to her own, but whether such identification meant that she understood herself as a representative type of New England is another matter. While I believe that she may well have shared Increase Mather's sense of the larger providential meaning of the war, I tend to agree with those critics who read her narrative as an act of memorialization, a witnessing of trauma, and a work of devotion. She professed that her reason for writing was to honor the Lord and "His wonderfull Power . . . in preserving us in the *Wilderness,* while under the Enemies hand" and to express gratitude for "His goodness in bringing to my hand so many comfortable and suitable Scriptures in my distress."[41]

My focus will be on this second motive—Rowlandson's desire to bear witness to the solace she received by means of Scripture. Rowlandson's text rehearses a familiar model for reading, one that showcases orthodox biblical exegesis while at the same time exhibiting the subtle forms of interpretive autonomy it could foster. Even before she receives a physical copy of the Bible from her captors, verses of Scripture, long rehearsed in memory, visit her with comforting messages. Removed from the world she knew, Rowlandson is left alone with her Bible. Her reading practice is similar to Hutchinson's: profoundly aware of her creaturely helplessness, she can only wait patiently for God's guidance. At times her suffering is so extreme that she cannot find any words to lament her pain or to pray for relief; only God can give her voice: "I cannot express to man the affliction that lay upon my Spirit, but the Lord helped me at that time to express it to himself." That relief often comes in the now-familiar form of divinely directed reading: "I opened my Bible to read, and the Lord brought that precious Scripture to me, *Jer.* 31:16: *Thus saith the Lord, refrain thy voice from weeping and thine eyes from tears, for thy work shall be rewarded.*" The effect is immediate and sustaining: the verse is "a sweet Cordial" when she is "ready to faint," and its power is enduring. She records that "many and many a time have I sat down, and wept sweetly over this Scripture." Another verse from Isaiah, "*For a small moment have I forsaken thee, but with great mercies will I gather thee,*" becomes a mantra promising God's return even in this context of his abandonment. Time and again the appropriate Scripture—particularly from Psalms—"presents itself" to her, "stilling" her spirit, giving instruction, and sometimes even speaking for her. When she is bereft of speech, she relies on the words of David, Job, or Daniel to give voice to her own grief.[42]

As many scholars have noted, the Bible also provided Rowlandson with ready voices for working through feelings that were stigmatized or unacceptable within her Puritan community: hostility toward her husband for failing to protect her, guilt about stealing food from an "English" child, vengeful smugness at the death of a papoose, unredeemable grief at the loss of her family and especially of her dear babe. In one memorable passage Rowlandson voices bitter disappointment at the inability or the unwillingness of the colonial soldiers to ford the Bacquaug River to rescue the captives. She recounts a "strange providence of God in preserving the heathen," exhaustively cataloging the difficulties they faced. These Indians carried "all they had, bag and baggage" and "all their luggage," including their captives. Many among them were "old and young, some sick and some lame," with many squaws, many "with Papooses at the backs," and with some carrying "their old decrepit mothers." This litany of burdens turns, however, on this rhetorical dime: "yet they got over this river." The army, by contrast, came after them "on that very day," and "yet this river put a stop to them."

Her anger at her countrymen is barely veiled below the surface of the text; her providential explanation does little to exculpate them. "God did not give them courage or activity to go over after us; we were not ready for so great a mercy as victory or deliverance." While the second clause suggests pious self-doubt and submission to God's chastening hand, the concluding scriptural citation leaves no doubt that the war is God's just punishment of a fallen generation: "*Oh that my people had harkened to me and* Israel *had walked in my ways, I should soon have subdued their Enemies, and turned my hand against their Adversaries.*"[43] Here biblical citation rides within and alongside a more personal indictment. Like Hutchinson before her, Rowlandson finds a way to articulate her personal rage, but always through the words of Scripture and always by means of indirection—what we might characterize as a strategy of innocence. Rowlandson's narrative of war, death, and abandonment—the complete and utter shattering of her daily life—never explicitly criticizes the leadership of the Puritan patriarchs. Rather her captivity and redemption are cast within a plot suggesting the equal and identical suffering of all members of the larger community. Perhaps because of her particular historical moment, perhaps because of her tactics of indirection, perhaps because of her undisputed position as a "goodwife," Rowlandson succeeds in giving voice to her frustration and despair with the standing order even while she is touted as speaking for it. The sufferings of David give her latitude to speak indirectly of her desire for revenge in the same breath that she praises the God of the Puritan fathers. Importantly, this biblical passage provides the comfort of explanation and the promise of a comic resolution within the well-defined grooves of a cherished and familiar narrative.[44]

Ultimately, however, neither the Bible nor rescue nor restoration to the Puritan community proves entirely adequate to soothe Rowlandson's shattered spirit. Extreme suffering, at least for a time, has wounded her beyond cure. Again, however, Scripture gives her the words to bear witness to her pain: "the dregs of the Cup, the Wine of astonishment, like a sweeping rain that leaveth no food, did the Lord prepare to be my portion." In the end, for Rowlandson, living in and through the Bible is expressed not in the terms of Mather's grand typology but in the terms of heartbroken endurance in the face of unremitting grief and suffering. It is expressed by patience, by guarded hope, and by a final and silent repose within the scriptural promise of deliverance: "I have learned to look beyond present and smaller troubles, and to be quieted under them, as *Moses* said, *Exod.* 14.13. *Stand still and see the Salvation of the Lord.*"[45]

The Eloquence of Mercy Short

Her material circumstances, educational background, and social status mark Mercy Short as very different from the women here discussed. Yet, in this brief history of gendered reading practices and the textualization of women's bodies, she clearly deserves a place. While official histories of the Antinomian Controversy sought to reduce Hutchinson to a corporeal sign, Mercy Short originally comes into historical view as nothing more than a suffering body. In March 1690 Short witnessed the violent deaths of her mother, father, and three siblings during an Indian raid; she was held captive for eight long months. Soon after she was redeemed, Short fell victim to a form of extreme suffering that Cotton Mather diagnosed as demonic possession. We have no direct access to Short's words or thoughts; her story is known only through Mather's record of his treatment of her possession. In that mediated narrative the scene of reading provides us with the only glimpse we have of Short's interiority.

Elsewhere I have argued that Short relived her real-world captivity symbolically in this episode of spiritual bondage, imagining herself beset by Satan and by evil spirits that often took the form of "Tawneys."[46] Seeking sanctuary in Mather's home, Short was surrounded by Mather and his congregants throughout her affliction. They kept a vigil with her, praying for her release and witnessing her suffering. Seemingly deprived of her own agency, Short was subject to sudden fainting spells "wherein shee lay for Dead many hours together." At other times she "fell into violent fits," being "Tortured and Harassed by Evil spirits." She claimed that she was sometimes forced to swallow pins and poisons, and that at other times she was prevented from eating at all. She was pinched, suffocated, rendered deaf and blind, taunted, tempted, and belittled by these cruel specters. While Rowlandson's pain often left her unable to find the proper words to express her sorrows, Short was rendered physically mute through much of her ordeal, able to communicate only by gesture.[47]

Confined to her bed throughout her torment, Short kept a Bible close by her side. She never relinquished interpretive authority over her experience; rather, by relying on the communicative and totemic power of the Bible, she sought through it to understand and to convey the source of her suffering. In one memorable instance, while Mather was preaching to the small group gathered around her, Short physically assaulted him and "tore a leaf of his Bible." The text from which Mather preached was Mark 9, describing Christ's successful exorcism of an evil spirit so violently torturing a young boy that "he foameth, and gnasheth with his teeth, and pineth away" (Mark 9:18). I would contend that Short's attack was not a random hysterical act and that through it she made legible the yearning and frustration engendered in her by a text that spoke directly to the source of her affliction but left her still in want of cure. Her mute gesture becomes eloquent for those with ears to hear, eyes to read.[48]

Time and again Short directed the efforts of her attending ministers by paging through the Bible, turning down leaves that gave voice to her travail and that instructed them about how to help her. Mather often voiced wonder at Short's uncanny skill: "But that which carries most of marvel in it, is, . . . in her Trances, a Bible Happening to ly on her bed, shee has taken it up and without ever casting her Eye upon it, shee has Turned over many Leaves, at last folding down a Leaf to a Text." The verses she selected sometimes illuminate the significance of her personal suffering; at other times passages hint at the larger, communal implications of Satan's presence in the New Jerusalem. According to Mather, Short always selected "the most pertinent Place that could bee thought of, and from thence Argue[s] against the Wretches that molested her." When Short's senses were restored, Mather asked how she came to those passages; her answer was the by-now-familiar claim of passive yet inspired reading: "shee told mee, her manner was to turn the leaves, till twas darted into her mind that she had the place; and there she folded." Given that Short had memorized Bible verses from an early age and had heard it preached through many times, we must credit her selection of these texts as deliberative communicative acts.[49]

The Bay Psalm Book, too, was engraved on Short's memory, affording another powerful tool for communicating. Mather reports that, "calling for a Psalm-book, shee has, in the Dark, turned over many Leaves, and at length, without Reading a Syllable, shee has turned down a Leaf to a Psalm, advising us to go sing it, on her behalf. I do affirm That no man living ever could have singled out Psalms more expressive of, and suitable to, her circumstances, than those she pitch'd upon." The most touching and eloquent of her surrogate speeches is Psalm 102, which Short described as "a fitt psalm for my Condicion." This text, "a prayer of the afflicted when he is overwhelmed," begs the Lord to abide in times of trouble.[50] The Psalmist's complaint poignantly reflects Mercy Short's own despair:

> My heart is smote, & dryde like grasse,
> that I to eate my bread forget:
> By reason of my groanings voyce
> my bones unto my skin are set.
> Like Pelican in wildernes,
> like Owle in desart so am I:
> I watch & like a sparrow am
> on house top solitarily.[51]

Short chose her text carefully; the passage may stand as a self-portrait as well as a personal prayer. Her grief and despair, periods of starvation, physical pain, and spiritual isolation are compactly and movingly expressed. "Like Pelican in wildernes"—what image could more eloquently reference Short's captivity and her subsequent feeling of displacement within the Puritan community? I would submit that on some level of consciousness Short was engaging in an act of self-typologizing here, using the same reading conventions deployed by Hutchinson and Rowlandson before her. To be sure, the evocation of a pelican in wilderness is a more humble, more ordinary type than the ones discussed in this essay. But the image also has powerful symbolic and typological resonance. In fable the female pelican saves her young by tearing open her breast, feeding them with her blood. In a Christian context the pelican types Christ's sacrifice and our redemption through him, emphasizing the intimate and constitutive relationship between suffering and salvation. As such, it preaches hope in the context of travail, joy amid agony. Not as Daniel facing down the leonine patriarchs nor as Israel redeemed from captivity but as a homely type of Christly sacrifice Mercy Short modestly yet poignantly reads herself in and through the Bible as a figure of redemption.

While Mather judged Hutchinson harshly and sought to restrain the aspirations of Zion's daughters, I believe he acquitted himself humanely in Short's case, sheltering her physically and spiritually and gathering the community to bear witness to her pain. To be sure, he and they appropriated her suffering for their own psychological and spiritual needs. First in her physical captivity and then in her spiritual possession, Short endured and then re-presented the traumas haunting every member of her community, many of whom had lost family members in Indian raids and all of whom worried about the larger providential meaning of these chastisements. Beset by political struggles with London and border wars with French and Native American allies, grieving the loss of the founding generation and a perceived decline in piety, and finally, bewildered by the "witchcraft" crisis at Salem, Mather's community perhaps discerned a pattern for their afflictions and the promise of a cure typed in the lived experience of Mercy Short. At the same time, they patiently kept watch with her as she followed out the painful work of self-understanding, making her heart known to itself again through the poetry of Scripture.

* * *

This brief history of women reading their Bibles suggests a persistent intimacy between lived experience and the reading of sacred texts, a homely and an inspiring way in which the Word was made to live and in which life itself became more legible to women readers. These stories also challenge modern presumptions about the repressiveness of Puritan culture, particularly with respect to women. Time and again the liberatory pulse at the heart of the Reformation opened a space for individuation, a democratization of reading, of knowing, and of believing. Intellectual and spiritual freedom was won and lost and found again by religious women in Puritan America. Yet, this was a deeply mixed history. Though women were encouraged to find personal inspiration in the Bible, their authority to discover its meanings was at times feared, disparaged, or opposed. Often the desire for communal stability worked to routinize piety, to socialize radical individualism, and to reinstate familiar patterns of deference. Sometimes, as in the case of Anne Hutchinson or Mary Dyer, this drift toward "order" combined with a more jealous safeguarding of patriarchal privilege. It is a matter to grieve that so often we can only glimpse the interior lives of these women by indirection, in contexts of controversy or crisis, and in texts written or transcribed by men with their own interpretive investments. This has also been a history in which some women have been humiliated for their ambitions or indentured to the symbolic machinery of the male gaze, and in which the interpretive energies of more women still have been routed into conventional domestic stereotypes.

An alternative ending, however, might focus on what we know of the continued vitality of Anne Hutchinson's spiritual experiment after she left Boston. Though Winthrop meant it as a criticism when he recorded that as she departed Hutchinson "gloried in her sufferings, saying that it was the greatest happiness next to Christ that ever befell her," we might read through his intent to discern a different history and conclusion of the controversy.[52] From the scraps we can glean, it seems that first in Rhode Island and then in Aquidneck, Hutchinson followed out the logic of her high spirituality. Refusing to compromise in order to remain, as Cotton had done, she became free to follow wherever the Spirit and her Bible led. In 1639, when Boston Church dispatched a delegation to Rhode Island with further admonitions for its "wayward" members, Hutchinson simply turned them away: "for our church she would not acknowledge it any church of Christs."[53] Suppose we say, then, not that she was banished but that she chose to step outside, step away from limitation—that her departure was an entry. Nathaniel Hawthorne speculated that in seclusion perhaps she found repose.[54] A transcription of a letter attributed to her in these years puts the matter differently. There Hutchinson celebrated her continued certainty that God was the "*Author*" and "*Maintainer*" of "*the True Light*" that shone through her to irradiate Scripture, prophesying with and through the words of Solomon that this light "*shall break forth more and more unto the perfect Day.*"[55]

We, who inherit the winner's archive, might propose that in rejecting the church's delegation Hutchinson also declined the history that besmirched her and refused a set of doctrines that to her seemed to tether spirit to gendered flesh. In addition, we might imagine that in a theology in which bodies and perhaps even individuated souls dissolved into pure spirit, death too may have lost its sting. True grief was emptiness, the absence or the loss of animating spirit, or at least so it would seem to Mary Dyer, Margaret Fell, Sarah Edwards, Anne Lee, and a host of female mystics who were to find in this sort of radical spiritism an antidote to earthly hierarchies, an incitement to self-expression as the fruit of self-annihilation, and a liberation from worldly constraints inhering within a Protestant tradition that at the same time provided the enabling conditions for transcending them.

Notes

I wish to thank Heidi Brayman Hackel and Catherine E. Kelly for their patience and insight, as well as for the inspiration the original conference brought to all the participants. The readers for the press offered timely and astute provocations to reflection. At a critical point Carla Mazzio generously read and commented on this essay. I would especially like to thank Lisa Ruddick for her invaluable insights; as always, she stands as the very type of collegial generosity. In addition, I want to thank my students who, over the past thirteen years, in the various incarnations of my courses "Typologies of Gender in Puritan America" and "Women, Writing, and Spirituality," have shared and deepened my appreciation for our paradoxical position as modern readers: hoping, in some sense, to stand prepared but passive before these texts, allowing them to speak through us, while also registering and accounting for our own powerful but distorting desires for readerly identification.

1. Neal Salisbury, ed., *The Sovereignty and Goodness of God, Together with the Faithfulness of His Promises Displayed: Being a Narrative of the Captivity and Restoration of Mrs. Mary Rowlandson and Related Documents* (Boston: Bedford/St. Martin's, 1997), 90. The passage from Cartwright is quoted in David D. Hall, *Worlds of Wonder, Days of Judgment: Popular Religious Belief in Early New England* (New York: Alfred A. Knopf, 1989), 22. In these opening paragraphs I am indebted to Hall's first chapter, "The Uses of Literacy," which provides an eloquent account of the enabling conditions for literacy in New England, the centrality of the Bible in everyday life, and the convergence of oral and print cultures in literacy acquisition. See also Hall, "Readers and Writers in Early New England," in A *History of the Book in America*, vol. 1, *The Colonial Book in the Atlantic World*, ed. Hugh Amory and David D. Hall (Cambridge: AAS and Cambridge University Press, 2000), ch. 4. E. Jennifer Monaghan's pioneering work on the intersections of gender and literacy acquisition has also been essential. In "Literacy Instruction and Gender in Colonial New England," in *Reading in America: Literature and Social History*, ed. Cathy N. Davidson (Baltimore: Johns Hopkins University Press, 1989), 53–80, Monaghan shows how the connection between oral and print culture was instantiated in the method of reading instruction, which relied on an oral alphabet and skills of memorization. As she points out, writing literacy for males was

mandated soon after 1642, though women of status often gained access to writing instruction. The 1642 Literacy Act is quoted in Monaghan, "Literary Instruction," 62.

2. Hall, "Readers," describes the range of cultural contexts and modes of engagement with Bible study; see esp. 122–124.

3. Beginning with "Typology in Puritan New England: The Williams-Cotton Controversy Reassessed," *American Quarterly* 19.2 (summer 1967): 166–91, and continuing in *The Puritan Origins of the American Self* (New Haven, Conn.: Yale University Press, 1975) and *The Rites of Assent: Transformation in the Symbolic Construction of America* (New York: Routledge, 1993), Sacvan Bercovitch pioneered the study of American Puritan typology, detailing how this brand of religious tribalism ripened into claims of manifest destiny. The distinction he makes between allegorical and historical typological modes is relevant here. As he points out, Roger Williams insisted that historical types, abrogated by Christ, must now be understood allegorically, signifying "a-temporal states of the soul" (175). Cotton (and Hutchinson) argued the continued relevance of the prophetic dimension of types: "Cotton proclaims the literal-spiritual continuity between the two Testaments and the colonial venture in America . . . delineating a form of typology which links past, present and future in a developmental historiography" (Bercovitch, "Typology," 175–76). Barbara Keifer Lewalski, *Protestant Poetics and the Seventeenth-Century Religious Lyric* (Princeton, N.J.: Princeton University Press, 1979), traces personal applications of recapitulative or correlative types. See also Janice Knight, "Learning the Language of God: Jonathan Edwards and the Typology of Nature," *William and Mary Quarterly*, 3rd ser., 48.4 (1991): 531–51, for discussion of the generative blending of these liberal and conservative typological modes. See Theodore Dwight Bozeman, *To Live Ancient Lives: The Primitivist Dimension in Puritanism* (Chapel Hill: University of North Carolina Press, 1988), for a counterview of the prophetic dimension of Puritan typological practices.

4. "Preface to the Reader," Salisbury, *Sovereignty*, 65. Though signed only "Ter Amicam," most scholars attribute the preface to Rowlandson's text to Increase Mather. Teresa Toulouse, "The Sovereignty and Goodness of God in 1682: Royal Authority, Female Captivity, and 'Creole' Male Identity," *English Literary History* 67.4 (winter 2000): 932, is among the many scholars supporting this position.

5. Short's possession is narrated in Cotton Mather, "A Brand Pluck'd Out of the Burning," in *Narratives of the Witchcraft Cases, 1648–1706,* ed. George Lincoln Burr (New York: Scribner's, 1914), 286. This text will hereafter be cited as Mather, *Brand.*

6. The scholarship on Hutchinson and the Antinomian Controversy is both impressive and vast. For a selected bibliography of recent scholarship, readers should consult David D. Hall, *The Antinomian Controversy, 1636–1638: A Documentary* History, 2nd ed. (London: Duke University Press, 1990), 445–47. This volume collects primary documents of the Controversy, including trial transcriptions; Winthrop's *A Short Story of the Rise, reign, and ruine of the Antinomians, Familists & Libertines;* and Thomas Weld's "Preface." For amplification of many of the arguments made here, readers should consult Janice Knight, *Orthodoxies in Massachusetts: Rereading American Puritanism* (Cambridge, Mass.: Harvard University Press, 1994). Analyses of the broad cultural and theological stakes of the Controversy include Andrew Delbanco, *The Puritan Ordeal* (Cambridge, Mass.: Harvard University Press, 1989); Louise Breen, *Transgressing the Bounds: Subver-*

sive Enterprises among the Puritan Elites in Massachusetts (Oxford: Oxford University Press, 2001); Michael P. Winship, *Making Heretics: Militant Protestantism and Free Grace in Massachusetts, 1636–1641* (Princeton, N.J.: Princeton University Press, 2002), and more recently Michael P. Winship, *The Times & Trials of Anne Hutchinson* (Lawrence: University Press of Kansas, 2005). For the importance of gender in the Controversy, including the lawfulness of Hutchinson's speech, see especially Susan Howe, *The Birth-Mark: Unsettling the Wilderness in American Literary History* (Middletown, Conn.: Wesleyan University Press, 1993); Sandra Gustafson, *Eloquence Is Power: Oratory and Performance in Early America* (Chapel Hill: University of North Carolina Press, 2000), 19–33; Jane Kamensky, *Governing the Tongue: The Politics of Speech in Early New England* (New York: Oxford University Press, 1997); Mary Beth Norton, *Founding Mothers and Fathers: Gendered Power and the Forming of American Society* (New York: Knopf, 1996); Lad Tobin, "A Radically Different Voice: Gender and Language in the Trials of Anne Hutchinson," *Early American Literature* 25.2 (1990): 253–70; and Bryce Traister, "Anne Hutchinson's 'Monstrous Birth' and the Feminization of Antinomianism," *Canadian Review of American Studies* 27.2 (1997): 133–58.

7. John Winthrop, *"A Short Story of the Rise, reign, and ruine of the Antinomians, Familists & Libertines,"* in Hall, *Antinomian Controversy,* 263, 265 (hereafter cited as Winthrop, *"Short Story"*); Thomas Weld, "Preface" to Winthrop's *"Short Story,"* in Hall, *Antinomian Controversy,* 207 (hereafter cited as Weld, "Preface").

8. Weld, "Preface," 209. Winthrop, *"Short Story,"* 269, 253.

9. "A Report of the trial of Mrs. Anne Hutchinson before the Church in Boston," in Hall, *Antinomian Controversy,* 383 (hereafter cited as "Church Trial"); Winthrop, *"Short Story,"* 253.

10. Norton, *Founding Mothers,* 374–88, offers superb discussion of the Controversy as a "crisis in the system of gendered power." Michael Ditmore, "A Prophetess in Her Own Country: An Exegesis of Anne Hutchinson's 'Immediate Revelation,'" *William and Mary Quarterly* 57.2 (April 2000): 349–92, provides the fullest and best account of Hutchinson's exegetical practice, detailing the biblical sources of her revelation, as well as her use of prophetic types. Composed early in 2001 for the Corvallis conference and drawing on my years of teaching these documents, this essay was drafted before I had the benefit of Ditmore's superb essay. My argument is consonant with his at a number of points, and I wish to acknowledge fully his precedence. Winship, *Making Heretics,* 166–211, examines Hutchinson's testimony in careful and full detail. Despite many points of agreement with Winship, I differ with him over the larger cultural origins and stakes of the Controversy.

11. "The Examination of Mrs. Anne Hutchinson at the Court of Newtown," in Hall, *Antinomian Controversy,* 315–16 (hereafter cited as the "Court Trial").

12. Ibid., 312.

13. Norton, *Founding Mothers,* offers a particularly fine discussion of the issues of private speech and public discourse raised by the trials. For a lucid analysis of the doctrinal divisions and theological stakes of the Controversy, see William K.B. Stoever, *"A Faire and Easie Way to Heaven": Covenant Theology and Antinomianism in Early Massachusetts* (Middletown, Conn.: Wesleyan University Press, 1978). For discussion of the implications of differences over indwelling and increated graces, see also Knight, *Orthodoxies,* chs. 3, 4.

14. "Church Trial," 319.

15. Ibid., 327.

16. Winthrop's *"Short Story,"* a polemically charged account of the two trials,

differs on key issues with the extant transcripts of the civil and church trials. Among these differences are the timing of the taking of oaths, the content of Cotton's testimony, and the disputes over lawful revelations. The timing of the oaths bears significantly on Hutchinson's possible motives in making her confession and also, to my mind, on the degree to which Cotton remained a target of inquiry. Winthrop reports that Cotton's testimony "did in a manner agree with the testimony of the rest of the Elders," on which the accusing ministers "confirmed their former testimony" with an oath. It is only then, with the case against her ostensibly sealed, that Hutchinson is provoked "to speake her mind," offering what seemed to Winthrop a desperate admission of her "immediate revelations" (*"Short Story,"* 271). The court transcript records a different scenario. Though marred with gaps and textual defacements at crucial points, the transcript records Cotton corroborating Hutchinson's memory of the crucial conversations ("Church Trial," 334). His testimony is then brought under scrutiny by some of the ministers (as his opinions on revelation were to be challenged later the same afternoon), with Cotton maintaining the substance of his account ("Church Trial," 335–36). It is at this point, well before the ministers submit to an official oath about Hutchinson's supposed slander, that she interrupts the questioning of Cotton with unsolicited testimony concerning the foundation of her opinions. In this account the ministers submit to an oath only after her "revelations" seem to seal her fate ("Church Trial," 346). Norton, *Founding Mothers,* 374–99, superbly tracks many of these differences between the two versions, with an eye to exposing Winthrop's patriarchal bias. Though her commentary of the crucial difference in the timing of the oaths and how they impact speculation on Hutchinson's motives is compelling, she does not consider the significance of the interrogation of Cotton in prompting Hutchinson's speech.

The loss of the original transcript of the civil trial, Winthrop's polemical revision of key testimony, differences between extant versions concerning the order of events, and the presence of obliterations, overwrites, and blanks at crucial moments in the testimony urge caution when reading the documentary evidence in this case. Foucault's reflections on politics of preservation and omission in the constitution of archives, along with the material circumstances of transcription, editing, and erasure, are especially relevant here, given the thinness of the documentary record concerning Hutchinson's life and opinions and what we know of the subsequent shaping of partisan histories of the Controversy. Despite her central importance, no documents in Hutchinson's own hand have survived, at least that have been discovered. The trial documents allude to sets of notes supposedly written by Hutchinson, but no manuscripts remain (though part of a letter thought to have been drafted by Hutchinson is quoted in S. G., *A Glass for the People of New-England, in which They may see themselvs and Spirit, and if not too late, Repent and Turn from their Abominable Ways and Cursed Contrivances* [London, 1676]. See discussion in n. 55 below). I dissent from Ditmore's speculation that this gap in the textual record suggests that Hutchinson may not have gained writing skills or had antipathy to print, a conclusion that sorts well with Patricia Caldwell's claims about her embeddedness in oral culture ("The Antinomian Language Controversy," *Harvard Theological Review* 69 [1976]: 355n13). In addition, while I agree with Winship that these references, instead, offer strong evidence of her writing literacy, I draw a quite opposite conclusion from his sanguine inference that "had Hutchinson written something for publication, there is a good chance it would have been published" (Winship, *Making Heretics,* 257n43 and 300n10). The paucity of the extant archive, it seems to me, sorts better with Susan Howe's compellingly suspicious reading of the politics of erasure embedded in the Controversy (Howe, *Birth-Mark*).

17. "Church Trial," 341.

18. I remain suspicious, as well, of the generative potential of the process of interrogation in provoking or allowing Hutchinson this space of soliloquy. To be sure, the act of such witnessing is highly consistent with Hutchinson's expressed self-confidence and proven pedagogical commitments; the prophetic vision she pronounces is resonant with views she espouses throughout her two trials and with the scanty evidence we have of her views after exile. However, Hutchinson's own sense of the faulty, mutable nature of human speech (as she declares "*I doe acknowledge my Expression to be Ironious but my Judgment was not Ironious*" ["Church Trial," 361]), her insistence that the *order* in which statements are made is crucial to their meaning ("that was the thing that I do deny for they were my words and they were not spoken at the first as they do alledge" ["Court Trial," 331]), and her estimation of the potential distortion of opinions under pressure ("*I did not hould any of thease Thinges before my Imprisonment*" ["Church Trial," 372]) would urge caution in our analysis of statements made in this climate of crisis. Caldwell, "Antinomian Language Controversy," offers an early and eloquent analysis of Hutchinson's profound sense of the expressive inadequacy intrinsic to our human condition.

19. "Church Trial," 336–37.

20. See Knight, *Orthodoxies,* 196–97. Both Winthrop and Dudley draw the parallel to Münster: "These disturbances that have come among the Germans have been all grounded upon revelations, and so they that have vented them have stirred up their hearers to take up arms against their prince and to cut the throats of one another" ("*Short Story,*"275; "Court Trial," 343). Winship, *Making Heretics,* 183–84, concludes that Hutchinson was guilty of charges of conspiracy against the state. I would argue instead that this was an early and a deeply partisan dispute, the outcome of which determined what positions would become understood as heretical and which groups would be labeled as dangerous to the state.

21. Conversely, it might be argued that the position favored by her opponents, that graces are inherent, preserved a more personalized sense of identity that, in turn, sustained material hierarchies of social status and sexed bodies. Additionally, it might be argued that Hutchinson's "mortalism," her repudiation of personalized resurrection—either of the body or of the individual soul—is not only the logical extreme of her high valuation of the indwelling spirit, tending to a realized eschatology, but might also be viewed as a mode of transcending the culturally ordained limitations of gendered embodiment. Paul's dictum that it is "not I, but the Christ that liveth in me" was deployed by countless radical sectaries to challenge patriarchal biases of the standing order. See Margaret Fell, *Women's Speaking Justified, Proved and Allowed of by the Scriptures,* (London, 1667): "the Church of Christ is represented as a Woman; and those that speak against this Woman's speaking, speak against the Church of Christ. . . . *Those that speak against the Power of the Lord, and the Spirit of the Lord speaking in a Woman, simply by reason of her Sex, or because she is a Woman, not regarding the Seed, and Spirit, and Power that speaks in her; such speak against Christ and his Church,* and are of the Seed of the Serpent" (4, emphasis added). This denial of the body as a strategy for overcoming gender constraints was realized most fully in sects embracing celibacy, especially the Shakers, who forwarded Anne Lee as the female messiah.

22. "Church Trial," 340. See Ditmore, "Prophetess," 353–59, for an extended and excellent discussion of Cotton's views on revelation. The record of Cotton's testimony on lawful revelation, though defaced in two key places, clearly defends Hutchinson's practice: "though the word revelation be rare in common speech and we make it uncouth in our ordinary expressions, yet notwithstanding, being understood in the scripture sense I think they are not only lawful but such as christians may receive and God bear witness to it in his word, and usually he doth express it in the ministry of the word and doth accompany it by his spirit, *or else it is in the reading of the word in some chapter or verse and whenever it comes it comes flying upon the wings of the spirit*" ("Church Trial," 340, emphasis added). This defense of "readerly" revelation was central in the Controversy, and a site where critical distortions in Winthrop's version become visible. In Winthrop's *"Short Story,"* Cotton's testimony is crucially abridged, omitting his defense of revelation through private reading and, in effect, rewriting Cotton's defense of Hutchinson into a condemnation (*"Short Story,"* 274). In the trial transcript, portions of testimony on the status of revelation offered by Cotton, Hutchinson, and Winthrop himself are obliterated ("Church Trial," 336–41).

23. "Church Trial," 337. Though Hutchinson identifies with biblical patriarchs rather than female types, I would argue that her testimony to this point describes an acceptable use of recapitulative typology. Drawing on theories that abjection or "feminization" of the soul was normative in Puritan conversion doctrine, Ditmore finds that "Hutchinson's reliance on male scriptural models involves a rhetorical gender reversal"; he concludes, "Hutchinson's 'error,' therefore, was not simply, as her latter-day feminist advocates have maintained, her manlike arrogance in daring to speak her own mind, but that in speaking her mind she adopted the rhetorical pose of an aggressive male in a culture that valued the submissive female; additionally, she personally appropriated scriptural models generally considered off limits" (Ditmore, "Prophetess," 374–75). I agree that criticism of her haughtiness might have rested on her use of patriarchal models, but even after the controversy women such as Mary Rowlandson continued to identify safely with the male types of Daniel, Job, and David. Moreover, rather than preceding and informing the Controversy, as Ditmore claims, I would suggest that a "redemptive pattern" that was "enfigured as humiliation . . . a self-sacrificing subjection to authority and community (whether to divinity or its agents)" (Ditmore, "Prophetess" 374) was not originally "paradigmatic," as Ditmore asserts, but may instead have been an outcome of the crisis. I am in accord, however, with Ditmore's analysis of the implications in Hutchinson's shift from recapitulative to prophetic typological readings of Isaiah and Daniel, and of the stakes that shift implied for the sacralization of the Puritan mission. Ditmore is especially fine in making visible the specific biblical references implicit in Hutchinson's speech and in detailing "the assimilation of her voice into scriptural citation" (Ditmore, "Prophetess," 373–84). For an eloquent analysis of the implications of Hutchinson's doctrines for New England's prophetic identity, see the classic articles by J. F. Maclear, "New England and the Fifth Monarchy: The Quest for the Millennium in Early American Puritanism," *William and Mary Quarterly*, 3rd ser., 32 (1975): 223–60; and "Anne Hutchinson and the Mortalist Heresy," *New England Quarterly* 54 (1981): 74–103.

24. "Court Trial," 337–38. Winthrop's version of Hutchinson's final words includes a more explicit threat to the state (Winthrop, *"Short Story,"* 273) that is missing in the trial transcript ("Court Trial," 338). See also Ditmore, "Prophetess," 377–81, for a finely grained analysis of this part of the testimony.

25. "Court Trial," 342; Winthrop, *"Short Story,"* 275.

26. "Church Trial," 355–56.

27. "Church Trial," 338. Again, Winthrop's *"Short Story"* presents a more rebellious Hutchinson, who claims, "you have *no* power over my body, neither can you do me any harme" (*"Short Story,"* 273, emphasis added). Amy Schrager Lang, *Prophetic Woman: Anne Hutchinson and the Problems of Dissent in the Literature of New England* (Berkeley: University of California Press, 1987), rehearses subsequent attempts to discredit Hutchinson and tracks her cultural legacy. Howe, *Birth-Mark* (15–20), is especially powerful in revealing the centrality of gender to the Controversy and the degree of rhetorical violence visited upon Hutchinson by Puritan men. See Tobin, "Radically Different Voice," and especially Traister, "Anne Hutchinson's 'Monstrous Birth'" on the strategic gendering of the Controversy and the ways in which the image of corrupted maternity was used in the scapegoating of Hutchinson.

28. Weld, "Preface," 202.

29. Cotton Mather's account of the Controversy entitled *Hydra Decapitata*, appears in *Magnalia Christi Americana,* ed. Thomas Robbins (New York: Russell and Russell, 1702; repr. 1985), vol. 2, ch. 3, 508–22; the quote is from 516.

30. This condemnation of Weld's and Winthrop's tactics is made by the author of *Mercurius Americanus* (1645) in Charles H. Bell, ed., *John Wheelwright*, Prince Society Publications (Boston, 1876), 188–228, 196. This pamphlet is a defense of Wheelwright, once attributed to him but now thought to be written by his son. It is certainly no defense of Hutchinson: "In spirituals indeed she gave her understanding over into the power of suggestion and immediate dictates, by reason of which she had many strange fancies, and erroneous tenets possest her" (197). However, the pamphlet also indicts Weld and Winthrop for the hypocrisy and callousness of their attacks on Hutchinson.

31. Weld, "Preface," 214.

32. In making this observation, the author of *Mercurius* also sarcastically observes: "I question not his learning, &c. but I admire his certainty, or rather impudence: did the man obtestricate?" (*Mercurius Americanus*, 196). I take this to be an error in the printed text; the context suggests that he is challenging Weld's knowledge of obstetrics.

33. Weld, "Preface," 218–19. Weld also suggests that the destruction levied against them was the result of an unnatural dominance of women in the Hutchinson family line. While genealogy was conventionally traced through the male line, here a purely female lineage is described and is, to Weld's delight (we cannot help but feel), obliterated: "*The Indians set upon them, and slew her and all her family, her daughter, and her daughters husband, and all their children*" (ibid., 218). This providential linkage of Hutchinson's death with the success of New England is inscribed in Edward Johnson's account in *The Wonder-Working Providence of Sion's Saviour, in New England* (New York: Charles Scribner's Sons, 1910), book 2, ch. 12, which lingers with some relish over the massacre and implicitly links it with the providential founding of Harvard College. See Howe, *Birth-Mark*, as well as Lang, *Prophetic Woman*, for condemnations of Johnson's calumny.

34. See Knight, *Orthodoxies*, ch. 4.

35. Michael McGiffert, ed., *God's Plot: Puritan Spirituality in Thomas Shepard's Cambridge* (Amherst: University of Massachusetts Press, 1994), 149, 212. Among those scholars surprised by the pathos of the narratives is Charles Cohen, in *God's Caress: The Psychology of Puritan Religious Experience* (New York: Oxford University Press, 1988).

36. Shepard, *God's Plot*, 213, 150, 153–54, 165, 169–72.

37. My reflections on Rowlandson's text here will hold no surprises for scholars in the field. Indeed, the best of recent criticism has focused on the ambivalence evidenced in Rowlandson's text, as well as the centrality of typological imagery to her expressions of these divided emotions. Rather, I intend these remarks to suggest the continuity of women's deployment of biblical types throughout the century. Salisbury's *Introduction* to Rowlandson's text, for example, discusses many of the issues I touch on here, pointing the reader to robust scholarly work on each. His selected bibliography (Salisbury, *Sovereignty*, 173–76) charts the scholarship on Rowlandson. Most congenial to my own understanding of Rowlandson's text are Howe's *Birth-Mark*, 89–130, and Mitchell Breitweiser's *American Puritanism and the Defense of Mourning* (Madison: University of Wisconsin Press, 1990). Howe brilliantly reveals the subversive power of the text, in which Puritan typological self-understanding is both evoked and unmade. Breitweiser's text records a similar pattern of corrosive ambivalence around the project of loss and mourning. In his account, the foreclosure of grief within a Puritan theology that required abjection produces intolerable psychological conflict for Rowlandson, resulting in moments of resistance and textual subversion. Also essential to an understanding of Rowlandson are the many fine articles by Teresa Toulouse, including "The Sovereignty and Goodness of God in 1682: Royal Authority, Female Captivity, and 'Creole' Male Identity," *English Literary History* 67.4 (winter 2000): 925–49; and "'My Own Credit': Strategies of (E)valuation in Mary Rowlandson's Captivity Narrative," *American Literature* 64.4 (December 1992): 655–76. For a superb recent account of the war, see Jill Lepore, *The Name of War: King Philip's War and the Origins of American Identity* (New York: Vintage, 1999).

38. Joseph Rowlandson, "*The Possibility of God's Forsaking a people, That have been visibly near & dear to him,*" in Salisbury, *Sovereignty*, 154.

39. "The Preface to the Reader," in Salisbury, *Sovereignty*, 65.

40. Ibid., 65–66.

41. Rowlandson, *Narrative*, in Salibury, *Sovereignty*, 82. Throughout the text Rowlandson borrows whole verses, signaling with such phrases as "now, may I say with David," Job, Daniel, etc. Some scholars believe this persistent citation indicates that her narrative was either edited by the ministers who brought it forward into press or was in less direct ways shaped by or pressed into the service of orthodoxy. I believe that while Rowlandson may have supplemented or amplified the place given to Scripture in this retrospective account, there is no reason to doubt that it provided a sustaining explanation for her suffering and proffered the hope of deliverance.

42. Rowlandson, *Narrative*, 78, 90.

43. Ibid., 79–80.

44. This passage serves as a centerpiece for many critics, including Howe (*Birth-Mark*) and Breitweiser (*American Puritanism*), who explore moments of subversion within Rowlandson's orthodox discourse. Rowlandson is so troubled by this particular failure of her countrymen that she recurs to it several times in the course of the narrative. When she enumerates the remarkable providences she "took special notice of in [her] afflicted time," for example, four of the five focus on the inadequacies of the soldiers. She recalls that the Indians "derided the slowness and dullness of the English Army" and again marvels at God's providence in making the river "impassable to the English," recurring to Psalm 81 to underscore that the Puritan community, guilty of "perverse and evil car-

riages," must reform and confess their utter dependence on God before general redemption will come (Rowlandson, *Narrative*, 105–6).

45. Rowlandson, *Narrative*, 112.

46. This section on Short is an abbreviated discussion of Janice Knight, "Telling It Slant: The Testimony of Mercy Short," *Early American Literature* (winter 2002): 39–69. Mather's *Brand* is composed of inseparable, yet somewhat distinct narrative structures—all mediated his act of transcription. We know only the sketchiest of details about Short—that upon her release in Boston she found herself in a strange town, with no family, no property, no friends, and presumably with no hope for bettering her circumstances.

47. Mather, *Brand*, 260.

48. Ibid.

49. Ibid., 275, 284, 276.

50. Ibid., 275.

51. *The Bay Psalm Book: A Facsimile Reprint of the First Edition of 1640* (Chicago: University of Chicago Press, 1956).

52. John Winthrop, *Journal of John Winthrop, 1630–1649*, ed. Richard Dunn and Laetitia Yeandle (Cambridge, Mass.: Harvard University Press, 1996), claims that "At Aquiday also Mrs. Hutchinson exercised publicly, and she and her party (some three or four families) would have no magistracy . . . Mrs. Hutchinson and some of her adherents happened to be at prayer when the earthquake was at Aquiday, etc., and the house was being shaken there, they were persuaded (and boasted of it) that the Holy Ghost did shake it in coming down upon them, as he did upon the apostles" (155). Winthrop also reported that after her excommunication Hutchinson declared to a detractor, "The Lord judgeth not as man judgeth, better to be cast out of the Church then to deny Christ" (Winthrop, "*Short Story*," 307). For a recent account of Hutchinson's last days, see Winship, *Times & Trials*, ch. 9.

53. See Hall, *Antinomian Controversy*, 392, for reports of Hutchinson's continued rejection of the judgment of the Massachusetts authorities.

54. Nathaniel Hawthorne, *Tales and Sketches* (New York: Library of America, 1996), 18–24. Hawthorne's view of Hutchinson in this "sketch" evidences a peculiar mix of admiration and contempt of the sort he lavished on Margaret Fuller and on his character Zenobia. He extols Hutchinson as a "woman of extraordinary talent and strong imagination" (19) and is critical of her persecutors. However, his ambivalence about strong women is in full view in his final paragraph: "Perhaps here she found the repose, hitherto so vainly sought. Secluded from all whose faith she could not govern, surrounded by the dependents over whom she held an unlimited influence, agitated by none of the tumultuous billows which were left swelling behind her, we may suppose that, in the stillness of Nature, her heart was stilled" (24).

55. These last words contained in S. G., *Glass for the People of New-England*, 137, supposedly transcribe a letter from Hutchinson to Leverett. This full passage reads: "If it were the True Light, in which you say I did once shine in, I am sure the Author thereof, and the Maintainer of it is God, and it shall break forth more and more unto the perfect day." Here, as in her trial, her words blend imperceptibly with Scripture: "But the path of the just is as the shining light, that shineth more and more unto the perfect day" (Prov. 4:18). I do not think that we can know whether *Glass* actually transcribes Hutchinson's words, but I believe these words fully resonate with what we know of her spirit.

Chapter 9

"With All Due Reverence and Respect to the Word of God": Aphra Behn as Skeptical Reader of the Bible and Critical Translator of Fontenelle

MARGARET FERGUSON

"Translation," Eve Sanders has written, "carved out an intermediary zone between reading and writing in which it was possible for [some early modern women] to claim position as [authors]."[1] I want to explore the intermediary zone that Sanders identifies in order to consider translation not only as a textual field in which we can discern traces of female authorship but also as a significant resource for students of the history of reading. Translation is often devalued in ideological schemes that privilege some kind of original creation and ownership of one's own literary property. Such schemes are already evident in early modern discourses about textual production—think, for instance, of Florio's famous dedicatory epistle in which he characterizes his translation of Montaigne's *Essais* (1603) both as a "defective edition" and as a species of writing "reputed femelle," as "are all translations."[2] While it is still easy to see translation as a defective or at least a secondary form of writing, some recent critics have invited us to theorize and historicize translation as a cultural act only partly interpretable with reference to modern or even early modern concepts of the (literary) author.[3] Danielle Clarke, for instance, has recently analyzed Mary Sidney's translation of Robert Garnier's *Marc Antoine* (*Antonius*, 1592) as a complex political intervention in which the translator is neither a "handmaid" to the original nor a rebellious subverter of it.[4] A romantic overvaluation of authorship considered as originality underlies the tendency to construe the relation between a translation and its (chief) original in terms of a Bloomian theory of agonistic influence. Although such a critical paradigm may work for part of the early modern terrain of translation—best, perhaps, for the type of translation John Dryden identified as "imitation" and wittily defined as that kind in which "the translator (if he has not lost that Name) assumes the liberty not only to vary from the words and sence, but to forsake them both, as he sees occasion"[5]—the paradigm is inadequate for many early ways of understanding the relation between translation and original, and for understanding the concept of "fidelity." As Luther's amazing theory and practice of biblical translation indicate, the notion of "fidelity," in Renaissance and Reformation contexts, may raise complex questions about a subject's competing allegiances; for Luther, fidelity to the German language and to his own vision of biblical truth takes precedence over any notion of fidelity to the Greek or Latin or even the Hebrew texts of the Bible.[6] Dryden's verb "forsake," when we consider it in relation to Aphra Behn's writing practice, turns out to have multiple meanings inflected by different textual traditions (classical and Judeo-Christian) and by the reader's awareness of the writing-subject's gender. Wives are enjoined by Genesis to forsake their parents in order to cleave to their husbands, but Ovidian nymphs are forsaken by their lovers (rarely also husbands) and Christ—a model available to both male and female writers—famously felt himself, on the cross, to be forsaken by his Father. As these examples indicate, we cannot ascribe a simple moral valence to a woman writer's act of "forsaking" her source.

Aphra Behn, whose various noms de plume arguably derive neither from her biological parents nor from her (alleged) husband,[7] made a somewhat paradoxical contribution to the volume of translations that Dryden presented to English readers. The paradox of Behn's contribution opens my path toward discussing other paradoxes in her (several) personae as translator. While Dryden's 1680 volume is a collection of translations of Ovid's epistles done in "several hands," the lone female contributor (Dryden somewhat ambiguously suggests) is also the only translator who does not actually know Ovid's original language: "I was desir'd to say that the Authour, who is of the Fair Sex, understood not Latine. But if she does not, I am afraid she has given us occasion to be asham'd who do."[8] Who "desired" him to say this? The coy phrasing invites skepticism.[9] Might Behn have known enough Latin to read it (as many modern academics do) with the aid of others' translations? She may well have desired not to reveal the whole truth and nothing but the truth about the nature of her education, which is a process that involves cultural appropriation in some of the same ways that writing does. In Behn's oeuvre there are no clear lines between original, imitated, adapted, and translated material.

The text on which I focus in this essay—Behn's translation, including a preface on "prose translation," of Bernard le Bovier de Fontenelle's

Entretiens sur la pluralité des mondes—seems to follow its original closely.[10] However, the question of the translator's fidelity is, as I hope to show, quite complex. To whom or what is Behn the translator—and theorist of translation—faithful? Her own statement on the matter goes as follows in her translator's preface: "I have endeavoured to give you the true meaning of the Author, and have kept as near his Words as was possible; I was necessitated to add a little in some places, otherwise the Book could not have been understood."[11] In this formulation Behn seems to place her work modestly in the second of the three categories of translation defined by Dryden. She offers neither "imitation," the most libertine mode of translation, as we have seen, nor what Dryden calls "metaphrase," "turning an author word by word."[12] Instead, like a good Anglican seeking the "via media," she is offering "paraphrase," which Dryden describes as "Translation with Latitude," that is, "where the Authour is kept in view by the Translator, so as never to be lost, but his words are not so strictly follow'd as his sense, and that too is admitted to be amplyfied, but not alter'd."[13] How exactly one can "amplify" a text without altering it is an interesting question, however—especially if among the amplifications is a preface that instructs the reader on what she/he should think about the translated work's merits in particular and, in general, about the enormously vexed relation between the New Science of Copernicus and Galileo, on the one hand, and God's divine Word, on the other hand.[14]

Fontenelle's text in its first edition, which Behn translated, consists of five dialogues or "conversations" between a learned and courtly male—the Fontenelle figure—and a high-ranking, curious, but somewhat naive and certainly badly educated "Marquise." Behn is critical of this figure; she also appropriates some of the Marquise's intellectual interests, particularly her fascination with the moon, for the persona of the female translator constructed in the preface. This text, which has only recently begun to be discussed by critics, advertises the translator's presence while completely failing to mention the fact that there is also a preface by the work's "author"—a preface that takes second place in the structure of Behn's book. Translation, like Eve, may be defective and secondary in the view of some early modern writers, but some women who were readers as well as writers did not accept such analogies.

Behn's translation of Fontenelle dramatizes several ways in which theories and practices of translation illuminate the historical emergence of the female reader in the early modern period. Translation is, to be sure, not the same as an act of reading either phenomenologically or materially; on the contrary, translation represents, in writing, multiple readings of a source text and, in many cases, other acts of reading as well that leave their traces in the translation as a written object. Because, however, translation points so interestingly to complexities in acts of reading that cross linguistic and cultural boundaries, and because translation is so central to an international field of early modern cultural debate sutured (and fissured) by theological, political, and sexual problems pertaining to ideas about fidelity, it seems worthwhile to discuss what one prolific early modern woman writer has to say on the topic of translation. Her reflections lead us toward questions about the workings of censorship—including self-censorship—in the practice of translation considered as the representation (not the same as a record) of layered acts of reading. Her reflections also raise questions about the relative prestige of different languages and about the competition between science and religion as sources of cultural authority. Moreover, and more practically, her take on science and religion focuses attention on both phenomena as sets of texts aimed at, and bought by, particular groups of gendered readers with particular kinds of education and hence different amounts of linguistic capital.

Modern anglophone critics and translators usually refer to Fontenelle's work (now shelved under the category science fiction in one Berkeley bookstore) as *Conversations on the Plurality of Worlds.* Mary Baine Campbell describes it as a "tremendously dense, witty, and also smug proto-Enlightenment dialogue [on cosmology] . . . that put the plurality of worlds on every European coffee table (including some Russian ones)."[15] The first of the work's many French editions appeared in 1686; later editions were amplified and corrected as Fontenelle the "amateur" scientist learned more about his subject. Ironically, it was this work of popular science—married, one critic has suggested, to the genre of romance—that got him elected, in 1691, to the post of secretary of the Académie des Sciences.[16] Behn's translation, which would buy her no such prestigious position, came out with remarkable speed in 1688, in a year when she desperately needed money.[17] She remarks at the end of her translator's preface that she would have preferred to give her readers "the subject" of the "plurality of worlds" "quite changed and made my own," but she had "neither health nor leisure" to do so (86). Instead she hopped on the bandwagon of Fontenelle's engaging synthesis of astronomical ideas drawn not only from Copernicus and Galileo but also from Kepler (*Somnium,* 1634) and from Cyrano de Bergerac, who explored hypothetical worlds on the moon and the sun in texts of 1657 and 1662.[18]

The long title of Behn's 1688 volume stresses that in her preface, at least, she is offering her English reader something "Wholly new":

A Discovery of New Worlds.
From the French.

Made English
By Mrs. A. Behn.
To which is prefixed a Preface, by way of Essay on Translated Prose: wherein the Arguments of Father Tacquet, and others, against the System of Copernicus (as to the Motion of the Earth) are likewise considered, and answered: Wholly new.

Behn or her printer changes Fontenelle's title in a way that dramatizes her project's affinity to New World travel narratives. For one critic, this change occludes the text's status as a scientific treatise while suppressing "both the conversational quality of [Fontenelle's] text and its uncomfortably provocative idea about the possible existence of many other worlds."[19] It seems to me, however, that an English text purporting to represent a "discovery of new worlds" (in the plural) would not necessarily have seemed tamer or even less "scientific" than the original title stressing "conversations" about "other worlds." Behn's title recalls, after all, not only works such as Sir Walter Raleigh's *A Discoverie of Guiana* (1595), which provocatively likened a new world landscape to a female body that "hath yet her maidenhead";[20] Behn's text might also have reminded English readers of texts such as John Wilkins's *Discovery of a World on the Moon* (1638) and perhaps also of John Milton's *Paradise Lost* (1667). Milton's angel Raphael "sails between worlds and worlds" on his descent from heaven to meet Adam and Eve, and Raphael opens Adam's mind (but not Eve's) to the possibility that his universe is Copernican rather than Ptolemaic; it is Milton's Satan, however, who most explicitly recalls (or anticipates) the figure of the New World discoverer as he seeks first to "spy" and then to destroy God's "new created World."[21]

Any description of a world different from that limned in the Bible could lead readers astray, as Behn slyly acknowledges when she praises Thomas Creech for translating Lucretius and for thus lifting the prohibitions on women imposed by their education and, implicitly, by Christianity. Most women lacked knowledge of classical languages, and this denied them access to the "Divine Mysteries" of ancient epics: "We are forbid all grateful Theams, / No ravishing Thoughts approach our Ear," writes Behn, arguably alluding to Milton's portrait of Satan bringing a false dream of temptation to the ear of the sleeping Eve.[22] In Behn's revisionary scenario of the biblical ur-story of the Fall, Creech becomes a revalued version of Milton's Satan, beneficently freeing latter-day Eves from their fetters:

So thou by this Translation dost advance
Our Knowledge from the State of Ignorance;
And Equallst Us to Man! Oh how shall We
Enough Adore, or Sacrifice enough to Thee! ("To the Unknown

Daphnis on his Excellent Translation of Lucretius," 1682, in *Works*, 1:26, lines 41–44)

In the preface advertised as "wholly new," she undertakes the task of defending Copernicus's new system of astronomy against Ptolemy's old one and against those who say that "this new Opinion was expressly contrary to the holy Scriptures, and therefore not to be embraced; nay, it was condemned as Heretical" (78). No one in England in 1688 was in danger of Galileo's fate for hewing to Copernican teachings, but the Church of England had not officially embraced them. Behn does so both in her translator's preface and in her decision to bring Fontenelle's dialogues to English readers. She does so in part, I suggest, because in Copernicus's system she arguably finds allegorical support for a newly complex relation of equality between earth and moon (both often figured as female) and a sun traditionally figured as male—and, to ordinary vision, as moving around a stationary earth. The Copernican system, as expounded by Fontenelle in a series of dialogues between a male philosopher who purports, like the sun, to enlighten a noblewoman who allies herself with the night and the moon, offers fruitful matter to a writer concerned to revise the traditionally stable hierarchy in which male is superior to female as author is superior to translator. Behn, I argue, wishes to destabilize such hierarchies with the help of Fontenelle and Copernicus.

She begins by acknowledging that "the Novelty of the Subject in vulgar Languages" is one of her motives for undertaking the translation of Fontenelle's dialogues about astronomical matters most often debated in Latin treatises. Other motives include the "General Applause" the French original has garnered and the appealing (and unusual) fact that Fontenelle introduced "a Woman as one of the speakers . . . for I thought an English Woman might adventure to translate any thing, a French Woman may be supposed to have spoken" (*Works*, 4:73). The female translator here opens space for a nationalist competition with Fontenelle's marquise and with his text more generally. She admits, however, that she found the translator's task "not so easie as I believed at first" (73). There is a parallel, I suggest, between the difficulties of translation and the difficulties of believing in a scientific system that counters the evidence of a stationary earth and a moving sun given by the body and particularly by the human eye. Emphasizing the theme of difficulty, Behn claims, implausibly, that Italian and Spanish are both "closer" to English than French is, and thus French is "of all the hardest to translate into English" (74). The argument lacks persuasive force, but it does have wit, especially when it encompasses the foibles of the French people in its (rather low) estimate of their language. The French, Behn remarks, are so enamored of the sound of their language that they "will go against all the Rules of Sense and Grammar" rather than produce a sound they consider ugly. The example she selects shows the French breaking a rule of grammatical gender to produce an acceptable sound effect: "Speaking of a Man's Wife, they say, son Epouse, whereas in Grammar, it ought to be sa Epouse; but this would throw a French Man into a Fit of a Fever" (75).

The translator's tone, here and throughout the preface, is urbane, and evidently designed to reassure the reader that this writer can weigh evidence on both sides of an argument with cool rationality even as she is using her rhetorical skills to win a contest. She does not, however, show her full hand about the nature of the contest and its stakes. Though she seems to be scoring easy points against the French, she is also, I would suggest, setting the stage for her later arguments in favor of an "allegorical" reading of the Bible to support the ideas of Copernicus over those of Ptolemy. The French way of breaking a rule in order to achieve an effect "against all the Rules of Sense and Grammar" foreshadows the way that the Copernican system apparently breaks rules of common vision, and common sense—and of a literal reading of the Bible—for the sake of a higher truth.

Behn's aim of challenging conventional hierarchies of value and ways of seeing is also apparent, early in her preface, when she presents the cultural difference between the French and English languages in terms of the cultural relativity of ideas of personal beauty—specifically, the fact that "what we think a Deformity, they may think a Perfection; as the Negroes of Guinney think us as ugly, as we think them" (76). Here she seems to degrade and distance the French—England's age-old rival and erstwhile conqueror—while also adopting the position of cosmopolitan tolerance that Montaigne had famously limned in his essay on cannibals. She also anticipates and obliquely allies her writerly perspective with the view that Fontenelle's Marquise expresses on the first night of her conversations with the philosopher. Despite her own "fairness," which Fontenelle praises, she finds a beauty "of a brown Complexion" "more charming" and "a true Emblem of the Night" (94).

From differences of opinion about languages and complexions, Behn moves to differences of opinion that her readers may have about the merit of the specific work she is choosing to bring to England from France—a place you might think is just across the channel but which she has already begun to suggest is "another world," as far from England as West Africa and perhaps wonderful rather than inferior. She offers a brief critical assessment, a "Character," as she calls it, of the text she is translating and also of its male French producer, who, she remarks with apparent disapproval, writes "as if the universe he is describing were entirely the product of Nature"; he "says not a word of God Almighty, from the Beginning to the End; so that one would almost take him to be a Pagan" (77). Pagans, we know, abound in Africa, but do they also inhabit England's old rival France, which was marked, as England was, by deep rifts between Catholics and Protestants? By her criticism and choice of epithet, Behn establishes, on the surface at least, a judicious, almost ethnographical perspective on a text she has distanced from her readers as if she were using the scientific instrument of the telescope. The rhetorical gesture that separates Behn and her English readers from alien pagans, however, masks a problem inherent in translation, a potentially pleasurable problem: it involves an erasure of boundaries, a promiscuous mixing of the kind Behn will explore in many of her fictions that deal with erotic liaisons that cross lines of hair or skin color, of social status, of nationality, and of religion. Behn seems well aware of the censorious comments that she may prompt by merging her writerly identity with that of a Frenchman who may be (mis)taken for a pagan. In the dialogues her "I" will indeed become at times indistinguishable from that of her male Author. When the Marquise asks for "some sensible Sign, by which we might discover the turning round of so vast a Body [as the Earth]," the philosopher, here a composite version of Fontenelle/Behn, replies: "The Motions (answer'd I) which are most natural to remove, are the least perceptible" (110).

In the second part of her translator's preface, Behn seems to extend her critique of Fontenelle as insufficiently Christian, but she also continues the task of making common cause with him on potentially dangerous matters of religion and science. Her defense of Copernicus and his followers against literal readers of the Bible swiftly turns into a defense of the Bible—or rather, a defense and illustration of a certain way of *reading* the Scriptures that allows (English) reverence to marry (French or foreign) skepticism. Behn's argument and method of allegorical reading preserve the Scriptures from the appearance of contradicting the findings of modern science. Behn takes Copernicus's part, she says humbly, only "as far as a Woman's reasoning can go" (78); and she deploys a similar modesty formula, the one cited in my title, when she intervenes in learned debates about the Scriptures. "With all due Reverence and Respect to the Word of God," she writes, "I hope I may be allowed to say, that the design of the Bible was not to instruct Mankind in Astronomy, Geometry, or Chronology, but in the Law of God" (79). Neither of Behn's modesty formulas fully hides the audacity of her undertaking, for despite repeated assertions that she is venturing to say "nothing but from good Authority" (85), her way of citing authority produces something she is quite aware may be judged "too Bold" (85). What she sets out to do is not only to show that certain scriptural passages held to confute a Copernican cosmology can in truth be interpreted as supporting it; she also ventures to tell us what God's true "design" was in producing the Bible. His design, as she describes it in the passage quoted above, is an important but severely limited pedagogical one: not aiming to instruct his people in "Astronomy, Geometry, or Chronology," God, as Behn describes him performing his authorial act, focused solely on teaching his readers his law, to "lead us to Eternal Life; and the Spirit of God has been so condescending to our Weakness, that through the whole Bible, when anything of that kind [that is, pertaining to science] is mentioned, the Expressions are always turned to fit our Capacities, and to fit the common Acceptance, or Appearances of things to the Vulgar" (79).

Her account of God's authorial design draws an uncanny line of resemblance between his verbal practices and those she describes as governing Fontenelle's cosmological dialogues as well as her own work as a translator. Recall the passage quoted earlier in which she professes to have translated her source closely except when "I was necessitated to add a little" in order to make the work understood, in order to translate the esoteric, that is, into something exoteric. To Fontenelle, she ascribes exactly the same aim of turning his expressions to "fit the Capacities" of the vulgar reader: his "Design," she writes, is to treat the astronomical part of "Natural Philosophy in a more familiar Way than any other hath done, and to make every body understand him" (77). She seems highly self-conscious about the fact that such translation entails kinds of "turning" or troping that may have serious intellectual consequences.[23] Indeed, immediately after stating her own aim to give us the "true meaning of the Author," she acknowledges that her work may require accommodations to the reader: "I was necessitated to add a little in some places" so that the book could be understood. The examples she offers are not self-evidently supportive of her claim, however: one example is of how she added a Latin word that *differs* from what English readers might ordinarily have expected; the second example is of how she has "retained" a French word rather than anglicizing its orthography or finding an English equivalent. Significantly, both of her examples of the translator's ostensibly truthful and helpful art consist of words connoting kinds of *turning;* both call attention to the translator's learning—over and beyond what she read in her source text—and to her creativity.

Her first example of what she as translator has added to her original is the word "axis"; the second is the French word *tourbillion.* In the case of "axis," she has indeed added a word to Fontenelle's French; when he describes the moon as turning "sur elle-même," for instance (Second "Entretien," ed. A. Calame, 54), Behn writes that the moon "turns upon her own Axis" (114). She repeatedly adds this foreign but not French word, which, as she explains, "is Axle-Tree in English, which I did not think so proper a Word, in a Treatise of this nature; but 'tis what is generally understood by every Body" (76). Her second example is even more perplexing because, as I noted, it shows her not adding but keeping a French word used by Fontenelle. This word was "very uneasie to me," she writes (76); it is "Tourbillion ["Tourbillon" in Fontenelle's text], which signifies a Whirl-wind, but Monsieur Des Chartes understands it in a more general sense, and I call it a Whirling; the Author hath given a very good Definition of it, and I need say no more, but that I retain the Word unwillingly, in regard of what I have said in the beginning of this Preface" (here she is evidently referring to her earlier comment that most translators avoid printing a French word in an English text "till use has rendered it more familiar to us" [75]).

This passage tortuously explaining and justifying her procedure with words connoting "turning" in a text that argues for recognizing the turning motions of the moon and the earth suggests that the practice of translation itself involves constant negotiations, on the translator's part, between the needs of the reader, on the one hand, and the demands of the original text on the other. Because no single "rule" of translation governs all of Behn's decisions about language, she herself is involved in a constant "whirling," we might say, between her source (and other authorities such as Descartes) and her readers. In this whirling, the question of the translator's agency and hence her degree of creativity is always problematic, as Behn suggests through formulations balancing active and passive aspects: "I was necessitated to add a little." Who or what is the higher authority invoked here but also left curiously unspecified?

Behn's persona in her preface is dramatically complex; she wishes, she confesses, she describes herself as being in difficult situations without hope of rescue: "If one endeavours to make [a French text] English Standard, it is no Translation. If one follows their Flourishes and Embroideries, it is worse than French tinsel" (76). Nonetheless, Behn's persona moves on, turning and mediating among alternatives: French and English at the beginning of the preface; and the Copernican and the Ptolemaic systems in the treatise's second (longer) part, which, as I have suggested, also engages with an opposition between religious fundamentalists, on the one hand, and (by implication) atheists or "pagans," on the other. From these oppositions she constructs a defense of allegorical reading and, by implication, of allegorical writing too as a via media among extremes.

Her preface works from beginning to end to ally the practice of translation to the dynamic epistemology of the new astronomy and its accompanying implications for the social order. In Christa Knellwolf's succinct formulation, "the major threat of the new theory, related to the dissolution of a single perspective and the subsequent impossibility of imagining a universe with the earth as its centre and rationale[,] . . . went hand-in-hand with changes in social order"; among these changes was "the perception of women's role in the propagation of knowledge."[24] Behn allegorizes a new role for women in general, and for the female translator in particular, by suggesting that the traditional relation between sun and moon, whereby "the Moon receives her Light from the Sun, which she restores again by Reflection" (83), is supplemented, in the Copernican system, by a more dynamic relation between moon and earth than has heretofore been acknowledged. Adherents of both astronomical systems agree, Behn writes, that "the Moon is the nearest Planets [*sic*] to the Earth, and subservient to it, to enlighten it, during the Night, in Absence of the Sun" (83). However, Behn's description of the moon makes its quality of subservience less and less visible. Indeed, she construes the moon as mysterious: its nature, movements, and powers are not yet fully known even to those who accept Copernicus's view of the universe. The moon becomes, in Behn's prefatory essay, an allegorical emblem for the scientific project understood as a quest to find, see, and understand that which exists but is not yet known: "[T]he Moon has other strange Effects, not only on the Earth it self, but upon all the living Creatures that inhabit it; many of them are invisible, and as yet unknown to Mankind" (83).

What are the moon's "effects" on "unknown" creatures? How might such effects be understood in relation to those effects that are "most apparent" but nonetheless unpredictable? The moon, whose powers are always relational, with respect both to the sun and to the earth, plays a key role both in Behn's preface and in Fontenelle's night-time dialogues; in her preface the moon figures not only the as-yet-unknown but also the translator's mediating role, with its potential for producing new knowledge rather than simply reflecting or conveying it according to the translator's conventionally subservient role in the universe of discourse.[25]

Fontenelle's dialogues gender the emergent domain of science as masculine while figuring the audience for a popular science as female. In this figuration, however, as Knellwolf rightly insists, "woman was not simply a figure for ignorance, any more than man was simply a figure for knowledge. Women occupied an ambivalent mediating role, and consequently were not entirely powerless."[26] In her own formulation, Knellwolf moves from discussing a textual figure of "woman" to discussing "women" who had the power to interpret "the figure of the marchioness in much more positive terms" than Fontenelle implies. Knellworth infers the existence of such historical readers both from her knowledge of French salon culture and from Fontenelle's addition in 1687 of a sixth "entretien" that seeks to stabilize the highly fluid relation between the marquise and the philosopher in the first five dialogues. The new dialogue shows the philosopher "no longer playfully patronizing" his female interlocutor but instead "demonstrating his superior authority."[27] Behn did not include this sixth dialogue in her version, perhaps because she did not see it in time or perhaps because it did not suit her purposes.

These arguably include complicating the boundaries that usually separate different types of textual authority. She presents God, Fontenelle, and herself as writers who all advance translation as a mediating—but also, potentially, socially leveling—activity requiring labors of interpretative reading. Translation, whether of classical or biblical texts, made materials heretofore readable by only a few available to the many. Opponents of biblical translation, of course, saw this as a key political as well as epistemological problem. The many might (mis)interpret translated texts in politically disruptive ways. Exploring different kinds of readers' ability to confer meaning and value on a variety of writerly projects including God's, Behn insists that she intends nothing unconventional and certainly "no Reflection on Religion by this Essay"; she leaves the political significance of her writing finally to the reader to assess. If her translation of Fontenelle is "approved of by the World," she may "hereafter venture to publish somewhat [that may] be more useful to the Publick" (85).

Her preface makes some surprising claims on behalf of vulgar readers, especially but not only those females who are represented (inadequately, in Behn's view) by Fontenelle's figure of an ignorant but curious Marquise. Behn's argument is tricky, however, in its political implications because she does concede an "esoteric" dimension—and hence a livelihood for the learned elite—to those parts of the Bible that deal with things "material to the Salvation of Mankind" but that do not deal with matters "indifferent," such as astronomy, geometry, and chronology. The problem is that her own analysis of the latter parts as "allegorical" makes the distinction between critical and indifferent matters in the Bible hard to grasp. Although she concludes her biblical exegesis with a pious bow to the authority of the learned and of the established church, she has herself asserted precisely the kind of allegorical reading she mentions, apparently disapprovingly, as a necessary product of the "Age" in which she lives: "We live in an Age, wherein many believe nothing contained in that holy Book, others turn it into Ridicule: Some use it only for Mischief, and as a Foundation and Ground for Rebellion: Some keep close to the Literal Sense, and others give the Word of God only that Meaning and Sense that pleases their own Humours, or suits best their present Purpose and Interest" (85).

Behn, I contend, belongs in that latter group, on the evidence of what she actually does with passages of Scripture. Her preface implies that giving the word of God a sense that pleases the humors of those who prefer Copernicus to Ptolemy is a relatively small price to pay to keep such people within the pale of religion at all. If there appears to be any contradiction between the divine words and what Behn regards as true science, the former, she decrees, shall be read as allegorical. She illustrates this point by choosing and interpreting, among others, a scriptural passage (from Psalm 19) about the sun that others had cited in support of a Ptolemaic theory of the universe: "In them hath he set a Tabernacle for the Sun, which is as a Bridegroom coming out of his Chamber; and rejoices as a strong Man to run his Race." Behn states that it is "most plain" that these words are "Allegorical": "Does not the Word *Set* impart stability, Fixdness and Rest, as much as the Words *run his Race*, and *come forth of his Chamber*, do signifie motion or turning round; Do not the Words *Tabernacle* and *Chamber* express Places of Rest and Stability? And why may not I safely believe, that this makes for the Opinion of Copernicus, as well as for that of Ptolemy? For the Words of the Scriptures favour one Opinion as much as the other" (82). Her technique of reading Scripture here (re)presents the Bible as agnostic on, indifferent to, sublimely undecided about the opposition between Ptolemaic and Copernican universes and, by implication, ideas about the male as active rather than passive.

Her strategy of reading the Bible as neither proving nor disproving either major theory of the universe contrasts strikingly with the use of Scripture to support a single correct view that we find in many of her major opponents' writing, both the representative Catholic she names (the Jesuit mathematician Father Andreas Tacquet) and the conservative English Protestants whom she tactfully does not name (among them, for instance, Alexander Ross, author of *The New Planet No Planet: or the Earth no Wandering Star, Except in the Wandering Heads of Galileans*, 1646). She uses Scripture to open a space for entertaining new hypotheses while remaining nominally faithful to the Bible's authoritative spirit if not its letter. She aims at saving the appearances of the national English religion while also delimiting its truths, or truth claims, into an area clearly separate from those ruled by empirical science. Although her discussion of the Bible is never overtly skeptical, her preface moves away from orthodoxy in some of the ways her poems do; consider, for example, her "paraphrase" of the Lord's Prayer, which elaborates as follows on the line "Lead us not into Temptation": "But if without some Sin we cannot move, / May mine proceed no higher than to love; /And may thy vengeance be the less severe, / Since thou hast made the object lov'd so fair" (*Works*, 1:171–74). The sin, the paraphrase suggests, is not really a sin at all, and the prose commentary works similarly to suggest that it is not really a sin or an error to believe in a view of the universe that appears to be contradicted by Scripture. Behn's reading works to distance us from the idea of the Scripture as God's voice and to stress instead the text's status as a material object. She lets us know that she has consulted "the best Edition of the English Bible, which is printed in a small Folio by Buck, in Cambridge" (83). Glossing Joshua's command that the sun should "stand still," she remarks that a marginal note in the English Bible puts an "asterism" by the word "stand" to inform even the non-Hebrew speaking reader that the original verb is "to be silent": "if it be so in the Hebrew, *be thou silent* makes as much for the Motion of the Earth, according to Copernicus, as for the Motion of the sun according to Ptolemy" (83).

Behn's prefatory argument could be paraphrased as follows: Render unto God the things that are his; by all means keep the things in the Bible that pertain to really important theological matters—but do not mind me if as a mere woman I expound a theory of allegory that blurs the line between the parts of the Bible that concern salvation—the Sun/ Son "moving," as it were, in his work for mankind—versus "indifferent" parts that concern astronomy, geometry, or chronology—matters that show the Sun/Son at rest (as it were) in his tabernacle. At those times the moon comes out to illustrate a different mode of enlightenment, one that calls the distinction between literal and figurative language into question. In her theological views as in her practice of translation, then, Behn appears to adopt a certain "latitude" as she quietly turns others' interpretations of biblical passages to serve her own purposes. Under the rubric of modesty and moderation, her text actively explores passages of Scripture that have generated doubt in previous readers; she mentions, for instance, Bishop Vitalis's perplexity about how Solomon could have begotten a son at the age of eleven as recorded in 1 Kings 14:21 (81). Citing authority selectively while also demonstrating her method of reading allegorically, she insists, in a perfectly orthodox way, that "the Letter of the Scripture does often kill, but the Spirit enlivens" (81). The Spirit, however, as her text figures it, seems quite often to be turning or whirling in an unorthodox direction.

Her way of reading the Bible to suit her purposes is not dissimilar from her way of reading Fontenelle's secular text. With the latter, however, she feels free, as she does not with the Bible, openly to voice disagreement. The meanings of her criticism may, however, be partly hidden. For all her interest in expanding the cultural territory of those readers traditionally seen as "vulgar," she is also and sometimes contradictorily interested in creating new secret societies, new elites limned in multiple media including spoken, handwritten, printed, and theatrically performed words. We have seen Behn criticizing her French original by calling Fontenelle a "pagan" even as she slyly changes his text—as Line Cottegnies puts it—to make his "covert skepticism more radical."[28] While it is hard to know what degree of prudence and/or irony may be lurking at certain points in her preface, it seems clear that her distancing gestures are part of a dialectic that includes also expressions of admiration: "The whole book is very unequal," she remarks; the "first, fourth, and the beginning of the fifth Discourses are incomparably the best" (77). The reader is thus enticed to proceed into the translation proper, to see for herself or himself what the "incomparable" parts look like (compared to the others). One of Behn's most interesting extended passages of mixed but enticing judgment on her source occurs in her description of Fontenelle's decision to introduce the Marquise in order to aid in his "design" of rendering science "familiar" to "everybody":

> For this End, he introduceth a Woman of Quality as one of the Speakers in these five Discourses, whom he feigns never to have heard of any such thing as Philosophy before. How well he hath performed his Undertaking you will best judge when you have perused the Book: But if you would know before-hand my Thoughts, I must tell you freely [note the paradoxical language of forced freedom], he hath failed in his Design; for endeavoring to render this part of Natural Philosophy familiar, he hath turned it into Ridicule; he hath pushed his wild Notion of the Plurality of Worlds to that heighth of Extravagancy, that he most certainly will confound those Readers, who have not Judgment and Wit to distinguish between what is truly solid (or at least, probable) and what is trifling and airy; and there is no less Skill and Understanding required in this, than in comprehending the whole Subject he treats of. And for his Lady Marquiese, he makes her say a great many very silly things, tho' sometimes she makes Observations so learned, that the greatest Philosophers in Europe could make no better. His way of Arguing is extremely fine. (77)

This passage holds up a contradictory mirror to Fontenelle's lady: she is at once made to say "silly" things and appears as a font of "learned" observations better than any made by Europe's male philosophers. Behn herself, preemptively shaping the reader's judgment, models a female reader who is skeptical of, indeed resistant to, the author's design even as she appreciates and appropriates it.

Neither a faithful handmaid to Fontenelle's text (in Dryden's terms, a maker of "metaphrase") nor a rebellious deviator from it (in Dryden's terms, an ambitious "imitator"), Behn may indeed fairly be called a translator, or reader, who paraphrases the original text—and who does so with richly paradoxical effects, reminding us that the root meaning of "paraphrase" is "saying-beside." Perhaps the best short way of describing Behn as a critical reader of Fontenelle and of many other male precursors, including Shakespeare and Ovid, from whom she borrowed extensively, is to think of her as entering into a quasierotic triangular relation not only with her source text but also with the new readers she hopes to gain through the work of translation. Behn's predecessor Katherine Philips had denounced "paraphrasers" as writers who exhibited a lack of modesty and fidelity toward the original they were claiming to translate.[29] Behn, it would seem, embraced the dubiously faithful role of the paraphraser—a moonlike role—partly because it encouraged a kind of translation in which the question of fidelity was never fully answered.

Notes

1. Eve Sanders, *Gender and Literacy on Stage in Early Modern England* (Cambridge: Cambridge University Press, 1998), 104.

2. Montaigne, *Essays*, trans. John Florio (London, 1603), sig A2ʳ.

3. See, for instance, Joseph Graham, ed., *Difference in Translation* (Ithaca, N.Y.: Cornell University Press, 1985); Yehudi Lindeman, "Translation in the Renaissance: A Context and a Map," *Canadian Review of Comparative Literature* 8.2 (1981): 204–16; and Glynn P. Norton, "Humanist Foundations of Translation Theory (1400–1450): A Study in the Dynamics of the Word," *Canadian Review of Comparative Literature* 8.2 (1981): 173–203. For further information on recent works dealing with women as translators, see Danielle Clarke, "The Politics of Translation and Gender in the Countess of Pembroke's *Antonie*," *Translation and Literature* 6. 2 (1997): n1.

4. See Clarke, "Politics of Translation," and also her *The Politics of Early Modern Women's Writing* (Harlow, U.K.: Longman, Pearson Education Imprints, 2001), 88–95. See also Douglas Robinson, "Theorizing Translation in a Woman's Voice," *Translator* 1.2 (1995): 153–75. His discussion of Behn on pp. 170–71 is interesting, but he errs in ascribing to Behn a bold "faithlessness" to her source text; the error arises because Robinson takes Fontenelle's "author's preface" to be Behn's original work.

5. Preface to *Ovid's Epistles, Translated by Several Hands* (1680), cited from *The Works of John Dryden*, ed. Edward N. Hooker and H. T. Swedenberg, Jr. (Berkeley: University of California Press, 1956), 1:114.

6. See "Defense of the Translation of the Psalms" and "On Translating: An Open Letter," in *Luther's Works*, ed. E. Theodore Bachmann (Philadelphia: Nulenberg Press, 1960), 35:177–223.

7. For Behn's biography, see Janet Todd, *The Secret Life of Aphra Behn*, (New Brunswick, N.J.: Rutgers University Press, 1977). For Behn's pen names, see M. Ferguson, "The Authorial Ciphers of Aphra Behn," in *The Cambridge Companion to English Literature, 1650–1740*, ed. Steven Zwicker (Cambridge: Cambridge University Press, 1998), 225–49.

8. *Works of John Dryden*, 119.

9. Elizabeth Spearing refers to Behn's "alleged ignorance of Latin," citing this passage; see "Aphra Behn: The Politics of Translation," in *Aphra Behn Studies*, ed. Janet Todd (Cambridge: Cambridge University Press, 1996), 155. See also Line Cottegnies, "Aphra Behn's French Translations," in *The Cambridge Compan-*

ion to Aphra Behn, ed. Derek Hughes and Janet Todd (Cambridge: Cambridge University Press, 2004), 221.

10. See Cottegnies's judgment that Behn's version of Fontenelle's *Entretiens* is "on the whole, very faithful" ("Aphra Behn's French Translations," 227). However, Cottegnies notes (227) that Behn "corrects" errors in its original and calls attention to one of those corrections (concerning the height of the atmosphere) in her preface.

11. Aphra Behn, *A Discovery of New Worlds*, in *The Works of Aphra Behn*, ed. Janet Todd (London: Willliam Pickering, 1993), 4:70–165. All quotations from Behn's version of Fontenelle and from her "Essay on Translated Prose" will be cited henceforth by page number in the text; this one comes from p. 76. For Fontenelle's original text, I have used the critical edition prepared by Alexandre Calame (Paris: Librairie M. Didier, 1966).

12. *Works of John Dryden*, 119.

13. Ibid.

14. See Clarke, "The Politics of Translation and Gender," 149–66.

15. Mary Baine Campbell, *Wonder and Science: Imagining Worlds in Early Modern Europe* (Ithaca, N.Y.: Cornell University Press, 1999), 144.

16. On Fontenelle's development as a scientist, see ibid. On the *Entretiens* as a "scientific romance," see Christa Knellwolf's important article "Women Translators and the Scientific Revolution," in *Translation and Nation: Towards a Cultural Politics of Englishness*, ed. Roger Ellis and Liz Oakley-Brown (Clevedon, U.K.: Multilingual Matters, Ltd., 2001) 65–119, esp. 87–91.

17. In the last decade of her life, her theatrical career stymied, Behn was forced to rely for her living on intermittent patronage and on what she could glean from those who printed her books. For her pleas to her publisher for money, see Todd, *Secret Life*, 324–25. Mary Ann O'Donnell suggests that Behn's translation was "rushed into print in competition with another translation," probably the one by Joseph Glanville printed in London in 1688. W. D. Knight had already published his translation, *A Discourse on the Plurality of Worlds*, in Dublin in 1687. See O'Donnell, *Aphra Behn: An Annotated Bibliography of Primary and Secondary Sources*, 2nd ed. (Burlington, Vt.: Ashgate, 2004), 216.

18. For discussions of Fontenelle's dialogue and its sources, see Nina Rattner Gelbart, introduction to *Conversations on the Plurality of Worlds*, trans. H. A. Hargreaves (Berkeley: University of California Press, 1990); Campbell, *Wonder and Science*, 143–49; Knellwolf, "Women Translators," esp. 86–102; and Erica Harth, "The 'véritables Marquises,'" in *Actes de Columbus: Racine, Fontenelle—Entretiens sur la pluralité des mondes, histoire et littérature: Actes du XXIe colloque de la North American Society for Seventeenth-Century French Literature, Ohio State University, Columbus, 6–8 avril 1989*, Biblio 17, 59, ed. Charles G. S. Williams (Paris: Papers on French Seventeenth Century Literature, 1990), 149–60.

19. Knellwolf, "Women Translators," 104.

20. See Louis Montrose, "The Work of Gender in the Discourse of Discoverie," *Representations* 33 (winter 1991): 1–41.

21. Quotations from John Milton, *Paradise Lost*, ed. Merritt Hughes, in *John Milton: Complete Poems and Major Prose* (New York: Odyssey, 1957), 5:268, 4:937.

22. Milton, *Paradise Lost*, 4:801–3.

23. I owe this observation about troping to a conversation with Jody Greene.

24. Knellwolf, "Women Translators," 96.

25. See ibid., 92, on Fontenelle's similar concern with whether translation from learned to popular representation modes might produce an "altogether different message."

26. Ibid., 101.
27. Ibid., 100.
28. Cottegnies, "Aphra Behn's French Translations," 229.
29. Katherine Philips, "Letter of Orinda to Poliarchus," September 17, 1663, cited in Robinson, "Theorizing Translation," 167.

Chapter 10

Female Curiosities: The Transatlantic Female Commonplace Book

Susan M. Stabile

Antiquities, or remnants of history, are when industrious persons, by an exact and scrupulous diligence and observations, out of monuments, names, words, proverbs, traditions, private records and evidences, fragments of stories, passages of books, that concern not story, and the like, preserve and recover somewhat from the deluge of time.

—*Francis Bacon,* De Augmentia Scientiae

She herself was a relic of the past!—and while the young hung with delighted attention, on her glowing and beautiful recitals of a by-gone age, and cherished deeply in their hearts, those lessons of wisdom, which had been the result of experience, the aged and middle-aged alike, were charmed with her eloquence.

—*Deborah Norris Logan's Obituary,* The Friend

The Curiosity Cabinet

Indian arrowheads and hatchets from Philadelphia's outlying pastures; an ancient iron coat of mail unearthed along the Susquehanna River banks; a sliver of William Penn's door frame at Pennsbury; a relic box comprised of wood fragments from Columbus's house in Haiti and from the mythical Treaty Elm under which Penn negotiated with the Lenape Indians; a bundle of Cherokee newspapers resisting Andrew Jackson's Indian removal policies; a transfer print of Nicolas Scull and George Heap's 1752 map of Philadelphia on white satin; a newspaper clipping recounting the oddity of Siamese twins; another announcing the October 1835 reappearance of Halley's comet of 1305; an engraving of the newly famous Fairmount Waterworks; pottery shards from a pre-Revolutionary punch bowl; wood chips from Charles II's arboreal hiding place during the Interregnum; a fireplace surround of colonial Dutch tile; George Washington's calling card; a dog-eared first edition of Benjamin Franklin's autobiography; a spring-loaded, gold snuffbox secreting a portrait of Napoleon beneath those of Maria Louisa and the king of Rome; an elaborate, miniature shell-work grotto; a random collection of old coins—these were some of the marvelous curiosities seen at Deborah Norris Logan's house at Stenton at the turn of the nineteenth century.

Antiquarian, belletrist, editor, and diarist, Deborah Norris Logan (1761–1839) was born in one century and grew old in another, outliving her parents, her siblings, her children, and most of her contemporaries by 1820.[1] As part of the elite class of Philadelphia Quakers that once governed the city, she was eagerly courted by local historians and archivists for her firsthand accounts of the Revolutionary War, the Continental Congress (which occasionally convened at her childhood home), and the "Founding Fathers." Logan frequently entertained local antiquarians in her library, where they "expatiated on old Books and papers and praised [her] industry in transcribing so much from them. . . . [they] discussed Characters and times by-past, and raked up from oblivion old anecdotes and things."[2] Local newspaper editors Robert Walsh (*National Gazette* [1819–36]) and Zachariah Poulson (*American Daily Advertiser* [1800–1840]) invited her frequent contributions on local history, political biography, and literary anecdotes. Fellow antiquarian John Fanning Watson consulted with her as he gathered information and advice for his romanticized *Annals of Philadelphia* (1830). As the first female member of the Historical Society of Pennsylvania, Deborah Logan contributed to the Penn Society's *Papers.* The Historical Society and other public archives doggedly solicited the treasure trove of manuscripts she hoarded at Stenton, including the voluminous correspondence between William Penn and his secretary, James Logan. After she carefully transcribed, annotated, and published the first of what was to be several volumes of this correspondence, Logan was requested as both a reader and an editor of forthcoming publications. As she remarks in her diary about the librarian and secretary of the American Philosophical Society: "This morning I rec'd a Book from my friend John Vaughan (an abridgment of the Life of Wm Penn) with a very polite and friendly note requesting that I would read it and offer any suggestions which I should think might improve another edition about to be undertaken . . . but really was ready to laugh at the thought of my poor judgment and slender information being in demand upon any occasion—and have wished that I really was the capable and intelligent person that they seem to take me for."[3] Despite her characteristic modesty, Deborah Norris Logan became one of the most illustrious female collectors, writers, and readers of the early national period.

At a time when public institutions for the preservation of American antiquities were proliferating (including the Philadelphia Athenaeum [c. 1814] and the Historical Society of Pennsylvania [c. 1824]), Deborah Logan purposefully established her home at Stenton as an anachronistic cabinet of curiosities.[4] As curiosity cabinets were both the European antecedents to public museums, on the one hand, and the temporary successors to the first museum attempts in the early United States, on the other, Logan's *Wunderkammer* was—and remains—a noteworthy anomaly.[5] Though equally active in the historic preservation and antiquarian movement of the early nineteenth century, Logan consciously resisted the Linnaean model of appropriating, classifying, and ordering collections for the "useful knowledge" of the general public. Instead she housed a random collection of objects, decorative arts, books, and manuscripts, which she generically described as "old-fashioned," "old-Style," or from the "Olden Times." Giving private, informal, and guided tours of what she fondly described as her "Old Establishment, so unlike modern things, the furniture, the China, the plate, the Library, all were objects of curiosity," Logan self-consciously pondered her responsibility in both preserving and manufacturing a uniquely American antiquity. "So unlike modern things," her house and its contents were relics with notable survival power. "My old castle," she writes, was "especially an object of great interest" to younger generations: "They had never seen Tiles placed round a chimney before. The clock, the magnifying Glass, the old dining room and its furniture, *all were objects of curiosity*."[6]

The early modern *Wunderkammer,* or cabinet of curiosity, was housed in the private closet of the collector, to be disclosed to intimate and select spectators. Typically comprised of natural (shells, fossils, botanical and mineral specimens) and artificial (coins, medals, antiquities, relics, and other manufactured objects) curiosities, the collection was considered a microcosm, encapsulating the phenomenal world in miniature.[7] As part of the imperial enterprise of the "Age of Discovery" when European explorers collected, cataloged, and displayed a variety of wonders from the New World, curiosity was both a human impulse and a material object; it was the "desire to see, learn, or possess rare, new, secret, or remarkable things, in other words, those things which have a special relationship with totality."[8] Taken out of their original contexts and placed in a new one, however, curiosities were inherently fragmented. Synecdochic in nature (or metonymic at best), such objects required the collector's classification and interpretation. In the absence of sufficient documentary evidence or provenance, then, curiosities were confirmed by texts. Objects became the subjects of reading and reading a coveted collection of wonders. Mimicking the early modern curiosity cabinet in her random, miscellaneous, and extensive collections, Deborah Logan accordingly established an analogous—and repeatable—experience of discovery: "Tho we did not find what we searched for" in an old trunk, she concedes, "yet I found many Books and fragments of Books which I was glad to *recover*." Another time she "*discovered* in a very old Box a treasure of Old Papers, many Books of Letters."[9] Unearthing these treasures, she rehearsed a kind of precolonial moment—the pleasure of discovery without the subsequent removal from her possession.

In this chapter I will examine how Deborah Logan's curiosity cabinet at Stenton provided a model for her transatlantic reading practices. Extracting excerpts from manuscript and printed sources in her commonplace books (one begun in 1808 and another containing collected pieces from 1815 to 1827) and diaries (1808–39), Logan enacted the imperial history of New World travel. Reading—as a complex process of curiosity, discovery, and collecting—was an act not only of exposing and investigating previously unknown knowledge but also of recovering and reframing what had been forgotten. A mode of exploration, reading (like curio collecting) was driven by curiosity—that "mark of discontent" that is "the sign of a pursuit of something beyond" what one has.[10] This same discontent, Logan remarked in 1828, epitomized the cultural backdrop for her reading: "What great changes have taken place. . . . It is hardly like the same world—for in addition to our own change from Colonies to Empire, and the astounding French Revolution which seemed for awhile to tear up the very foundations of society, there is the brazen career of Napoleon, and the astonish[ing] march of the human mind in various discoveries. Now this may be called perhaps the restless age of invention, activity, and innovation." Yet, "in this Country, I think, things and People, are forgotten (even unusually) soon."[11] In these passages Logan telescopes time into a single "Age of Discovery."

Blending the early modern discourse of wonder, awe, and marvel with the antiquarian passion of the nineteenth century, Logan pondered the place of the United States in world history. Looking to the past to explain the present, she sought evidence of a uniquely "American" antiquity for a country that was only a few decades old. Like the early modern traveler, the antiquarian was a kind of archaeologist who collected and studied past cultures in pieces. Her collection was based on randomness and variety; her method was to compile, compare, and contrast.[12] Taking fragments out of their original contexts, she documented objects with written (manuscripts and books), archaeological (ruins, relics, buildings, artifacts), and epigraphical (inscriptions on architecture and artifacts) evidence. Reading, therefore, was the material process of collecting and interpreting rarities.[13] The commonplace book and the diary were the cabinets for preservation and display.

The commonplace book, according to Samuel Johnson, was "a book in which things to be remembered are ranged under general heads."[14] Like curio collecting, commonplacing was topographical in scope and method.[15] As topoi (or "places in the mind" in Greek), commonplaces were imagined as metaphorical spaces (that is, cabinets) that gathered and arranged specific examples or *copia* (that is, fossils, botanical specimens, shells) under topical "heads" (that is, "Natural Curiosities"). Similar to curiosities, *copia* (including aphorisms, maxims, anecdotes, quotations, epigraphs, verse, and recipes) were collected for their variety, singularity, and abundance. They were taken out of their original contexts and given new significance when placed among other previously unrelated specimens.

Mixing Old and New World curiosities, Deborah Logan's red, leather-bound album (1808) situated information on Native Americans, William Penn, George Washington, Benjamin Franklin, and pre-Revolutionary female boycotts alongside Henry II's tomb at Fontevrand Abbey, Scottish travel writer James Bruce's Abyssinian travels, Italian explorer Giovanni Belzoni's excavations in Egypt, and British orientalist John Leyden's voyage to India. Lacking any apparent classification by topic, genre, or chronology, Logan's commonplace book highlights its compiler's selectivity. As its epigraph by Oliver Goldsmith states: "A [wo]man shews [her] Judgement in these Selections and [s]he may be often twenty years of [her] life cultivating that Judgement." The remainder of the book blends excerpts from American and European magazines (*New Monthly Magazine, New York Magazine,* the *Museum, Edinburgh Magazine)*; fair copies of Logan's own poems ("Recollections to My Husband," "Napoleon," "To Albanus George Logan, Esq.") and two by her cousin and fellow belletrist Hannah Griffitts ("The Female Patriots" and "To Sylvia"); and romantic verse by Samuel Taylor Coleridge ("Punishment's Prisons"), Percy Bysshe Shelley ("Paradise Regained"), and Felicia Hemans ("The Wreck").

The second commonplace book (1815–27), while including extracts of published works, mostly contains copies of Logan's own poetry. It includes "The Gazette's Reviewed" (1819), a poetic list of grievances against the politics of "the Democratic Press," which she "intended to have been inserted in the Village Record." She recopied "Recollections to My Husband" from her previous commonplace book (and diary) and added an array of generically titled "Sonnets," including one each on aging (1815), death (1821), and spring (1827). She composed a poem in response to reading Francis Bacon, "Lines Suggested by a Passage in Lord Bacon's Works." She included one of her odes to Washington,

"President of the United States"; a transcription of "Lines said to be written on the Wall of an apartment in the Philadelphia Prison where the Author [Charles Pryor] was confind"; and poems on Cleopatra, Napoleon, and the fourteenth-century Scottish king Robert the Bruce. Taken together, Deborah Logan's commonplace books illustrate her readerly tastes while allowing us, as readers, to visit the transatlantic places that once occupied her mind.

Her diaries, read as a kind of compendium to the commonplace book, form another material collection. A collection of writings written almost daily for over thirty years, these cumulative texts followed the antiquarian condensation of synchronic time.[16] Recording the present while nostalgically revisiting the past, Logan's diaries amplify her fascination with antiquities: "There is no describing the strange interest I take in antiquities. Life is full of amusement to a person of my turn of mind." In another diary entry she muses, "I still live in times that are past more than in the present." Beginning a new diary in June 1824 (having run out of pages in the previous one), she remarks: "it is not a new Work I am beginning but only a continuation of an Old one. Yet, I have a strange predilection for Old things: the New Book in which I now begin to write does not please me half so well as did the Old one which I have just filled and consigned to a shelf in the closet, besides my other 'Works.'"[17] Dating each entry, copying prose and verse from printed sources, composing her own poetry, and pasting newspaper clippings and cabinet pictures onto the carefully numbered pages, Logan created a collection much like a curiosity cabinet of Old and New World wonders. While each entry—as a separate object—has resonance, it is the accretion of and interdependence among these textual fragments that establish the diary as a collection. Each of the volumes, in turn, can be read as part of a larger whole. The diary as a collection becomes a collection of diaries, for it "relies upon the box, the cabinet, the cupboard, the seriality of shelves. It is determined by these boundaries."[18]

The diary likewise marks the boundaries of the diarist herself. According to sociologist Jean Baudrillard, "a given collection is made up of a succession of terms, but the final term must always be the person of the collector."[19] The collection, in other words, is an integration of objects and the compiler. Explaining the associative power of things, Logan explains: "I love to look upon objects that have met their eyes who are gone, the characters endeared to me by reading their integrity and value in the unintentional Records of themselves which they leave behind."[20] Given the diary's autobiographical function and material aesthetic, its entries serve as a metonym for the diarist, who expresses herself in parts. As Logan remarks, "I [read] passages out of my older Diary, they all flatter me by listening to these Books with interest."[21] Like all collections, Logan's diaries are what museum theorist Susan Pearce calls in another context the cumulative "acts of material autobiographies."[22] Diaries, then, are a mode of self-collection and display.[23]

Marked by and marking our lives, a collection thus palpably embodies the collector's taste and judgments. More personal than reading lists culled from a book catalog, a subscription library, or probate records, the commonplace books and diaries present a composite sketch of Deborah Logan as a reader (as well as a compiler) of "collections": miscellanies, anthologies, and gift books (collected verse and prose);[24] book reviews (collected interpretations);[25] almanacs (collected ephemera); periodical essays (collected manners and opinions);[26] anecdotes (collected characters);[27] letters (collected emotions);[28] biographies (collected lives);[29] newspapers and magazines (collected events);[30] and travel books (collected places).[31] Emphasizing their material resemblance to the wonder cabinet, moreover, many of these compilations were aptly titled "Cabinets," "Museums," "Repositories," or "Collections."[32] The literary objects they preserved were subsequently called "fragments," "relics," "pieces," or "selections," named either for their splintered form or for their extraction from previous texts. Occasionally reading other genres, Deborah Logan had a distinct predilection for reading other collections.

Though elite men and women alike kept diaries and commonplace books in the early national period—as part of their polite education, in preparation for coffeehouse or salon conversation, as an extension of reading circles, and/or as a method of scribal publication in their literary coteries—these genres, I would argue, are distinctly gendered.[33] Their fragmented form and content materially mimic the shape of women's lives. "I have not had a single hour alone in the Library to myself for several days," complains Deborah Logan in a representative diary entry; "housewifely business, a little Gardening, . . . and today preparing some little delicacies for the table (my husband expecting a few friends to dine with him tomorrow) have constituted my employments." She writes in another, "By myself very agreeably in the Library, the rest of the family being in town."[34] Even her obituary testifies to the domestic constraints on the female reader: "her well-regulated mind, conscientiously and faithfully attended to the performance of every duty—even to the minutest relations of domestic life. . . . In order that her literary labours might not interfere with the occupations of everyday life, she was for many years in the habit of rising long before day, and employing the early morning hours" in reading, transcribing, and writing. Her evening hours, conversely, were spent in collective reading activities as she recited to her domestic help and female relatives in the parlor or dining room.[35] A woman's diary or commonplace book, like her leisure time, captured stolen moments. However, if anthropologist James Clifford is correct in his assertion that "collecting has long been a strategy for the deployment of a possessive self, culture, and authenticity" in Western society, then women such as Deborah Logan explored texts as means of intellectual development and cultural independence.[36]

Independently maintaining her cabinet of curiosities at Stenton, Deborah Logan consequently became a local curiosity herself. She was, as one contemporary wrote, "a relic of the past." Though curiosity, as Barbara Benedict argues, was particularly transgressive for women during the long eighteenth century, transforming them from curious subjects into curious objects, Logan's status as a "relic" legitimated her as an antiquarian and a collector. Antiquarianism, as much of the contemporary literature attested, was largely considered a gentlemanly pursuit in the eighteenth and early nineteenth centuries. An extension of the Grand Tour, it was part of the upper-class male's breeding and education. However, frequently satirized as eccentric pedants anachronistically immersed in the useless rubble of the past and peeping toms peering into antique vessels, male antiquarians were dismissed as superannuated curiosities.[37] Aged women in the early Republic, on the other hand, confounded these gender stereotypes. Revered for their links to the past, they were living repositories of cultural memory, responsible for transmitting information to future generations.[38]

As a well-respected antiquarian, Deborah Logan not only played an informal role in the public management of the Loganian Library in Philadelphia[39] but also maintained a sizable library of books, periodicals, and newspapers in her home for the use of her social circle. "We had reference to Books, as so many were about us," she writes, "and with reading sometimes aloud, and our work, we passed the day agreeably."[40] She continuously lent books to male and female neighbors alike. "Old Absalom Williams," she notes in one diary entry, "has become a great reader and gets Books frequently from me, came down on that account to day. . . . I brought him other Books in exchange." "Folios, Millers Gardeners Dictionary, and Hills Eden," she comments in another, "delighted Elisabeth, with the 'Solitary Gardener' and others of our old books." Logan also saw her book and manuscript collection as a gift to posterity. She brought guests "up into the Library, talked to them of Books, shewed them things that I thought would interest them, and endeavored to impart some idea of the true pleasure which is received by the Mind from the love of elegant literature, and the consciousness that we are advancing in knowledge. I would rather be instrumental, tho in a small degree, in forming such a taste in an ingenious Youth." Momentarily concerned about accusations of pedantry, Logan concludes, "I hope [they] won't think I am a Blue Stocking."[41] Whether as a bluestocking or an antiquarian, Logan earned status as a colonial relic in the early Republic that only served to pique people's curiosity.

* * *

Shaped like a curiosity cabinet, the remainder of this essay will bring readers inside Deborah Logan's literary collections, which I divide into three parts: "The Ruin," "The Monument," and "The Relic." Each section—as material fragments and romantic commonplaces—combines a brief explication of one of Logan's poems, which I cull from her commonplace book (1815–27), along with a gloss on her antiquarian reading methods detailed in her diaries. The first part, "The Ruin," examines the analogy of reading and tourism through Logan's interest in the Egypt mania in the early nineteenth century. It presents, in other words, the act of reading as an act of discovery. Considering the antiquarian's use of epigraphical evidence in the second segment, "The Monument," I introduce Napoleon's tomb at St. Helena as a metaphor for the next phase in Logan's reading process: collection and transcription. Much like the antiquarian's collection of funereal inscriptions, note-taking, I argue, is a form of inscription. The monument (like the commonplace book) receives inscriptions (like transcribed extracts) that not only preserve the past but also arrest the reader's attention for future contemplation. The third section titled "The Relic" examines Logan's epic poem on the Scottish soldier and knight James Douglas's fourteenth-century pilgrimage to the Holy Land with Sir Robert the Bruce of Scotland's heart. Since transcribed texts, like corporeal relics, are partial, they require supplementation, or annotation—the final step in Logan's reading process. Linking historical annotation with personal genealogy, she ultimately writes herself into her collection. Annotation, then, is an autobiographical act, a mode of textual authority that leaves the reader's final mark on the texts she collects.

The Ruin

Deborah Logan begrudgingly remarks in her diary of March 1828: "this afternoon [I] had a visitor who entertained me with his Travels in Egypt. If I were a young man I certainly would visit the remoter shores of the Mediterranean, and *see* the Old World for myself. I don't think any bodys description can make you take in things quite like *seeing*." Wishing to see Egypt before the European treasure hunters began decimating tombs, unwrapping mummies, and breaking statues for unwieldy souvenirs during the collecting craze following Napoleon's plunder, Logan imagined herself as a romantic tourist.[42] She immersed herself in travel books, which transported her to the Egyptian landscape: "I have been 'In the Land of Egypt, and the eternal Pyramids' all afternoon," she writes in her diary. After taking a short break, she "continue[s] to Travel in Egypt. . . . The Ruins of the Works of art, are more imposing there, than in other countries." An unexplored landscape until opened by the reader, the travel book created the experience of seemingly unmediated observation. Logan thus employs what the theorist Michel de Certeau calls "the traveling eye"—the meditative or imaginary flights taking off from a few words on the page. "Readers are travelers," he explains; "they move across lands belonging to someone else, like nomads poaching their way across fields they did not write, despoiling the wealth of Egypt to enjoy it themselves."[43] Touring through books, readers in the early Republic moved between typographic spaces, creating and taking away meaning often unintended by the author. Inside and outside the text at once, the reader/tourist collected and domesticated knowledge of the foreign. They scribbled marginalia in books and copied extracts into commonplace books, annotating what appeared to be curious or obscure. The extracted transcriptions and imposed glosses, like cultural ruins carried home as souvenirs, accordingly enacted the fragmented experience of the tourist in a foreign land. The table of contents, commonplace heads, and footnotes that structured the book established a new frame of reference. Commonplacing, therefore, was a colonial practice of discovery.

As a metaphorical form of tourism, commonplacing was also a female practice, as Deborah Logan illustrates in her poem "The Ornaments of a Fashionable Piece of Furniture Suggests a Moral Lesson from the History of Cleopatra." Exchanging travel literature's familiar trope of the passive, feminine landscape as an unravaged virgin or suckling mother for that of the curious, female reader, the poem presents the domesticated spoils of Egypt in the dining room of a fictional female collector named Celia.[44] Much as did actual women of the early American Republic, Celia collected fashionable Empire-style objects, which boasted artificial ruins in such Egyptian motifs as sarcophagi, obelisks, scrolls, lions' and dogs' paw feet, lyre splats, and winged and caryatid supports. Lounging at the room's periphery on her ottoman throughout the poem,[45] Celia adopts the picturesque gaze of the romantic tourist, who first scans the scene at a distance, only to focus on its constituent parts: "It comprehends an extensive tract at each sweep. It examines *parts*, but never descends to *particles*."[46]

Celia accordingly looks across the room at the enormous and ornamental sideboard. Probably part of the American Empire or British regency period (1800–1825), the sideboard would have a wooden or marble top, which in the particular case of this poem, sat upon monumental pedestals in the shape of Egypt's most illustrious queen, Cleopa-

Figure 10.1. Sideboard similar to the one Logan describes in her poem "The Ornaments of a Fashionable Piece of Furniture Suggests a Moral Lesson from the History of Cleopatra." Mahogany, mahogany veneer, tulip, and white pine. Created by Joseph B. Barry, Philadelphia, Pa., 1808–15. Courtesy, Winterthur Museum.

tra. (See Figure 10.1.) The emblazoned queen grew in Celia's gaze until the image attained human—and then gigantic—proportions:[47]

> She lookd—for straight before her view
> (And as she lookd, the Image grew)
> From where the Dead in mummied state,
> Supports the massive Side-boards Plate,
> With graceful step and Regal mien
> Issued the form of Egypts Queen.

The tabletop on which Celia's household luxuries are displayed rests—like the bounty of an empire—on Cleopatra's shoulders. The queen's monumental body is incorporated into the body of the sideboard.[48]

More than a collector of Egyptiana, Celia is also a reader. As the poem opens, she is seen reading from Lord Byron's "potent page." Perhaps she is perusing his travel poem "Stanzas Written in Passing the Ambracian Gulf," in which he is reminded that "on these waves, for Egypt's queen, / The ancient world was won and lost." Or perhaps she is contemplating the fifth canto of *The Age of Bronze*, in which Lord Byron laments: "Egypt! For whose all dateless tombs arose / Forgotten Pharaohs from their long repose, / . . . While the dark shades of forty ages stood / Like startled giants by Niles's famous flood." Or maybe she bristles at his sardonic remarks about Cleopatra in *Don Juan*. Whatever the text, Celia quickly loses interest and begins daydreaming about Cleopatra. Repeating Byron's biases against Cleopatra in particular and the romantic travel narrative's orientalist depiction of Egypt in general, Celia sees Egypt as a luxurious, excessive, decadent, and calamitous female. The poem reduces the entire culture to ruins, while at the same time elevating Cleopatra to gigantic proportions: she is not just a woman but also an empire. However, aspiring women, the poem warns, like empires, eventually fall. The poem's speaker, then, uses the trope of antiquarian travel to moralize on female virtue. Playing with the notion of the ruin—as a material fragment resulting from imperial wars and treasure hunters, on the one hand, and as spoiled reputation, on the other—it ultimately collects Cleopatra as a ruin, a landmark bearing a lesson.

Domesticating Cleopatra's drive for empire, the poem underscores the parallels between Cleopatra's famous banquet for Marc Antony and Celia's Egyptian-inspired sideboard. Authors from Plutarch to Shakespeare, Deborah Logan well knew, had mythologized Cleopatra's four-day feast for its attendant material splendor: how she ornamented the walls with purple and gold tapestries, how she cultivated the floor until it was strewn knee-deep in roses, how she crushed and imbibed one of her pearl earrings in a goblet of wine, and how she gave away at the party's end the lavish gold and bejeweled dinner service. Most noteworthy, however, is the poem's reiteration of the queen's imperial(ist) body displayed at her original and Celia's subsequent feasts:

> The cearments burst, her limbs enfold
> With fine-wrought-fabric's drop'd with gold
> Her head, a beaming circlet graced.
> Her feet, with pearly sandals laced.
> All India's gems and Persia's art
> Were borrowed Splendour to impart.

As a mummy, Cleopatra's ornamented corpse signifies the multivalent meanings of consumption as both the ingestion of food and the acquisition of foreign luxuries. Given the booming consumer market for mummies flourishing in Europe from 1815 through the 1850s (that is, people literally consumed mummy for medicinal purposes and the promise of longevity), Cleopatra is a literal manifestation of the ruin: ancient material once literally alive.[49] Better than any tourist attraction, the mummy offered a new kind of spectacle and display: "it *embodied* the past in which it had participated, and to which it could offer [direct] access."[50] More palpable than the vicarious thrills gleaned from a travel book, the mummy was a material personification of antiquity.

The poem fittingly ends with Celia's internalization of the romantic tourist's gaze, which is preoccupied with decline, fragmentation, decay, and ruin. Identifying with Cleopatra and regretting her own decadent ways, Celia saves her reputation from ruin. Her view of the sideboard, in the end, becomes didactic: domesticating the scene of foreign travel and collection, Celia no longer seeks the fashionable, the curious, or the exotic. Instead she transforms the pearl that Cleopatra crushed, dissolved, and drank with vinegar into what the poem's speaker calls the "pearl of Contentment." The conservative rhetoric of domesticity as the panacea to excessive (that is, feminine) consumption at the poem's conclusion might seem at first glance to place the female collector—as tourist and reader—snugly back in her own dining room. However, when read within the larger context of Deborah Logan's commonplace book, the poem takes on another meaning. Placed near her transcriptions of other poems on Egyptian travel (including Thomas Campbell's "Belzoni's Address to a Mummy" and Felicia Heman's "A Traveller at the Source of the Nile"), the artificial ruin of Cleopatra's mummy on Celia's sideboard embodies the well-rehearsed topoi of consumption and digestion. As Ann Moss points out, commonplacing was metaphorized as "a well-stocked larder, with all sorts of goods and raw ingredients piled together at random within their separate storage areas, ready to furnish forth a beautifully appointed table."[51] Similarly the sideboard was a topos for the collection of commonplaces, while the banquet signified their elegant display. Describing her reading in gastronomic metaphors, Logan approximates the pleasures of Cleopatra's banquet: "I am famished as to Intellectual food"; "Amidst interruptions of every kind," it is impossible "to produce volumes of clear narration or well-digested thoughts"; "The recipe I suppose, for such a state, is to Read—Good Books of Course" and then "chew the cud of sweet and bitter thoughts."[52] A physical process much like digestion, internalizing extracts was a kind of intellectual buffet, and for the tourist, it was a movable feast.

The Monument

Having read more than three published biographies of Napoleon by November 1832, Deborah Logan became fixated on the meteoric rise and fall of this peculiar cultural curiosity.[53] "He was indeed an extraordinary Being that has passed like a fiery and sublime meteor across the horizon of our time," she writes. As comets remained superstitious and portentous curiosities to many in the early Republic, she believes that "Astrologers can calculate the nativities that have been . . . and I should like to know what were the Aspects of the Planets and which was Lord of the Ascendent" at the hour of Napoleon's birth. Surely, she concludes, "some Star of Malignant influence predominated." Without reliable astrological predictions, Logan relied instead on her antiquarian methods of collecting the past, approaching Napoleon's biographies as a form of (re)collection: "I look at what is written on the Subject of Napolean and his wars now as materials for future historians, it is not immediately after such a period that things are known and understood exactly as they were, Time develops many facts, and gives to objects their true bearing." Preserving history, material collections, she contends, ensure an archival mode of revisiting the past and, more important, reconsidering past preconceptions. On reading a biography, or collected life, of Napoleon, Logan writes: "It will be the fault of the Reader if he is not wiser and better for reading the Book. It has arrested many of my prejudices." Despite what she calls Napoleon's "inordinate ambition, the unjustifiable invasion of Spain, the Campaign of Russia, the horrors of conscription, and so many of his acts that it is needless to enumerate them," she admits, "yet I own I have parted with many of my prejudices, have condemned treatment which he received. And wished him to have been made as comfortable and happy as he could be when no longer able to disturb others."[54] More than a mode of curiosity and discovery, then, reading required transcription from texts for both preservation and future contemplation.

Materializing the importance of transcription as a mode of collecting unique topoi from a diversity of texts, Logan pasted into her diary a lithograph of Napoleon's tomb on the remote island of St. Helena (see Figure 10.2). Enclosed in a circle, the image portrays his modest tomb shaded beneath an emblematic funerary willow and a simple row of cypress trees.[55] Literally cut from its original text, the decontextualized image lacks an inscription; no date, no name, no epitaph offers explana-

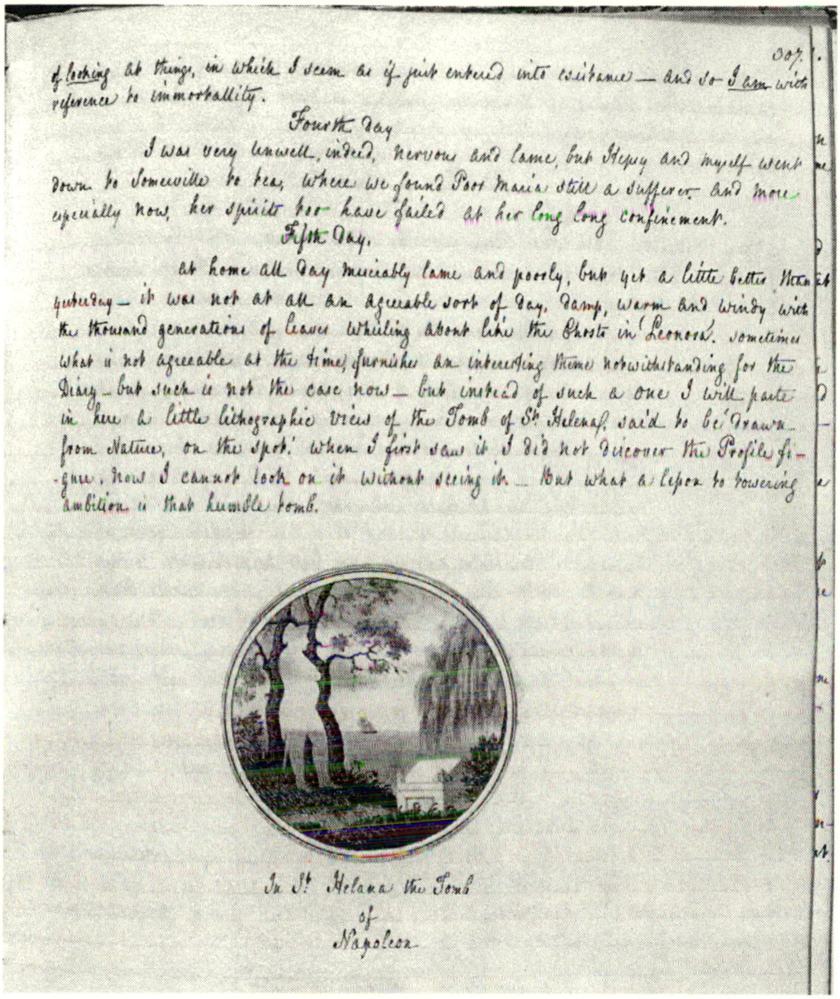

307

of looking at things, in which I seem as if just entered into existance — and so I am with reference to immortallity.

Fourth Day

I was very unwell, indeed, nervous and lame, but Hepsy and myself went down to Somerville to tea, where we found Poor Maria still a sufferer and more especially now, her spirits too have failed at her long long confinement.

Fifth Day.

At home all day miserably lame and poorly, but yet a little better than yesterday — it was not at all an agreeable sort of day, damp, warm and windy with the thousand generations of leaves whirling about like the Ghosts in 'Leonora'. sometimes what is not agreeable at the time, furnishes an interesting theme notwithstanding for the Diary — but such is not the case now — but instead of such a one I will paste in here a little lithographic view of the Tomb of St. Helena, said to be 'drawn from Nature, on the spot.' when I first saw it I did not discover the Profile figure, now I cannot look on it without seeing it — But what a lesson to towering ambition is that humble tomb.

In St Helena the Tomb
of
Napoleon

Figure 10.2. Lithograph of Napoleon's tomb pasted into the diary of Deborah Norris Logan. The Historical Society of Pennsylvania, Logan Papers, vol. 55 (13), Collection #380.

tion. Logan consequently provided one below the picture, carefully centering her script like an engraving carved into the cement slab:

In St. Helena the Tomb
Of
Napoleon

In the text preceding the lithograph and inscription, she further explains this most recent addition to her literary curiosity cabinet: it is a "little lithographic view of the Tomb of St. Helena, said to be '[taken] from Nature, on the Spot.' When I first saw it, I did not discover the disguise. Now I cannot look on it without seeing it.—But what a lesson on ambition is that humble tomb." Standing between the two cypress trees, as she noticed at second and third glance, is the hidden profile of a woman imperiously watching over Napoleon's grave. The visual game of hiding profiles of political figures in bouquets of flowers or branches of trees was in vogue throughout the early nineteenth century. Given the popularity of "flower language," by which different botanical specimens signified human virtues (and vices), printed profiles of the controversial Napoleon proliferated. An exercise in discovery (that is, finding the unexpected), the lithograph, I would argue, also suggests the importance of inscription (that is, recording the commonplace).

Napoleon's uninscribed monument along with Deborah Logan's corrective caption serves as apt illustration of the complementary process of reading and commonplacing. A monument is a written record, indication, evidence, token, or mark; it is the building, statue, or blank tomb on which an inscription is carved. An inscription is the accompanying legend, imprint, motto, dedication, superscription, or epitaph.[56] As Deborah Logan had read in John Weever's *Ancient Funerall Monuments* (1631), the monumental inscription describes a textual condition that preserves the past for future remembrance. The monument, like a blank diary or commonplace book, is "a thing erected, made, or written, for a memorial of some remarkable action, fit to be transferred to future posterities." However, once inscribed, it becomes a text, an extracted life briefly collected, for "Bookes and the Muses workes," according to Weever, "are of all monuments the most permanent."[57] Following the tradition of Elizabethan collectors, who transcribed and preserved funerary inscriptions in printed collections, nineteenth-century antiquarians had made it their business to collect inscriptions from funeral monuments, coins, coats of arms, and other heraldic devices.

Valuing these objects for their textuality, Deborah Logan understood that extracting inscriptions from the physical monument for inclusion on the manuscript page was requisite for their preservation. The art of transcribing, in other words, iterates the monumental gestures of inscribing. As Weever exclaims: "how barbarously within thee his Maiesties Dominions, they are (to the shame of our time) broken downe, and vtterly almost all ruinated, their brazen Inscriptions erased, torne away, and pilfered."[58] Commemorating the dead, monuments more importantly offer lessons for the living. Their pithy inscriptions arrest the reader, demand her perusal, and invite her interpretation. A part of the memento mori tradition that reminds the living to think about their own mortality, the monument is prescriptive: it tells us how to behave. At the same time, it is prospective: it anticipates how the past will be remembered in the future. Logan explains in her diary: "The only security against the accidents of Time and Barbarism is, to record present transactions, or gather the more ancient ones from the general Wreck. The most indistinct collections have this merit."[59] Echoing the antiquarian metaphors of John Weever in gathering inscriptions from the wreck of history, Deborah Logan demonstrates how compiling extracts had the happy effect of creating new texts. The diary and the commonplace book, as collections of past reading, became collections for future browsing.

Recovering Napoleon's unmarked and forgotten grave from the wreck of history, Logan twice commemorated him in her commonplace book with poems simply entitled "Napoleon." Written ten years apart, in 1815 and 1825 respectively, the poems illustrate the importance of inscription, of marking lives in slate as well as in ink. She composed the first poem in response to Napoleon's defeat at Waterloo and his subsequent exile to St. Helena in 1815. The second poem comes four years after his death, a time when Napoleonic objects and souvenirs were routinely scavenged by worshipping collectors.[60] Rather than trophy hunting for a celebrity relic, a resonant "piece" of the fallen Napoleon, Deborah Logan decided to put him back together, re-collecting his life through elegies. Like an inscription that invites repeated reading, or like the multiple biographies or the lithograph that offer multiple perspectives, the poems, too, illustrate Deborah Logan's changing responses to the meteoric hero as he rises and falls.

She accordingly begins "Napoleon" (1815) with the image of "an Eagle in his flight, / [Who] dared the Sun beam, and mock'd the gazers eye," only to send him plummeting by the end of the initial quatrain: "Mounting to dignity from height to height, / Till soon he fell in Ruin from the sky." Chronicling his legendary ferocity from Egypt to Russia, the poem laments his hubris. It then trades the emblematic medal of the French Order of the Great Eagle to which the poem first alludes, for "his sad Prototype," Prometheus, leaving Napoleon in "a long despair, / Chain'd to a Rock, and left to perish there." The noble eagle that formerly adorned his uniform would come to life, treacherously plucking the imperial wanderlust from his eyes.

The second elegy quickly spans the decade between Napoleon's exile and his death, picking up where the previous poem left off. No longer chained to a rock, the dead Napoleon lies peacefully on a pall. The poem's speaker walks into the room and bends reverentially over the corpse. After rehearsing the familiar postmortem physiognomy (the "haughty, stern and proud, / From his pale brow was fled"; "most calm was all his face"; "a solemn smile was on his lips"; "his eyes were closed in pensive grace"), she describes the corpse's ceremonial vestments. Rejecting the "vulgar" shroud, Napoleon essentially choreographed his own burial: "He had put Harness on to die, / The Eagle star shone on his breast, / His Sword lay bare his pillow nigh." Complementing his two-cornered, tricolored cockade, Napoleon's regalia were reportedly decked with ribbons and medals from the Orders of the Great Eagle, Reuin, and the Legion d'Honneur. Despite these honors, the speaker laments, the dead hero would have no lasting tribute at his grave:

> No sculptur'd pile our hands shall rear;
> Thy simple sod the stream shall have;
> The native Holly's leaf severe
> Shall grace and guard thy grave.

Placed in an embedded series of tin, mahogany, and lead coffins, Napoleon's unembalmed body was lowered into the ground and covered by an unmarked slab of cement. Since she could not have anticipated the removal and reburial of Napoleon's body beneath an elaborately inscribed monument in Paris nineteen years later, Deborah Logan created a monument with this poem.

Its concluding image of the tomb guarded by the native holly tree brings us back to the hidden figure in the lithograph. Perhaps seeing herself as the shadow woman inscribed in the trees, Logan, as antiquarian collector and commonplacer, assumed responsibility for preserving the past. As inked inscriptions, her poems become part of the more permanent monument of the commonplace book. Together they supply the elegiac epitaph missing from the curious image of Napoleon's tomb.

The Relic

On June 21, 1815, Deborah Logan spent "every spare minute up in the Library" while her husband was in town. Relishing such rare intellectual moments, she put them to good use: "I am almost ashamed to say, attempting to put into verse the History of Douglas's expedition with the Heart of King Robert Bruce—I fear even partiallity will blame me for not estimating my own weakness better—but it is designed only for her sight and is too long to transcribe here."[61] Written in a single day, her epic poem, "The Expedition of the Renowned Douglas and His Friends to Syria, with the Heart of King Robert Bruce," recounts how Sir James Douglas promised Robert Bruce (1274–1329), king of Scotland, to carry his royal heart to the Holy Land on his death, burying it at Golgatha on

Calvary's Hill. Bruce's final wish fulfilled a heraldic gesture he hoped to accomplish during his life. The poem recalls:

> How of the purposd hence to go
> Old Scotia's Lion there to show
> And lay the waning Crescent low
> Before the holy shrine.

Honoring the regal Scottish coat of arms, Douglas, "the guardian of his Sov'reigns heart," dutifully prepared for his pilgrimage:

> To fair Jerusalem's honored shrine,
> To place the Golden urn he bore,
> A Pilgrim, to that hallowed shore,
> Perform the vow so dreadly swore,
> And worship Love Divine!

Placing the silver and enameled casket of the deceased king's heart around his neck, Douglas departed with an impressive cohort of knights, squires, and gentlemen. Characteristically distracted along the way by the opportunity to join Alfonso XI of Castile's Crusades against the Muslims in Granada, the legendary "Black Douglas" was killed in a bloody battle in Seville. His body along with the encased heart of the king were returned to Scotland for burial: Douglas in his family vault at Bride's Chapel and Bruce in Melrose Abbey.

Transcribing a fair copy of the poem into her commonplace book on the following day, Deborah Logan noted in her diary: "Finishd my piece. the facts faithfully copied from Guthrie." Characterizing the poem as "my piece," she presents it as a tangible relic. Another curiosity, the relic (whether the withered finger, tooth, or toenail of a saint or the royal heart of a king) retains the materiality of its origins while accumulating symbolic associations in its new context. Because of its inherent partiality, on the one hand, and its vulnerability to decay and replication, on the other, a relic (like a monument) requires documentation.[62] Logan thus provides us with a telling metaphor for the third and final stage of her reading process: annotation. In culling relevant annotations from William Guthrie's ten-volume *History of Scotland* (1767), Logan not only authenticates her literary relic but also authorizes herself as an implied reader of another antiquarian text.[63]

Annotations, moreover, emphasize the complex relationship of the female collector to her collection. They show at once her initial alienation from and gradual power over her amassed relics. Since curiosities, I have argued, are taken out of unfamiliar or even exotic locales, they embody the collector's temporary estrangement in a foreign place during her (literal or metaphorical) travels. This, along with the relic's incompleteness, suggests the antiquarian's distance from the past. The accompanying annotation, it follows, is "always a testimony to alienation from a text, always represents a response to a prior culture from which one believes oneself distanced."[64] At the same time, annotations are particularly topographical, according to Jacques Derrida. They are the collector's framing devices. Placed below, beside, or between transcribed topoi, the reader's supplementary notations assume "a delimination in the space that gives it a paradoxical independence, a freedom, an autonomy. The footnote is also a text unto itself, rather detached, relatively decontextualized or capable of creating its own context."[65] Extracted curiosities, therefore, assume meaning in the collection only through their interdependence.

Reading herself into the text as an annotator, Deborah Logan essentially reshapes the manuscript and printed material to "complement her own subjectivity."[66] The two brief annotations within the poem as well as the additional documentation in her diary illustrate her increasing control over and identification with her collection. Logan cross-references her cursory footnotes (the first alluding to "Lastalryk, or Restalryk, the seat of the Logan's near Edinburgh" and the second to "Sir Robert Logan of Restalryk") with an elaborately detailed manuscript, "An historical account of the Ancient & honorable family of Logan of Restalrig near to Edinburgh, and other families of the name of Logan," which was written by Mr. George Logan at the request of James Logan's brother William Logan and dated May 16, 1753.[67] Transcribing the manuscript into her diary in 1808, Logan placed her own careful citations in cramped but readable script in the margins, imitating the genealogical marginalia in the early printed books from which they were gleaned: Raphael Hollinshed's *Chronicles of England, Scotland, and Ireland* (1577) and Alexander Nisbet's *A System of Heraldry* (1722).[68]

Read in the context of these annotations, Deborah Logan's poem ultimately celebrates Robert Logan of Restalrig, one of the knights who accompanied Douglas on his aborted journey until when "fighting valiantly against the Saracens in the Kingdom of Granada they were slain."[69] Since annotation is part of the antiquarian's attempt to collapse the distance between the past and the present, Logan shifts her focus from Robert Bruce's ancient coat of arms detailed in her poem to the Logan family crest emblematized in Hollinshed's and Nisbet's chronicles. She learned that it "carr[ied] piles, or passion nails for the antiquity of the name." After Robert Logan's participation in Douglas's Crusade, she further read, the Logan family crest was emended. According to Hollinshed: "added to their arms a mans Heart which our Heralds blazon thus, or, three passion nails, sable, instead of piles, conjoined in pint, piercing a mans heart in Base gules," the color red indicated on blazon by engraved vertical lines.[70]

The coat of arms thus provided a material gloss to Deborah Logan's poem on Scottish antiquity. Given the ancestral trajectory of the annotations in both the commonplace book and the diary, her epic poem is also an unexpected memoir of its author. Toward its conclusion the poem not only mourns Robert Logan's death but also marks his passage as a foreshadowing of his progeny's future passage to America: his "parting eye" looked to the West, to a "Land for Freedom famed, his Son's should see." Telescoping antiquarian time once again, Deborah Logan read the pilgrimage of the famous king's heart as the prehistory for the Logan family's emigration from Scotland to Pennsylvania. Exchanging a literal relic (the king's heart) for a metaphoric one (the poem itself), she traced Robert Logan's illustrious family tree to the branch that "settled in East Lothian, from whom the Logans of Stenton are descended." Amplified by its annotations, the poem swelled its antiquarian author's heart.

The Armchair Traveler

In this essay I have argued that Deborah Logan's reading practices—discovery, transcription, and annotation—were another material mode of female collecting in the early Republic. As textual analogies for the early modern *Wunderkammer*, her commonplace books and diaries rehearse the nineteenth-century penchant for antiquarianism—the acquisitive desire to unearth historical curiosities and rarities while at the same time trying to authenticate the origins of a distinctively American antiquity. Without a usable past, however, she necessarily explored transatlantic precedents, reading printed collections from Europe: miscellanies and anthologies, gift books and biographies, travel books and anecdotes, book reviews and magazines. A kind of armchair traveler, Logan transcribed extracts as she toured the books, adding annotations and literary responses to frame the compilations and to ensure the repeatable act of discovery through future reading. Reading, like curio collecting, was thus topographic in nature, allowing her to cross geographic, historic, textual, and gender boundaries as she vicariously followed Cleopatra, Napoleon, and James Douglas through Egypt, the island of St. Helena, and Scotland, respectively. Writing marginalia in printed texts and pasting printed texts into her manuscripts, she underscored the fluid boundaries between print and scribal publication for the early national female reader. As an aged woman in a new republic, she discriminatingly circulated or hoarded peculiar artifacts, oral histories, and other archives as cultural currency, making her an indispensable resource to her contemporary male antiquarians. However, like all collectors, Deborah Logan was ultimately outlived by her collection. "Originating within this life" (that is, constructed in one context) and "recapitulat[ing] [her] indefinitely beyond the point of death" (that is, accumulating meaning in another context),[71] Logan's literary curiosity cabinets are now part of the American antiquity she labored so long to create: "Will my Books and Diarys Survive me," she asks. "If they do, I should like them to convey a faithful view both of myself and of my venerable Old Mansion endeared to me by associations of many kinds."[72]

Notes

1. For a fuller biographical sketch, see Susan Stabile, *Memory's Daughters: The Material Culture of Remembrance in Eighteenth-Century America* (Ithaca, N.Y.: Cornell University Press, 2004), 1–9, 38–45.

2. Deborah Logan, manuscript diary, 11:61, Historical Society of Pennsylvania (HSP). Hereafter the seventeen volumes located at the HSP will be cited by volume and page number. Her earlier diaries (1808–15), which are housed at the Library Company of Philadelphia (LCP), will be cited by date and page, following Logan's organizational method.

3. Logan, 6:77.

4. Other local cabinets of curiosity, which evolved into public museums, included The Library Company (c. 1740), the Pennsylvania Hospital (c. 1757), Dr. Abraham Chovet's cabinet (c. 1774), Pierre Eugene du Simitiere's "American Museum" (1782), and Charles Willson Peale's Museum (1786–1827). See Murphy D. Smith, *A Museum: The History of the Cabinet of Curiosities of the American Philosophical Society* (Philadelphia: American Philosophical Society, 1996); Joyce Henri Robinson, "An American Cabinet of Curiosities: Thomas Jefferson's 'Indian Hall' at Monticello," in *Acts of Possession: Collecting in America*, ed. Leah Dilworth (New Brunswick, N.J.: Rutgers University Press, 2003), 16–41; and Joel J. Orosz, *Curators and Culture: The Museum Movement in America, 1740–1870* (Tuscaloosa: University of Alabama Press, 1990).

5. At the same time that Deborah Logan was collecting what I would consider "artificial" curiosities or antiquities, other women were specifically collecting "natural curiosities," as Susan Scott Parrish argues in *American Curiosity: Cultures of Natural History in the Colonial British Atlantic World* (Chapel Hill: University of North Carolina Press for the Omohundro Institute of Early American History and Culture, 2006).

6. Logan, 15:200; 16:46.

7. On the early modern *Wunderkammer*, see Joy Kenseth, ed., *The Age of the Marvelous* (Hanover, N.H.: Dartmouth College, Hood Museum of Art, 1991); and Anthony Allen Shelton, "Cabinets of Transgression: Renaissance Collections and the Incorporation of the New World," in *The Cultures of Collecting*, ed. John Elsner and Roger Cardinal (Cambridge, Mass.: Harvard University Press, 1994), 177–203.

8. Krzysztof Pomian, *Collectors and Curiosities: Paris and Venice, 1500–1800*, trans. Elizabeth Wiles-Portier (Cambridge: Polity Press, 1990), 9. For another view on curiosity, see Barbara Benedict, "The 'Curious Attitude' in Eighteenth-

Century England: Observing and Owning," *Eighteenth-Century Life* 14 (November 1999): 59–98.

9. Logan, 13:194; 1:58.

10. Barbara Benedict, *Curiosity: A Cultural History of Early Modern Inquiry* (Chicago: University of Chicago Press, 2001), 2–3.

11. Logan, 6:199.

12. For discussions of antiquarianism, see Rosemary Sweet, *Antiquaries: The Discovery of the Past in Eighteenth-Century Britain* (New York: Hambledon and London, 2004); Martin Myrone and Lucy Peltz, eds., *Producing the Past: Aspects of Antiquarian Culture and Practice, 1700–1850* (Brookfield, Vt.: Ashgate, 1999); Thomas DaCosta Kaufmann, "Antiquarianism, the History of Objects, and the History of Art before Winkelmann," *Journal of the History of Ideas* 62 (2001): 523–41; Stuart Piggott, *Ruins in a Landscape: Essays in Antiquarianism* (Edinburgh: University Press, 1976); and Arnaldo Momigliano's groundbreaking work, including "Ancient History and the Antiquarian," *Journal of the Warburg and Courtauld Institutes* 13 (1950): 285–315.

13. Though recent theorists of collecting associate the collector with the author, I will argue for the provocative parallels to the female reader in the early national period. See, for example, Mieke Bal's comparison of collecting to narratology in "Telling Objects: A Narrative Perspective on Collecting," in *Cultures of Collecting*, 97–115; and Walter Benjamin's "Unpacking My Library: A Talk about Book Collecting," in *Illuminations: Essays and Reflections*, ed. Hannah Arendt (New York: Shocken, 1968), 59–67.

14. Samuel Johnson, "commonplace book," *A Dictionary of the English Language* (London, 1755).

15. On commonplacing, see Stabile, *Memory's Daughters*; Susan Miller, *Assuming the Position: Cultural Pedagogy and the Politics of Commonplace Writing* (Pittsburgh: University of Pittsburgh Press, 1998); Ann Moss, *Printed Commonplace Books and the Structuring of Renaissance Thought* (New York: Oxford University Press, 1996); Peter Beal, "Notions in Garrison: The Seventeenth-Century Commonplace Book," in *New Ways of Looking at Old Texts: Papers of the Renaissance English Text Society, 1985–1991*, ed. W. Speed Hill (Binghamton, N.Y.: Renaissance English Text Society, 1993), 131–47; and Mary Thomas Crane, *Framing Authority: Sayings, Self, and Society in Sixteenth-Century England* (Princeton, N.J.: Princeton University Press, 1993).

16. A collection is synchronic in its ahistoric combination of elements from different places and time periods, which when brought together form a cohesive and unified set.

17. Logan, 11:20; 6:64; 7:1.

18. Susan Stewart, *On Longing: Narratives of the Miniature, the Gigantic, the Souvenir, the Collection* (Baltimore: Johns Hopkins University Press, 1984), 157.

19. Jean Baudrillard, "The System of Collecting," in *Cultures of Collecting*, 12.

20. Logan, 10:128.

21. Ibid., 14:140.

22. Susan Pearce, *On Collecting: An Investigation into Collecting in the European Tradition* (New York: Routledge, 1995), 95.

23. Russell Belk discusses the collection as an extension of the collector in "Collectors and Collecting," in *Interpreting Objects and Collections*, ed. Susan M. Pearce (New York: Routledge, 1994), 317–26.

24. These are what might be considered the published versions of the commonplace book. Like early modern verse miscellanies, these collections during

the romantic period shared the aesthetic principles of variety and abundance with the manuscript commonplace book. Though it would seemingly be commodifying the commonplace book into a ready-made text, readers could transcribe selections into their own manuscript books. For a rich discussion, see Barbara Benedict, "Literary Miscellanies: The Cultural Mediation of Fragmented Feeling," *English Literary History* 57 (summer 1990): 407–30; and Benedict, "The 'Beauties' of Literature, 1750–1820: Tasteful Prose and Fine Rhyme for Private Consumption," in *1650–1850: Ideas, Aesthetics, and Inquiries in the Early Modern Era*, ed. Kevin Cope (New York: AMS Press, 1994), 1:317–46.

25. As canned synopses of the latest publications, reviews such as the *North American Review* and the *Edinburgh Review*, according to Deborah Logan, are inherently biased. Finding an eighteenth-century precursor, "The Compendious Library or Library Journal Reviv'd" (1752), she writes: "After having been conversant in modern Reviews and collections How did this work appear to me? Why it was quite a Refreshment, and has confirmed me in what I had long suspected, that actual improvements in many of the Walks of literature were very problematical.—I like Old Books. I like the sensible, manly and serious Spirit of this Reviewer, and could not help contrasting it with the branching declamation, party prejudices and Quizzical turn of some articles which I have lately read. The Preface should be read to point out the duty of a Reviewer.—But I have done" (Logan, 9:117–18).

26. Her choices of eighteenth-century essay collections include the *Rambler*, the *Tatler*, and the *Spectator*.

27. Among her favorite anecdotes are those collected from Alexander Pope's literary circle, which are mentioned frequently in Samuel Johnson's *Lives of the Poets*. Johnson quotes liberally from the unpublished version of Joseph Spence's *Anecdotes, Observations, and Characters, of Books and Men* (1820), which Deborah Logan read with great delight.

28. She read several of the British bluestocking and French salonierre's published letters, including those of Anna Seward and Madame Sevigne.

29. She read biographies more than any other genre: William Haley's *Life of Romney* (1809), Thomas Moore's *Memoirs of the Life of Sheridan* (1825), and William Tudor's *Life of James Otis* (1823) are just a select few.

30. While she read such magazines as the *Gentleman's Magazine, Blackwood's Magazine*, and the *Museum*, Logan also subscribed to several newspapers, including Zachariah Poulson's *American Daily Advertiser*, Robert Walsh's *National Gazette*, and Elias Boudinot's *Cherokee Phoenix*. The newspapers escalated, however, into an unwieldy collection: "What a treat they must have been when People got them only once a week! or when the old Settlers only received them with the Annual Ships!" (Logan, 7:25).

31. Her travel reading included James Boswell's account of Johnson's *Tour of the Hebrides*, John Griscom's *A Year in Europe* (1824), and John Davy's *An Account of the Interior of Ceylon and of Its Inhabitants with Travels in the Island* (1821).

32. Easily accessible Philadelphia publications included *The Cabinet; or Philosopher's Masterpiece* (1824), *The Historical Cabinet* (1834), *Ladies' Literary Cabinet* (1819–22), *The Lady's Cabinet Album* (1832), *The Lady's Cabinet of Polite Literature* (1809), *American Museum* (1789–99), *Repository and Ladies' Weekly Museum* (1800–1806), *Museum* (1822–23), *Columbian Museum; or, Universal Asylum* (1793), and *Ladies' Literary Museum, or, Weekly Repository* (1817–18).

33. On women's reading circles, see Mary Kelly, "'A More Glorious Revolution': Women's Antebellum Reading Circles and the Pursuit of Public Influ-

ence," *New England Quarterly* (June 2003): 163–96. On coteries, see Stabile, *Memory's Daughters.* On men's practices, see Kevin Berland, Jan Kirsten Gilliam, and Kenneth A. Lockridge, eds., *The Commonplace Book of William Byrd II of Westover* (Chapel Hill: University of North Carolina Press, 2001); and Kenneth Lockridge, *On The Sources of Patriarchal Rage: The Commonplace Books and the Gendering of Power in the Eighteenth Century* (New York: New York University Press, 1992).

For relevant discussions of women's reading in the late eighteenth and early nineteenth centuries, see Cathy Davidson, *Revolution and the Word: The Rise of the Novel* (New York: Oxford University Press, 2004); Cathy Davidson, ed., *Reading in America: Literature and Social History* (Baltimore: Johns Hopkins University Press, 1989); Linda Kerber, *Women of the Republic: Intellect and Ideology in Revolutionary America* (Chapel Hill: University of North Carolina Press, 1980); Barbara Ryan and Amy M. Thomas, eds., *Reading Acts: U.S. Readers' Interactions with Literature, 1800–1950* (Knoxville: University of Tennessee Press, 2000); Martyn Lyons, "New Readers in the Nineteenth Century," in *A History of Reading in the West,* ed. Guglielmo Cavallo and Roger Chartier (Amherst: University of Massachusetts Press, 1999); and Susan Matthews, "Women Writers and Readers," in *Romantic Writings,* ed. Stephen Bygrave (New York: Routledge, 1996).

34. Logan, 2:158; 2:161.

35. The diary is replete with examples of her recitations: "Read to the family in the evening in Bensons Life of Christ" (1:56); "In the evening I read to the Girls Rittenhouse's Oration of Astronomy" (5:16); "I then went into the dining room and with Mary and Susan for my audience Read some Serious Poetry and several Chapters in St. John's Gospel" (6:108); "after the Candles were lighted, and we had set in to amuse ourselves with reading 'Comus'" (6:112b); and "In the evening I was beginning to read the 4th Book of Paradise Lost to Sarah and Elizabeth" (6:73).

36. James Clifford, "Collecting Ourselves," in *Interpreting Objects and Collections,* 260. See also Clifford, "On Collecting Art and Culture," in *The Predicament of Culture* (Cambridge, Mass.: Harvard University Press, 1984), 215–52.

37. Benedict, *Curiosity,* 119; Obituary of Deborah Logan in *The Friend* (Philadelphia, 1839); Sweet, *Antiquaries,* xii.

38. For discussions of age and gender, see Teri Premo, *Winter Friends: Growing Old in the New Republic, 1785–1835* (Urbana: University of Illinois Press, 1990); and Stabile, *Memory's Daughters,* 129–77.

39. James Logan donated his private collection of some twenty-six hundred volumes as a trust for the public in 1754 and opened the Loganian Library in 1760. His descendants arranged for the then four-thousand-volume library to be incorporated with the Library Company of Philadelphia in 1792.

40. Logan, 5:124.

41. Ibid., 11:240; 13:30; 7:5.

42. Many critics discern between independent traveling and choreographed tourism, the latter becoming popular in the 1820s with the rise of the published guidebook. See, for example, James Buzzard, *The Beaten Track: European Tourism, Literature, and the Ways to Culture, 1800–1918* (Oxford: Clarendon Press, 1984).

43. Michel de Certeau, *The Practice of Everyday Life* (Berkeley: University of California Press, 1984), 170, 174.

44. On the trope of the feminine landscape, see Annette Kolody, *The Lay of the Land: Metaphors as Experience and History in American Life and Letters* (Chapel Hill: University of North Carolina Press, 1975). For recent discussions of gender,

travel, and colonialism, see Sara Mills, *Discourses of Difference: An Analysis of Women's Travel Writing and Colonialism* (New York: Routledge, 2003); Mary Louise Pratt, *Imperial Eyes: Travel Writing and Transculturation* (New York: Routledge, 1992); and Meyda Yegenoglu, *Colonial Fantasies: Towards a Feminist Reading of Orientalism* (New York: Cambridge University Press, 1998).

45. Celia's Eastern-inspired ottoman suggests a fascination for and fear of the luxurious, exotic, and feminine East, as the literary critic Edward Said aptly theorizes in *Orientalism* (New York: Vintage, 1979). See, too, Caroline Winterer's intelligent discussion of the neoclassical sofa and the recumbent female figure as markers of luxury and effeminacy in the early American Republic in "Venus on the Sofa: Women, Neoclassicism, and the Early American Republic," *Modern Intellectual History* 2.1 (April 2005): 29–60.

46. William Gilpin, *Three Essays on the Picturesque*, in *The Picturesque: Literary Sources and Documents*, ed. Malcolm Andrews, 3 vols. (East Sussex: Helm Information, 1994), 2:15.

47. Egypt was appreciated by romantic travelers for its wonder rather than resonance, for its singularity rather than typicality, for its giganticism rather than sublimity, according to Nigel Leask, *Curiosity and the Aesthetics of Travel Writing, 1770–1840: "From an Antique Land"* (New York: Oxford University Press, 2002), 108. See, too, Diego Saglia, "Consuming Egypt: Appropriation and the Cultural Modalities of Romantic Luxury," *Nineteenth-Century Contexts* 24.3 (2002): 317–32.

48. As the curator Wendy Cooper points out, the craze for the Egyptian style in American architecture and furniture—particularly dining room furniture—was evident as early as 1808. By 1810 the Philadelphia cabinetmaker Joseph B. Barry advertised his Egyptian-inspired furniture in the *Aurora Daily Advertiser.* For a further discussion, see Wendy Cooper, *Classical Taste in America, 1800–1840* (Baltimore: Baltimore Museum of Art and Abbeville Press, 1993), 130–42; and Donald Fennimore, "Egyptian Influence in Early Nineteenth-Century American Furniture," *Magazine Antiques* 137 (May 1990): 1190–201. I would like to thank Laura Keim, curator of Stenton Museum, for sharing these references with me.

49. Derived from the Persian word *mumnia*, meaning "pitch" or "bitumen," *mummy* referred not only to the preserved Egyptian corpse but also to the substance used in embalming, as Brian Fagan illustrates in *The Rape of the Nile: Tomb Robbers, Tourists, and Archaeologists in Egypt*, 3rd ed. (Boulder, Colo.: Westview Press, 2004), 27–42.

50. Susan Pearce, "Bodies in Exile: Egyptian Mummies in the Early Nineteenth Century and Their Cultural Implications," in *Displaced Persons: Conditions of Exile in European Culture*, ed. Sharon Ouditt (London: Ashgate, 2002), 54–72.

51. Moss, *Printed Commonplace Books*, 225.

52. Logan, 16:65; 10:99; 6:77.

53. Among the biographies she discusses in her diaries are Sir Walter Scott's nine-volume *Life of Napoleon* (1827) and Count Emmanuel de Las Cases's eight-volume *Memorial de Sainte Helene* (1823).

54. Logan, 6:114; 7:106; 6:115–16; 6:114, 127.

55. Since the French and English were at an impasse over the inscription on Napoleon's tomb (the former desiring "Napoleon" and the latter "Bonaparte"), the tomb was never inscribed.

56. "Monument," "Inscription," in *Oxford English Dictionary* (New York: Oxford University Press, 2006).

57. John Weever, *Ancient Funerall Monuments* (London: Thomas Harper, 1631), 1, 3. Logan was reading and transcribing from this work by Weever in June 1815, as her diary indicates (1:103).

58. Weever, *Ancient Funerall Monuments*, 10–11.

59. Deborah Logan, manuscript, June 10, 1814, Stenton.

60. On Napoleonic collecting, see Stuart Semmel, "Reading the Tangible Past: British Tourism, Collecting, and Memory after Waterloo," *Representations* 69 (winter 2000): 9–37, and Judith Pascoe *The Hummingbird Cabinet: A Rare and Curious History of Romantic Collectors* (Ithaca, N.Y.: Cornell University Press, 2005).

61. Logan, 1:108.

62. Ibid. The relic's vulnerability to decay or even manipulation further illustrates the importance of antiquarian documentation. As artificial curiosities, secular relics in the early Republic were often physically enhanced, changed, or even improved: they were copied, imitated, and reproduced. As the historian David Lowenthal points out, duplicated relics were called "facsimiles": while "copies" would imitate existing or lost originals, "forgeries" pretended to be the originals. Such textual terminology (i.e., the printed facsimile, the manuscript copy, the forged hand) accentuates the relic's value as a collectible literary curiosity. See David Lowenthal, *The Past Is a Foreign Country* (New York: Cambridge University Press, 1985), 263–362.

63. Ralph Hanna III, "Annotation as Social Practice," in *Annotation and Its Texts*, ed. Stephen A. Barney (New York: Oxford University Press, 1991), 181. The implied reader, according to the Reader-Response School of Criticism propounded by Wolfgang Iser, is a literary construct. Unlike the actual reader, the implied reader is written into the structure of the text.

64. Hanna, "Annotation as Social Practice," 178.

65. Jacques Derrida, "This Is Not an Oral Footnote," in *Annotation and Its Texts*, 194.

66. Barbara Benedict, *Making the Modern Reader: Cultural Mediation in Early Modern Literary Anthologies* (Princeton, N.J.: Princeton University Press, 1996), 47.

67. Logan diary, 1808, 18.

68. Raphael Hollinshed, *Chronicles of England, Scotland, and Ireland* (1577; repr. London: J. Johnson, 1808); Alexander Nisbet, *A System of Heraldry: Speculation, Practical, with the True Art of the Blazon*, 2 vols. (Edinburgh: T & A Constable, 1816).

69. Logan diary, 1808, 18–19.

70. Ibid., 20–21.

71. Baudrillard, "System of Collecting," 17.

72. Logan, 6:199.

Part IV
Afterword

Chapter 11

Reading Outside the Frame

Robert A. Gross

This brief afterword by a male reader comes at the close of a volume of learned essays composed almost entirely by females and focusing on women's historical encounters with texts. It thereby depends on what has come before, taking its agenda from the contributors and developing its terms and themes from their central concerns. There is surely historical justice in that circumstance, for it reverses the gender roles that governed literary transactions in the Western world for centuries. As this collection demonstrates powerfully in its sweeping survey of books and reading from the Renaissance to the dawn of the Industrial Revolution, women were obliged to engage texts, whether in manuscript or print, through a male frame. Who wrote virtually all the books they read but men? Who controlled access to literacy and schooling? Who enjoyed a room of his own? Worse still, early modern women, even in the privileged circles of the aristocracy, could seldom take up a book with open minds and confident spirits. They were burdened by male-constructed stereotypes designed to circumscribe their reading and curb their ambitions. The very male authors who deigned to address female readers belittled their audience as feather-brained show-offs interested only in passing pleasures or idealized them as pious souls submissive to God and his masculine representatives on earth. Men prescribed what women should read, how they should read, and what value their reading contained. If the printing revolution set in motion by Johannes Gutenberg unsettled traditional hierarchies, it took a while to affect the social relation between the sexes. Printing served the cause of patriarchy.

Or so it presumed. In the face of all these obstacles, this volume documents persuasively, women asserted their wills, affirmed their desires, and ensured their presence in the republic of letters, even when they had to depend on works composed by men. Reading became a treasured activity in women's lives, perhaps even, in Mary Kelley's words, "a constant." If any generalization is warranted from this collection, it is surely that men have constantly tried and failed to confine women's minds by controlling their reading.

Women of the early modern era entered the world of letters at a severe disadvantage. Everywhere, in Protestant and Catholic lands alike, a literacy gap divided the sexes. In the elite classes, to be sure, daughters as well as sons often learned to read; the skill was an ornament of privilege for some, a religious duty for others. However, the cultural premium resided in the education of boys, who went off to school for instruction both in the basics—writing and arithmetic—and in the advanced subjects that gave access to the classical tradition; their sisters remained at home for lessons in domestic skills. Not that female education was altogether neglected: Boarding schools for privileged girls were fashionable in seventeenth- and eighteenth-century England, offering tuition in the same sophisticated arts of needlework, music, dancing, and writing that would be conveyed to their colonial counterparts across the Atlantic. Nonetheless, women lagged well behind men in the ability to write, and they were shut out of the classical training that became an arduous rite of passage for the future leaders of the British Empire. Such exclusions had the effect of barring women from independent cultural leadership. Without the ability to write, most women were consigned to the silence that Virginia Woolf once imagined as the inevitable fate of Judith Shakespeare, "the wonderfully gifted sister" of the bard who, had she existed, would have faced opposition at every turn to the cultivation of her genius and ultimately would have died of despair at her own hand. The bulk of the literature they read was written by men and available mainly under male aegis. Books were expensive, their prices kept artificially high by monopolistic publishers. The female readers of Shakespeare portrayed by Sasha Roberts were favored by patriarchal fortune. The folio edition studied by Lady Anne Merrick in 1638 had been issued fifteen years earlier at a price that removed Shakespeare from the popular audience that once flocked to his plays and snapped up his playbooks. So canonized, for a century and a half Shakespeare became a luxury good for the elites in church, state, and trade—and for the ladies who shared in their privilege.[1]

These barriers to female participation in literary culture were hardly impregnable. The implicit narrative in this collection is progressive, with women steadily gaining visibility and influence in the republic of letters from the sixteenth through the eighteenth centuries. At the heart of this process were three interrelated developments: (1) growing access to the world of books, evident in expanded schooling for girls and rising rates of written literacy; (2) a new demand for literature addressing the concerns of women and expressing their interests; and (3) the multiplication of texts and genres intended to serve the female market and paving the way for the rise of women writers. The dynamic of change was evident as early as the sixteenth century, when Marguerite de Navarre, in Ian Moulton's telling, took the medieval genre of the *novelle*, with its titillating treatment of female sexuality by such male writers as Boccaccio, and turned it into a serious reflection on the fateful choices awaiting women in affairs of love, courtship, and marriage. Such "female literature"—works dedicated to or written by women—developed in tandem with the press, especially in England during the tumultuous era of the civil war and the commonwealth, when censorship relaxed and dissenters of all sorts put forth their opinions in print. Upon these foundations were built the literary careers of such exceptional seventeenth-century figures as Aphra Behn, playwright, poet, translator, and path-breaker for the many female authors who entered the publishing marketplace from the mid-eighteenth century on to satisfy the swelling demand for imaginative works addressed to women's circumstances and needs. In the fictional genre of sentiment renamed the *novel*, women readers embraced a genre of their own.

Female authorship often struggled to develop within a male frame. In her practice of translation, Aphra Behn "paraphrased" male authority, inserting her own notions into the text even as she professed "fidelity" to the original. Likewise, Deborah Logan, the assiduous Quaker collector of relics from "olden times," whose voluminous commonplace books and diaries are the focus of Susan Stabile's chapter, assembled her literary corpus from the works of others. Extracts from writings, mostly by men, filled the pages of her books. Her initiative lay in changing the contexts: the originals now resided in a setting defined by her unfolding interests and given meaning by the annotations she inscribed for future reference. What men brought forth the women remade. At times gentlewomen fashioned literary forms of their own, such as needlework samplers, that were inaccessible to men. A rare soul, such as Ann Hutchinson, dared to challenge the highest male authorities of the land with a sophistication in argument equal to their own—a harbinger of future generations of learned women in the early American Republic.

The foregoing narrative should be familiar to students of women's history on both sides of the Atlantic. It is a story of male power and female resistance whose trajectory is twofold: one line of development culminates in female demands for equality and public participation; the second traces the creation of women's institutions and subcultures. Within this framework the history of books and reading rehearses well-known themes in social history. Seen from the perspective of the female reader, the world of books reproduces the structural inequalities and the contests of power running through Western society down to the modern era. For all its promise of fresh insights, the history of the book mainly reveals a new arena for an old struggle. It annotates the received wisdom and reprints commonplaces about the past.

Does culture simply mirror society? Or does it exercise an independent force in the shaping of social life, including gender relations? The *maître* of book history, Roger Chartier, has recently insisted that reading does not map the divisions of early modern society. Books of all sorts circulated throughout the ranks of the preindustrial order; "no reading matter was exclusive to any one group." Even Spanish tales of chivalry, designed for aristocratic entertainment, made their way into the hands of curious workers, craftsmen, and merchants. The physical form of texts altered in the downward passage; for the popular market, printers issued cheap booklets—single- or double-sheet pages folded and sewn into octavo format and illustrated with crude woodcuts. So adapted and popularized, romances were read aloud in rural settings far from court circles, an evening's amusement even for illiterate peasants. Thanks to the ingenuity of the book trade, print overcame social distinctions and forged cultural connections between the elite and popular classes. Yet, difference persisted, according to Chartier. If people read the same works, they did not necessarily read them in the same ways. Reflecting their positions in the social hierarchy, different groups developed distinctive reading practices, by which they "appropriated" texts—that is, gave them meaning—in terms pertinent to their circumstances. The challenge for the historian of reading is thus to "discern the ways in which different readers used and read the same texts."[2]

Taking a cue from Chartier, we might view the female reader from an altered perspective. Instead of concentrating on male exclusions and female challenges, we might ask why, if they held all the cards in the realm of culture, men ever wanted women to sit at the table and join the game. Why encourage and foster female literacy? Such education was costly, both in time and money. It took women away from household duties. It gave them access to male discussions about church and state. It enabled independent spiritual lives. It put female experience on view and encouraged women to assert their own demands. It might prompt readings and uses of texts—say, the Bible or the Declaration of Independence—at odds with those discerned by men. It could discomfort a male-dominated world.

Despite all these disadvantages, men in the privileged classes of the early modern era did not monopolize the written and printed word. Rather, reading developed into a heterosocial practice joining men and women together in select social circles. It could serve either sacred or secular ends. Protestants took to heart Paul's avowal that there is "neither male nor female" in Christ. On that principle they determined that everyone should read the gospel: "all ages, all sexes, all degrees and callings, all high and low, rich and poor, wise and foolish," in the words of the Elizabethan cleric Thomas Cartwright. Bible reading was not only a daily ritual in Puritan households conducted by the family patriarch but also a duty incumbent upon all members for the sake of their souls. It united husbands and wives, parents and children in sociability even as it subjected them to religious discipline. Through constant "intensive" reading of Scripture, the godly read themselves into the divine plan and construed their lives in its metaphoric terms. The trouble with Ann Hutchinson, as Janice Knight shows, is that she deployed Scripture all too well, until she dropped her guard and drifted away from the sacred Word. *Sola scriptura* was a stringent rule of Puritan faith.[3]

Politeness rivaled piety as a spur to female reading. Storytelling, dramatic readings, and literary talk animated social gatherings among the elite. At tea tables and salons, in country houses and town assembly rooms, men and women took texts of all sorts—manuscript poems of their own composition, printed playbooks and novels, ancient history as told by modern writers in vernacular languages, contemporary newspapers and periodicals—and made them the stuff of conversation and the medium of courtship. Displays of refinement and wit were tests of gentility; a gentleman's standing was affected by the performance of his wife. No wonder, then, that fathers invested in the schooling of their daughters, whose literary "accomplishments" ornamented the parlors and enhanced their prospects of good marriages. Female literacy was thus integral to class status in the upper reaches of society. In illustration of Thorstein Veblen's *Theory of the Leisure Class,* elite males ostentatiously competed for status by releasing their female dependents from the necessities of household work and supporting them in the pursuit of nonutilitarian arts. Educated women added aesthetic value to the genteel home. In a widely read manual of conduct, the Reverend John Bennett counseled young ladies that men "provide the furniture; *you* dispose of it with propriety. *They* build the house; *you* are to fancy and to ornament the *ceiling.*" That advice was offered in 1795; Martha Stewart was waiting in the wings.[4]

The connection between reading and social distinction can be made too tight. In the drive to expose the cultural pretensions of the privileged, a historian is tempted to miss a central point. As a shared pastime among women and men, reading became a valued site for the cultivation of more informal, mutual, affectionate relations between the sexes. Its practice played a significant part in the eighteenth-century rise of the companionate family—a development urged by the many novels of sentiment that filled the leisure hours of the genteel. Seen in these terms, the story of the female reader is not reducible to existing class and gender divisions. It constitutes critical evidence in its own right: an independent realm of cultural activity that helped to fashion a new mode of social life. In the history of books and reading lie important clues for social history.

Were common texts read in different ways, as Roger Chartier proposes? Not necessarily. Ann Hutchinson was as orthodox as her erstwhile mentor, the Reverend John Cotton, in her spiritual decoding of the Bible and her mastery of Puritan typology. Aphra Behn followed an approved method of "Translation with Latitude" recommended by the poet John Dryden. Deborah Logan organized the extracts in her commonplace book according to rules originally set by humanist scholars centuries before. Why should they have broken with customary practices? They were intent on participating in the religious and cultural life of their times, just as young ladies such as Charlotte Forten and Bessie Lacy at the academies of antebellum America developed the ambition to be learned women. "Serious study serves to harden the mind for more trying conflicts; it lifts the reader from sensation to intellect," Hannah More advises in *Strictures on Female Education.* Forten and Lacy would have had it no other way.[5]

Reading, we might then argue, ran against the fault lines of Western society on both sides of the Atlantic world. In its shared practice men and women undercut the patriarchal order. Yet, as the essays in this volume suggest, that generalization is too facile. The common activity of reading was conducted on unequal terms. Throughout the early modern era and down to the early nineteenth century, men were characteristically the producers of culture, women the consumers. Denied access to the skill of writing, many women were placed in the passive situation of reading texts they could never produce on their own. Like Judith Shakespeare, the only mark most would leave on the historical record was an *X.* Their more privileged sisters repeated, paraphrased, annotated, and memorialized the words of male authorities. But in increasing numbers from the mid-eighteenth century on, women staked claims to knowledge and participated in print culture with greater confidence and competence. Witness the rising numbers of female authors not just in fiction and belles lettres but also in spheres once reserved for males: Catharine Macaulay in history, Madame de Staël in philosophy, Hannah Adams in religion. The passion for reading inflamed even the chambermaids of Vienna, according to one unhappy male observer in 1781: "they play the part of sentimental souls, demand the rights to *belles lettres,* read comedies and poems conscientiously, and learn entire scenes, passages or verses off by heart." Like the female readers of Revolutionary America, they claimed a representation in the republic of letters that was denied them in the realm of state. In the succeeding generation female authors and genres, abetted by profit-minded booksellers, emerged to meet that demand.[6]

The rise of female readers and authors is, then, a central element in the reading revolution of the eighteenth century. A vast new constituency for the printed word, women, both as producers and consumers, drove the expansion of print culture throughout the Atlantic world. As they found their voices in print, they could envision and identify with a larger sisterhood and subject male-dominated institutions to systematic critique. Even as they were still commonly obliged to see themselves through a male gaze, they obtained the literary means to challenge the distorted mirror and to portray female lives on their own terms. They thus altered the culture as they struggled to define themselves. In that encounter surely lie the power and potential in the historical recovery of the female reader.

Notes

1. Ross W. Beales and E. Jennifer Monaghan, "Literacy and Schoolbooks," in *The Colonial Book in the Atlantic World*, ed. Hugh Amory and David D. Hall, vol. 1 of *A History of the Book in America* (New York: Cambridge University Press, 2000), 380–81; David Vincent, *Literacy and Popular Culture: England 1750–1914* (Cambridge: Cambridge University Press, 1989), 11–13, 22–24; Rosemary O'Day, *Education and Society, 1500–1800: The Social Foundation of Education in Early Modern Europe* (London and New York: Longman, 1982), 186–90; Lawrence Stone, "Literacy and Education in England, 1640–1900," *Past and Present* 42 (February 1969): 72–73; Virginia Woolf, *A Room of One's Own* (New York and London: Harcourt, Brace, and World, 1957); William St. Clair, *The Reading Nation in the Romantic Period* (Cambridge: Cambridge University Press, 2004), 143–49.

2. Roger Chartier, "Reading Matter and 'Popular' Reading: From the Renaissance to the Seventeenth Century," in *A History of Reading in the West*, ed. Guglielmo Cavallo and Roger Chartier, trans. Lydia G. Cochrane (Amherst: University of Massachusetts Press, 1999), 269–83, quotations 270, 272.

3. David D. Hall, "Readers and Writers in Early New England," in Amory and Hall, eds., *Colonial Book in the Atlantic World*, 119; Naomi Tadmor, "'In the even my wife read to me': Women, Reading and Household Life in the Eighteenth Century," in *The Practice and Representation of Reading in England*, ed. James Raven, Helen Small, and Naomi Tadmor (Cambridge: Cambridge University Press, 1996), 162–74.

4. John Bennett, *Letters to a young lady, on a variety of useful and interesting subjects, calculated to improve the heart, to form the manners, and enlighten the understanding. In two volumes*, 2nd ed. (London: printed for T. Cadell, Jr., and W. Davies, 1795), 1:168–69.

5. Hannah More, *Strictures on the Modern System of Female Education. With a View of the Principles and Conduct Prevalent among Women of Rank and Fortune. In two volumes*, 5th ed. (London: T. Cadell, Jr., and W. Davies, 1799), 2:183, quoted in John Brewer, "Reconstructing the Reader: Prescriptions, Texts and Strategies

in Anna Larpent's Reading," in *Practice and Representation of Reading in England,* 235–36.

6. Reinhard Wittmann, "Was There a Reading Revolution at the End of the Eighteenth Century?" in *History of Reading in the West,* 291; Cathy N. Davidson, *Revolution and the Word: The Rise of the Novel in America* (New York: Oxford University Press, 1986).

Notes on Contributors

Heidi Brayman Hackel, formerly of Oregon State University, has joined the faculty at the University of California at Riverside. The author of *Reading Material in Early Modern England: Print, Gender, and Literacy* (2005), she is currently working on a cultural history of deafness, muteness, and manual gesture in early modern England.

Bianca F.-C. Calabresi is Haarlow-Cotsen Postdoctoral Fellow at Princeton University. She has published articles on alphabetical literacy and on rubrication in early modern Europe and is currently at work on a book entitled "The Female Narcissus: Renaissance Women's Writing Technologies."

Margaret Ferguson, University of California at Davis, is the author of *Dido's Daughters: Literacy, Gender, and Empire in Early Modern England and France* (2003). Her many contributions to the study of early modern women and to feminist approaches to the early modern period include coediting *Rewriting the Renaissance: The Discourses of Sexual Difference in Early Modern Europe* (1986) and *Women, Property, and the Letters of the Law in Early Modern England* (2004). She is currently working on a book on Aphra Behn's translations and imitations.

Robert A. Gross holds the James L. and Shirley A. Draper Chair of Early American History at the University of Connecticut. He is the author of *Books and Libraries in Thoreau's Concord* (1988) and *The Minutemen and Their World* (1976; twenty-fifth anniversary edition, 2001). He is a member of the general editorial board of *A History of the Book in America*, sponsored by the American Antiquarian Society, and coeditor with Mary Kelley of the second volume in the series, *An Extensive Republic: Books, Culture, and Society in the New Nation, 1790–1840* (forthcoming).

Mary Kelley, Ruth Bordin Collegiate Professor of History, American Culture, and Women's Studies at the University of Michigan, is the author of *Learning to Stand and Speak: Women, Education, and Public Life in America's Republic* (2006) and *Private Woman, Public Stage: Literary Domesticity* *in Nineteenth-Century America* (1984). She is an editor of the writings of Margaret Fuller and Catharine Maria Sedgwick. She is a member of the general editorial board of *A History of the Book in America* and the coeditor with Robert Gross of the forthcoming volume 2 of that history.

Catherine E. Kelly, University of Oklahoma, is the author of *In the New England Fashion: Reshaping Women's Lives in the Nineteenth Century* (1999), which was awarded the James J. Broussard First Book Prize by the Society for Historians of the Early American Republic. Her essays on provincial life, social networks, class, and gender have appeared in the *Journal of the Early Republic* and the *American Quarterly*. She is currently writing a book on early national visual culture.

Janice Knight, University of Chicago, is the author of *Orthodoxies in Massachusettes: Rereading American Puritanism* (1994), which was awarded the Thomas J. Wilson Prize by Harvard University Press and the Ralph Henry Gabriel Prize by the American Studies Association. She has published essays on Puritan religious culture in *William and Mary Quarterly* and *Early American Literature.* Her current project focuses on the intersections of gender, performance, and religious emotion in early America.

Mary Ellen Lamb, Southern Illinois University, has published widely on early women readers and writers in such journals as *English Literary Renaissance, Criticism,* and *Critical Survey.* She is the author of *Gender and Authorship in the Sidney Circle* (1990) and coeditor of *Oral Traditions and Gender in Early Modern Literary Texts* (Ashgate, forthcoming). Her most recent book, *The Popular Culture of Shakespeare, Spenser, and Jonson* (2006), places women's "old wives' tales" at the center of early modern popular culture.

Ian Frederick Moulton, Arizona State University, is the author of *Before Pornography: Erotic Writing in Early Modern England* (2000) and the editor and translator of Antonio Vignali's *La Cazzaria* (2003). He is currently researching a book on dialogues dealing with love and sexuality in sixteenth-century Western Europe.

Sasha Roberts taught at the University of Kent in Canterbury. She wrote *Reading Shakespeare's Poems in Early Modern England* (2003), coedited *Women Reading Shakespeare, 1660–1900: An Anthology of Criticism* (1997), and edited a special issue of *Critical Survey, Reading in Early Modern England* (winter 2000). Her many published essays include work on manuscript circulation and early modern visual arts.

Susan M. Stabile, Texas A&M University, is the author of *Memory's Daughters: The Material Culture of Remembrance in Eighteenth-Century America* (2004) and several articles on early American women's journals, garden books, and literary coteries. Her current project is an unconventional biography of Deborah Norris Logan (1761–1839) and Logan's nostalgic collection of "American antiquities."

Caroline Winterer, Stanford University, is the author of *The Mirror of Antiquity: American Women and the Classical Tradition, 1750–1900* (2007) and *The Culture of Classicism: Ancient Greece and Rome in American Intellectual Life, 1780–1910* (2002).

Index

Acknowledgments

This volume had as its origin a conference organized at Oregon State University and funded in large part by the Thomas Hart and Mary Jones Horning Endowment for the Humanities. While the volume has grown and shifted considerably since that first gathering, the excitement and sense of discovery that distinguished those early conversations have shaped and guided this collection. For their insights at the conference, we are grateful to all the participants but especially to those speakers whose work is not represented explicitly in this volume: Janice Radway, David Scott Kastan, and Eve Rachelle Sanders. Fredrika Teute provided invaluable help early on, identifying and linking scholars on both sides of the Atlantic. Anita Helle gave insights, leads, and cheer even in the midst of a volume of her own. Paul Gilje offered astute advice during the publication process. Robert and Mary Jo Nye, with their characteristic and enormous generosity, opened up the possibility of the conference itself. We also extend our thanks to Jerry Singerman and Erica Ginsburg at the University of Pennsylvania Press, who guided the project from inception through production, and Patricia Coates, whose careful editing improved the manuscript.

Other critical support for this volume came from University of Oklahoma Vice President for Research Lee Williams and from the Oregon State University Center for the Humanities. We are grateful to our home institutions for material support and to the many archives and research centers from which we jointly carried on the work of the volume. Heidi first explored transatlantic interdisciplinarity with Steve Hackel, whose expertise, generosity, and love have undergirded this project. Rich Hamerla offered Cathy endless good humor and more than a few reality checks; he also gave the volume its last and best name.

If scholarly debts are a pleasure to acknowledge, our dedication of this volume speaks to the tragedy and loss that can also accompany a long project. We dedicate this volume to the memory of one of our fellows in this project, Sasha Roberts, and to the joy with which she embraced scholarship, friendship, and life.

Breinigsville, PA USA
25 October 2009
226414BV00001B/8/P

9 780812 220803